THE PARENTING OF CHAMPIONS

THE PARENTING OF CHAMPIONS

*Raising Godly Children
in an Evil Age*

J.R. LUCAS

Wolgemuth & Hyatt, Publishers, Inc.
Brentwood, Tennessee

© 1989 by J. R. Lucas. All rights reserved
Published March 1990. First Edition
Printed in the United States of America
97 96 95 94 93 92 91 90   8 7 6 5 4 3 2 1

Wolgemuth & Hyatt, Publishers, Inc.
1749 Mallory Lane, Suite 110, Brentwood, Tennessee 37027.

Library of Congress Cataloging-in-Publication Data

Lucas, J. R. (James Raymond), 1950–
    The parenting of champions : raising godly children in an evil age
/ J. R. Lucas. — 1st ed.
        p. cm.
    ISBN 1-56121-016-1
    1. Parenting — Religious aspects — Christianity. 2. Family —
Religious life. I. Title
BV4526.2.L82 1990
248.8'45 — dc20   90-30179
                                                                          CIP

To Pamela Kay,
my lovely wife and untiring helpmate,
a growing champion and faithful collaborator
in parenting and in the writing of this book
(Proverbs 31:29)

To Laura Christine,
my eldest daughter and wise encourager,
a joyous presence and kindred spirit
who has brought me comfort
from the very first day
that God spoke her into being
(1 Thessalonians 2:19)

To Peter Barrett,
my eldest son and special friend,
a golden gift to me and a strong leader
in our family for many years to come
(1 Timothy 4:12)

To David Christopher,
my youngest son and gentle compadre,
an irreplaceable spirit and teacher
of the meaning of love and affection
(1 Thessalonians 3:9)

To Bethany Gayle,
my youngest daughter and bright light,
a delightful heart and enthusiastic enlivener
of my coming middle age
(Philippians 1:3)

To Maryl Jan,
my spiritual daughter and covenant friend,
a crystal-clear speaker of truth
and a tender heart
who always encourages me
by her life and love
(2 John 1)

CONTENTS

PREFACE

Praise the LORD!
Blessed is the man who fears the LORD,
*   who finds great delight in his com-*
*   mands.*
His children will be mighty in the land;
*   each generation of the upright will be*
*   blessed.*

(Psalms 112:1–2)

Are you trying to raise decent kids? It just won't be enough.

It won't be enough for you. Having "decent" kids won't be enough to satisfy that deep longing you have in your heart for your children to be really special, to make a major difference in the world in which God has placed them, and to be an outstanding blessing to those around them — and to generations yet unborn.

And it won't be enough for your kids. Being decent, just staying out of major trouble, won't be enough to keep them from being affected or even engulfed by the evil age that surrounds them. The spirit of the age speaks too loudly and parades too attractively. Even if your children don't go up in flames, they can be reduced to ineffectiveness in the kingdom of God.

This is why, first, this is a book on *parenting,* and not a nuts-and-bolts book on child-rearing. The purpose of this book is to start a change in you that can *become* a change in your children. I will try to show you how to relate to God rightly so that your children can too. I will attempt to show you how you can become what you need to be to carry out your great task. I will encourage you to know in your experience the deep reality of being a child of God, so that the beauty of that relationship can overflow into your relationship with your children.

And this is why, second, this is a book on parenting *champions*. By champions I don't mean someone who necessarily achieves worldly fame, wealth, or power; but I *do* mean someone who becomes famous with God and those around him, someone who is rich toward God, someone who has godly wisdom so that he has great power and increasing strength (see Proverbs 24:5).

A *champion* is "any person . . . receiving first prize or place in competition." You and I and our children are in a race. Paul told us that we should "run in such a way as to get the prize" (1 Corinthians 9:24). When my children are standing before Jesus as He tests the quality of their work (see 1 Corinthians 3:12–15), I want to be standing someplace nearby so that I can hear Jesus give them a hearty "well done!" I would like you to have the same experience with your children — and my guess is that you would too.

A *champion* is also "a combatant, a fighter — especially one who acts or speaks in behalf of a person or cause — a defender." We are in the midst of a fierce spiritual war (see Ephesians 6:10–18). There is only one thing for us and our children to do: "Fight the good fight of the faith" (1 Timothy 6:12). Our children need to be tough — God's way — and ready to act and speak up for Him and His kingdom. The Goliaths today are many, but you can raise Davids to bring the giants down.

And this is why, third, this book was written about parenting champions in an *evil age*. We have moved in our day from a sinful age (which all ages are) to an evil age, an age which mocks God and ignores His commands and promises. So many parents around us seem to have lost control of their children to peers, ungodly celebrities, all forms of media, and the spirit of unbounded "independence" that pervades what is left of Western civilization. Perhaps this has even happened to you.

And what has been the all-too-frequent response?

Many Christians and Christian groups, instead of being the salt of the earth, have either made a pietistic retreat into their homes and churches or have become virtually indistinguishable from the secular morass that surrounds them. This withdrawal into irrelevancy or descent into slime has allowed the culture to disintegrate even further, which will in turn bring even greater pressure on the family.

Many parents, in fact, are beginning to feel that the whole matter of parenting is out of their control. Even if they put their children in Christian schools and other Christian activities, they often see their children drawn to the ever-louder beat of the secular drum. Not a few of these children even resent or mock their Christian surroundings. Other children are quieter, but then seem to run away from their parents and their faith when they get away from home.

Too often Christian authors, teachers, and leaders have not been much help. Too many of them are telling parents to "hang on" and "just try to get your children through." Somehow, a message to "hang on" through your children's adolescent years until they are old enough to get out on their own is not a very lofty view of what you can accomplish as a parent. Hormones don't have to win. It *is* tougher to raise outstanding children than it was in other times and places, but you have an awesome God who is anxious to prove you "more than conquerors" (Romans 8:37).

I don't want you to just survive parenting, or end up saying, "Well, we gave it our best shot." I want to elevate your vision of your ministry as a parent. You can do better than just keeping your kids away from drugs or promiscuous sex (although those things are certainly important!). This book deals with the very essence of what it means to be a Christian parent, any one of whom could, with God's help, raise Christian champions. But you can't expect to have champions unless you *dedicate* yourself to parenting champions, and then learn how to do it.

And this is the key: *You.* This book will ask you to act like and be a champion as the primary way of teaching, or discipling, your children to act like and be champions. Although there are methods and techniques to be found in these pages, they are only secondary to the major point: If you, the parent, aren't recklessly committed to the Lord and living as a Christian champion, then there's not much that you can do to get your child to be one either.

One final thought: This book is written for *Christian* parents. There is no way to accomplish this noble task without knowing God as your Father, Jesus as your Lord, and the Holy Spirit as your Guide. If you're not a Christian, you can get some value from the principles, because reaping what you sow is as certain as water running downhill. If you aren't a Christian, I still encourage you to read on, if only to get a first taste of the potential that you are missing.

Most of all, I don't want you to say, "You know, that book really had some good ideas," and then forget you ever read it (is there anything as sad as a good, but unused, idea?). Take your time with this book. Read a section and apply it; each section is a tool. Discuss each section with your spouse. Don't feel as though you have to read and apply the whole book at once.

And here's my hope: that you will actually get off your easy chair and *do* something. Not talk about doing it, or think about doing it, but for our God's sake to actually *do* it — *now!* One principle or thought at a time.

Your kids are waiting.

PART 1

A CALL
FOR HIGH VISION

1

PARENTING CHAMPIONS: A VISION FOR PARENTS

*Where there is no vision, the people are
unrestrained,
But happy is he who keeps the law.*
(Proverbs 29:18, NASB)

You can do it.

That's right. You can really do it. Not you in general, but you specifically. You, the person reading these words, can accomplish what many of the "notables" of our day and of history have failed to accomplish. In the midst of a very evil age, you can parent champions.

Champions. The word has such an exquisite ring to it. Wouldn't that be something? Wouldn't you love for people to come up to you and say, "You mean that boy is *your* son?" Or, "How on earth did you raise *that* lovely young lady?" Wow! You could put out somebody's eye with the buttons popping off your shirt.

Don't settle for anything less.

I want to encourage you to lift up your eyes to the shining, snow-covered mountain of victory in Christian parenting. *You* can be a Christian champion. Your *children* can be Christian champions. You can make it to the top of that mountain together.

This is a day in which some very discouraged Christians are beginning to ask some very discouraging questions. But they are really very old questions, ones that have been asked by God's people in other times and places as cultures began to disintegrate: "Many are asking, 'Who can show us any good'?" (Psalms 4:6). "When the foundations are being destroyed, what can the righteous do?" (Psalms 11:3). As we see our culture decline with breathtaking speed, it is only natural to ask these questions.

But we who are believers are to rise above the merely natural and find our way with God's help to the *super*natural. In the first place, apathetic Christianity (what a contradiction in terms!) allowed things to get where they are now. Our whining is not only pathetic — it's misplaced. We are a little like the man who killed his parents, and then threw himself on the mercy of the court because he was an orphan! Several generations of Christians have allowed our culture to die, and now they want the non-Christian world to "give our families a break."

But there will be no break given by this post-Christian culture; no mercy asked, no quarter given. Whatever is recovered for the kingdom of God is going to have to be recovered as it was lost: One value, one principle, one family, one child at a time. *Your* family. *Your* child.

You can do it.

Good Christians

Given the spiritual assaults on the culture and the family, it *is* the most natural thing in the world to go into a survival mode when thinking about your role as a parent.

It's easy today to feel that as long as you can get your kids through, as long as they come out as "good Christians," that's the best you can do. It's a kind of "Custer's last stand" approach to parenting.

Other "good" Christians will often agree that it's very hard today to do even this small thing, since the days are so very, very evil. We can easily persuade ourselves that helping to save our children from the pit and giving them a halfway decent start in life is, in the midst of incredible godlessness, somehow enough.

It is not enough.

It has never been enough — not in any age or place. This "mind-your-own-business," "plod-through" Christianity has never been sufficient to do the job that God needs to have done. But in this age and place, it's not only not in the ballpark, it's not even near the ticket booth. While the evil age drives many parents and counselors to accept mediocrity as the best they can expect, wise parents will understand that the *evil age itself* is one of the main reasons to raise a champion.

If you were preparing your child to go on a walk through some lush, shady field, you might send him off with a canteen of water and a sandwich. But if you had to prepare your child to walk through a barren, scorching desert, you would certainly send him on his way with all of the provisions for strength that you could think of and that he could carry. You would prepare him for the actual journey that he needed to make. This age is *not* a shady field!

God is clear that He wants powerful, mighty ambassadors to represent His life to the world. All children surely have certain gifts and specific abilities in which they can and must excel for God, and we must surely help them to develop these areas. But there isn't much that can be said for stopping here and using these kinds of things to show the world that your children are "good Christians," even while they exhibit little character and make no real impression on the age. Adequate Christianity is not Biblical. Whoever and whatever and wherever you are, the demand in Scripture is for *astonishing* Christianity — and the demand is no less for your children.

Look at history. Look at how much has been accomplished through the efforts of such a very small number of people. What on earth would happen if every Christian parent would chuck this willingness to be satisfied with adequacy, and choose instead to raise a spiritual giant of God? A generation of such giants would leave even this sinful world changed dramatically.

If we know Jesus as our personal Savior, we already have eternal life. We are already in the kingdom of God, for "our citizenship is in heaven" (Philippians 3:20). We have a God of power, a Savior of power, a Spirit of power, and a Word of power. We have a bigger chunk of God's omniscience available to us in Scripture than many of us know what to do with. So why are we so lifeless? Why do we and our children so often act just like everyone else? Why do we behave as though we have such a surplus of ignorance? Finally and most importantly, why don't we have power?

I'm sure that God knows the answer to these questions. I'm equally sure that He would rather not know — that He would rather see us living out the power that we already have in Christ.

We can be powerful if we choose to be. The Bible says: "Blessed is the man who fears the LORD, who finds great delight in his commands" (Psalms 112:1).

We know from Scripture that fear of the Lord defines a wise man, and that such a man increases in strength, attacks and destroys the strongholds of the worldly, and stands immovable against the raging of a world that pretends to be strong but is enslaved by its own weakness. These things are exquisite in themselves, but this psalm has a series of promises, and the first one is this: "His children *will be* mighty in the land; each generation of the upright will be blessed" (v. 2).

What a promise! Isn't it fabulous? Please note that it's not a promise that his children will be mighty in heaven (which they, of course, will be), but that they will be mighty *in the land!* Right here and now, you can leave a legacy of power that will continue to change the world long after you've made your voyage to your home country. Your own children may be the very reason, in fact, that the world doesn't destroy itself in their lifetime.

How do you get in on this promise? How, you are asking, can I produce mighty children? How can my children have it all? The answer was given before the promise was described. All of God's promises, both for blessing and cursing, are conditional. This wonderful promise is no different.

First, *you* have to fear the Lord. It's quite interesting that the promise is based on *your* fear of the Lord, not on your children's fear of the Lord. The reason is very simple: The best way for your children to learn the fear of the Lord is through being discipled by you as *you* become a God-fearing man or woman (see Nehemiah 7:2).

The second condition for the promise is that you find "great delight in his commands." God has, in a single verse, given both the beginning and ending methods of successful parenting. It starts with the fear of the Lord and ends with finding His commands delightful. He wants you to find them true, and He wants you to obey them in His strength. But this isn't enough. He also wants you to find them delightful — and not just a little delightful, but *greatly* delightful. As John reminds us: "This is love for God: to obey his commands. *And his commands are not burdensome,* for everyone born of God has overcome the world" (1 John 5:3–4 emphasis added). Contrary to so much of the teaching we hear today, God *is* interested in our taking His commands seriously. And also contrary to this teaching, His commands aren't the way to slavery; they're the way to freedom and victory. Not survival, but *overcoming the world!*

What's the bottom line? You as a parent have an ironclad promise that if you think and do certain things, your children will be mighty. Not adequate, not out of trouble, but *mighty.* God has put their outcome partly in your hands. But if you don't take everything that God says and then joyously and immediately put it into practice, God is telling you not to be surprised when your children grow up to be ninety-eight-pound spiritual weaklings. And if you're not satisfied with the puny lives that your children will be leading, don't blame it on God or Satan or the world or the evil age. You'll be able to conduct your entire investigation by looking in a mirror.

One of the difficulties you're going to have in training a champion who can truly conquer in this evil age is that you yourself may have grown up in an easier time. Your training might be totally inadequate to deal with what *you* are facing today, much less with what your children are facing. You'll have to let God retrain and restrengthen you before you can do anything for your children. But you must do it, for yourself and them — and you must do it quickly.

It's all too easy to give your children just enough "religion" to inoculate them from the life of power. You can leave them with a life that looks good in a suit, but then wrinkles as the pressure comes. You can manipulate them so that they have too much "religion" to keep them from seeing their weakness and need for God, and too little true religion to allow them to stand.

Only a change in *your* life, only being a man or woman of God, will allow you to be a successful parent and your child, a champion. Don't settle for too little. It's easy to do, and you'll hate yourself for it.

Even if your children are "good Christians."

Maybe especially.

The Starting Point

Many Christian parents teach their children that the highest gift that God has bestowed on them is their personal salvation from the penalty of sin, through the shed blood of the Messiah on the cross. This is certainly the first blessing, the fundamental gift from God upon which all other blessings are based. Without salvation, your children are just wandering prey, lost and bleeding, waiting to be destroyed by the merciless father of lies.

But is salvation the *highest* possible blessing? Or is the highest blessing justification before God? Could it be the wisdom and power to walk a sanctified life? Or the authority that God has given us on earth? Do you think it might be our deliverance from the full curse of the law (see Deuteronomy 28:15–68; Galatians 3:13)? How about our acceptance by the Lord? Or could it be the good works and related rewards that He has stored up for us? This is a tough question for the simple reason that God has given us so much even though we deserved execution and hell.

But none of these are the *highest* blessing from the hand of God. These are juicy and fabulous, to be sure, but the best is better than all of this. At the point of salvation, God becomes your *Papa,* your Daddy, and you become His child.

It doesn't get any better than that.

How do we know this? "Yet to all who received him, to those who believed in his name, he gave the right to become children of God" (John 1:12). Did you get that? You have a *right* to become God's child, and your children have the same right. This is such an awesome blessing that God actually uses it to define the magnitude of His love for us (see 1 John 3:1).

There are so much Scripture verses on this subject that it's hard to be selective, but here are a few:

- Ephesians 1:3–8 — In love, God planned our adoption. An adopted son in the first century received absolute sonship and had all the rights of a natural son.

- 2 Corinthians 6:16–18 — Our adoption is God's plan and His decision. God wasn't forced into adopting us.

- Hebrews 2:11 — Jesus agrees with the Father and is not ashamed to call us His brothers!

- Romans 8:15 — This adoption has the Spirit of sonship. There's no fear, just love and affection as we cry out, "Papa!"

- Galatians 3:26–4:7 — We own the whole estate, because our Father owns everything. We have the *full* rights of sons. In fact, it's because He has adopted us as sons that He gives us of His Spirit. We aren't flesh of His flesh — we are *spirit of His Spirit* (and someday we will have a spiritual body like Jesus' — 1 Corinthians 15:42–44). We are heirs of God and joint heirs with Jesus, His Son, our Brother.

God didn't have to offer all of this to us — but praise Him, He did! And if you and your children don't grasp this intimate relationship with God as a loving Father, you and they will *never* be able to grasp and accept all of the wonderful blessings of God that He wants to shower upon you in this life. These things just won't make sense. Why would God want to listen to me? Why would He care? Why would He rescue me? Why would He want to *honor* me, for goodness sake?

Because He is your *Papa*.

Your children *can* settle for less. They *are* His children if they're truly saved, but they can live as though they aren't very close to Him and largely miss enjoying their relationship with their heavenly Father. They can go back to "those weak and miserable principles" (Galatians 4:9) that deny the fatherhood of God — but why on earth would they?

One reason — perhaps the main reason — is that their parents never teach them and show them how to simply rest in the lap of their heavenly Father and "live it up" as a child of the mighty Creator God.

Your children want their father to have certain characteristics. They want him to be available, approachable, gentle, appreciative of their time with him, rejoicing in them, a teacher, respected by others, a powerful personality, balanced so they know where they stand, protective, just and fair, worthy of imitation, worthy of their attempts to please him, full of pleasant surprises and blessings, and willing to give up all for them.

God is all of these things to your child, even when you as a father are stumbling around in the dark and trying to find the starting line. Teach your children often and deeply about their perfect Father; most important of all, let your children see in your walk and life that this God is, without question, their father's Father and mother's Father.

The thing we all want the most from our fathers is love and the commitment that goes along with it. In fact, the first three things we want from our fathers is love, and then love, and finally love, always. No backing down, in spite of our mistakes and flaws. God is that kind of father. And He doesn't just want to *treat* you as though He is a father and have you *act* as though you are His son—He *is* your father, and you *are* His son!

Teach your children that even if they blow it, even if they make some terrible mistake, that God won't cast them out (see John 5:24). He may have to discipline or even punish them severely (see Hebrews 12), but even then His love is the driving force. No loving father looks for ways to drop the hammer on his son or daughter. And our heavenly Father is the most loving of them all.

Look at the story of the lost son in Luke 15. This is usually used to describe an unsaved person coming to God. But that can't be the only way to look at this story, because the young man is already a son at the beginning of the story, and unsaved people simply aren't children of God! This is, in fact, the ultimate "blown" relationship between a father and his son. Does the father hate the son, look for ways to nail him, hate to see him come back, and give him a crummy place in the pigpen (which is the best that the world had for him)?

No way.

The father sees his son coming back and is filled with compassion. He *runs* to his son, hugs him and kisses him, accepts the repentance even as he cuts his son's speech short, showers him with the best blessings of his house, begins a celebration (with a fattened calf that it almost looks as though he's been saving for the occasion), pleads with the brother to love and forgive (a real lesson for the families and the church), and gives *no hint* that the sonship had ever changed.

It *is* important for us to note that this father didn't go chasing all over to find his son. There does come a time when a father has to let his children reap what they sow and not get in the way of God's discipline and even punishment of these children. There comes a time when parents are instructed to bring a rebellious child to the elders for handling. But the point of fatherhood is that, if it's real, it can never go away.

Even when we are prodigals, God never stops being the prodigal's Father. In fact, He is a prodigal Father, since *prodigal* also means "yielding abundantly; luxuriant." He is totally committed, loving, compassionate, forgiving. Somehow, find a way to convey this to your children. Work on it creatively. After giving them the truth of the Word of God, there is perhaps no better thing to do than to treat them as God has said He wants to treat you.

In *Knowing God* (InterVarsity, 1973), J. I. Packer hits home with this truth:

> God adopts us out of free love, not because our character and record show us worthy to bear His name, but despite the fact that they show the very opposite. We are not fit for a place in God's family; the idea of His loving and exalting us sinners as He loves and has exalted the Lord Jesus sounds ludicrous and wild—yet that, and nothing less than that, is what our adoption means. . . . There are no distinctions of affection in the divine family. We are all loved *just as fully as Jesus is loved* [emphasis mine]. It is like a fairy story—the reigning monarch adopts waifs and strays to make princes of them—but, praise God, it is not a fairy story: it is hard and solid fact, founded on the bedrock of free and sovereign grace. (pp. 195–196)

Can you grab hold of this? Can you convey it to your children? No task is more worthy for you to undertake for yourself or for your saved child. "How great is the love the Father has lavished on us, that we should be called children of God! And that is what we are!" (1 John 3:1).

Amen!

Thank you, *Papa*.

Son of Nun

Once you've gotten hold of the reality of the mighty God of creation being your very own Papa, and begin walking in that reality, and start to convey this to your own children through your words and example, you will be demonstrating that you are related to the Father "from whom his whole family in heaven and on earth derives its name" (Ephesians 3:15). You'll be taking on the family resemblance, looking more and more like your Father.

Ultimately, there's no family except God's family. If you understand this, you're ready to affect history, for one of the joys of Christian parenthood is the prospect that your principles and values and goals can be carried through many generations by your descendants.

Many parents figure that parenting is an important job, but that it's still peripheral to the real purposes that they're supposed to accomplish with their lives. To them, parenting is a job that must be discharged successfully, just like any other effort that they might undertake. They try to prepare their children to lead their own lives, and believe that their children will then work to achieve their own goals, on a separate path.

Friends, parenting isn't just another job on the long list of jobs that you've been assigned. This is a way to affect countless people to at least the third and fourth generations of your descendants. Note: Not *just* your descendants, but all people who come into *contact* with your descendants. A godly life, mixed with a fine job of parenting, can leave a mark on this world that is beyond your wildest hopes and dreams.

There are, of course, many obvious scriptural examples. Abraham believes God and the promise is carried through Isaac and Jacob and beyond in a very clear and interconnected fashion. David, a man of wisdom who conceives the temple, raises Solomon, a wiser man who actually builds the temple. Timothy is encouraged by Paul to remember the sincere faith "which first lived in your grandmother Lois and in your mother Eunice" (2 Timothy 1:5). This principle works with the wicked as well, as can be seen by reading about the later kings of God's people. With few exceptions, each one is worse than any who preceded him, but his behavior is always compared to that of his rotten ancestors.

God is telling us: This isn't a job — this isn't an eighteen-year duty — this is not simply a good work to finish and then set aside. This is how you will be remembered in the actual, real world for generations. He's saying: Be careful how you live and what your children see. He's telling us to do what few human beings ever do: Look ahead to posterity. He wants us to think about what we would see if we were to come back again, fifty years after our death.

Most people, I think, would be pretty overwhelmed.

Scripture tells us, "A good name is more desirable than great riches; to be esteemed is better than silver or gold" (Proverbs 22:1). This doesn't just mean your reputation; without doubt, this also actually includes your name and the images and ideas that your name will raise. This is clearly a heritage that will be passed on to your children and is immeasurably more important than any material trinkets that you might leave to them.

If you have any doubt that your good (or bad) name will be preserved through your children, why do you think Scripture says that the father of a wise man can answer anyone who treats him with contempt (see Proverbs 27:11)? Or that there is no joy for the father of a fool (see

Proverbs 17:21)? Or that anyone who would lead God's people must be judged on the basis of his children's lives and behavior as well as his own (see 1 Timothy 3:4–5; Titus 1:6)?

And a good name is not something that just happens to Christians, like winning a door prize. Scripture says: "Let love and faithfulness never leave you; bind them around your neck, write them on the tablet of your heart. *Then* you will win favor and a good name in the sight of God and man" (Proverbs 3:3–4, emphasis added).

So it's pretty clear that the value of your name and ideas and convictions is in your own hands, as you walk a life of love and faithfulness — or a life of leaking values and wastefulness. How this is passed on to your children is also in your hands, even after they've become adults. And how you will be remembered is up to you, including any wickedness, which will cause your name to rot (see Proverbs 10:7).

Everything you are and do will speak in some way loud and clear, and perhaps for centuries. Since there have only been 125 or so generations on earth since creation, you can affect a large portion of history for good. Thousands — tens of thousands — of people can be influenced by your godly descendants, by the children and grandchildren and great-grandchildren who are, in some wonderful way, in your body right now (see Hebrews 7:9–10).

So if you want greatness, don't look for a promotion or fame or power or wealth. Look instead for godliness — and for a lot of time with your future mouthpieces, some of whose descendants you won't get to meet until they join you with the Lord.

One of my favorite examples of the efforts of a man of God living with power through his child is the scriptural example of Joshua son of Nun. Now, we have absolutely no account of the life of this man, this father called Nun. The only thing we know is that he is the son of Elishama and the father of Joshua. Most of the people listed in chronologies in Scripture are never again discussed, and if they are not discussed, their names are usually dropped. But here we have this person named Nun, who is himself not discussed, but whose name appears over twenty-five times.

And how does it appear? Always in conjunction with the name of his son, Joshua. Joshua is constantly referred to as "Joshua son of Nun." This can't be just for clarification of which Joshua we are talking about; it's not like there are many Joshuas leading the people into the Promised

Land. If this were so, it would be akin to the media's habit of referring to President Truman as "Harry *S.* Truman," to distinguish him from all of the other presidents named Harry Truman.

Where do you think Joshua came from? He was a powerful man of God, and one who must have been raised by another powerful man of God. God, I think, really believes in this business of blessing and cursing families, and in this case was showing in the story of Joshua the blessing that must have come in part through the faithfulness of his father. I believe that God was honoring the parent for the outstanding faith and values that were so evident in his son. He was reminding us of the son's starting point — a godly parent.

I would like to close this section with a portion of Psalm 119. These words, I'm sure, represent the kinds of thoughts that must have been in the heart of this man named Nun. They are the kinds of thoughts that must be in the heart of any parent who wants to be remembered and honored for many generations. These words are in that part of the Psalm in which all of the verses begin with the fourteenth letter of the Hebrew alphabet, the letter Nun.

> Your word is a lamp to my feet and a light for my
> path.
> I have taken an oath and confirmed it, that I will fol-
> low your righteous laws.
> I have suffered much; renew my life, O LORD, ac-
> cording to your word.
> Accept, O LORD, the willing praise of my mouth,
> and teach me your laws.
> Though I constantly take my life in my hands, I will
> not
> > forget your law.
> The wicked have set a snare for me, but I have not
> strayed from your precepts.
> Your statutes are my heritage forever; they are the
> joy of my heart.
> My heart is set on keeping your decrees to the very
> end.
>
> (Psalms 119:105–112)

So please—for our God's sake, for your sake, and for the sake of countless people yet unborn—do an excellent job of raising little Harold or Irene.

Son of *you*.

A Godly Seed

We know that we're in the family of God. God is our Father and we are His adopted sons. Jesus is not ashamed to call us His brothers. We're related by faith and blood, Jesus' blood, to all those who are saved by Jesus' work on the cross. In fact, God the Father wants us to be in the family tree of the heroes of the faith. In the words of Paul, we are "Abraham's offspring . . . He is the father of us all" (Romans 4:16).

Our Father is interested in a "godly seed," in spiritual children who will make Jesus known as the Lord of all of life. Our Papa wants us to be champions and He wants us to parent godly champions. He wants His family line to be continued.

So, if we are serious believers, how should these truths affect our thinking about families and children?

The "experts" tell us that there are too many people. We used to let God worry about that kind of thing, and even then we had a hard enough time just minding our own business. The psalmist said: "I do not concern myself with great matters or things too wonderful for me. But I *have* stilled and quieted my soul" (Psalms 131:1–2, emphasis added).

It's just too easy today to forget that "Sons are a heritage from the LORD, children a reward from him" (Psalms 127:3).

We talk about the "surplus population" in India and Africa, as though these people are a lumped mass of subhuman parasites. We sometimes sound as though we don't know whether we want to evangelize the world's people or eliminate them. We have fallen for the idea that these people are some kind of statistical accident or aberration. We actually believe the "social planners" when they tell us that men can control population growth and should decide what kind of people will be conceived or allowed to live.

Well, it just isn't so. Men don't control population growth, because men do not make babies (in spite of the overemphasis on the belief that men and women create life by means of sexual relations, an idea which, in many ways, eliminates the sovereignty of God). *God* makes babies, and He has fashioned each one of those immortal souls *from eternity* to be placed in a particular time and place and family. Even the social planners aren't accidents.

There is a most astounding passage in the book of Acts, chapter 17. God, through Paul, states the following:

> The God who made the world and *everything* in it is the Lord of heaven and earth and does not live in temples built by hands. And he is not served by human hands, as if he needed anything, because he *himself* gives all men life and breath and everything else. From one man he made every nation of men, that they should inhabit the whole earth; and *he determined the times set for them* and the *exact places where they should live.* (vv. 24–26, emphasis added)

It's pretty clear here who the Creator is and who gives men life and breath; it's no less clear that He has determined *from eternity* the number and makeup of those who have ever lived or who will ever live. It's as though He has a reservoir consisting of all those whom He has had the desire to create and love, and then searched through history to find the times (like now) and the places (like your city or town) where they should be placed — *exactly.*

With a little thought, you can see how God has worked these decisions in and through and around human decision making. Looking through history from His eternal vantage point, He has clearly seen who will decide to be open to His blessing totally, who will decide to limit His blessing, and who will decide not to have His blessing at all. God is big enough to allow for these human, free-will decisions and to still remain sovereign and capable of fulfilling the passage quoted above.

The question for you, though, is whether you'll be part of God's family planning or cling to your own. The result which you must face if you choose to limit or eliminate children from your marriage is that someone else may be getting the child who could have been well suited to you and the memory of your name.

Are there children in God's decreasing reservoir who would do so very well in your family? Are there children whom He's aching to put into your loving care? Are there children out there who really *belong* to you? Will you someday meet someone in heaven who is introduced to you as your *almost* son or daughter? Open your heart to God! He loves to work through His people, but the children He has created from eternity *will* find their way into His universe — with or without you.

However, this isn't a plea for big families per se. This is more basic than that; this is a plea to let God bless you. This is a plea for the family size that God has determined would be the best for you and these other immortal human beings. Have you ever said to God, "Lord, don't send me any more money! I just don't have room for any more of that blessing"? I doubt it, because we all really believe money to be a blessing. And so if children are really a blessing — and Scripture says they are — why do we tell God to keep His kids to Himself?

God knows the resources required to raise these children in both spiritual and practical ways and has never placed children in a situation that would hinder them from coming to the Lord. In fact, Paul concludes the passage in Acts 17 by giving the reason for God's careful placement: "God did this so that men would seek him and perhaps reach out for him and find him, though he is not far from each one of us" (v. 27).

This could be the most encouraging thing for you to ever know to help you move ahead in confidence with the good work of parenting: You as a parent can rest assured that if God gives you a child, that your home is the *very best* available place for that child to be, out of all the homes in all the countries in all the centuries that have ever been or that ever will be. It's been said that parenting is the only tough job that you can get without any prior experience, but this just isn't so. You have been made a parent precisely because of your experience, and you, of course, can rely on the experience of God to help you do the job.

And if you desire a big family, and the Lord blesses your desire, please enjoy it to the fullest! It's okay to get a kick out of it!

Many will tell you that you can't easily raise five or six or seven kids today. Listen, it's *never* been easy to raise five or six or seven kids. If you have lousy parenting principles, *one* might be too big a family. But if your principles are right, every one of yours can become a mighty man or woman of God. "Like arrows in the hands of a warrior are sons born in one's youth. Blessed is the man whose quiver is full of them. They will not be put to shame when they contend with their enemies in the gate" (Psalms 127:4–5).

One of the things that more and more Christians are becoming interested in is how to reclaim our culture — not just individuals — for Christ. Jesus told us to make disciples of *the nations*. How will we ever do it?

Perhaps the way can come through Christians having and raising many champions for Christ. Many Christians are complaining about the decline of morality, but *you* can actually do something about it in your own home. God can give you a godly seed. Working with God, you can develop a godly plant.

And what about the enemy? Well, with birth control, abortion, infanticide, euthanasia, and homosexuality, the wicked could largely kill themselves off in a generation or two. They have no desire for godly seed, so God lets their very planning and actions carry the seed of their own destruction.

What if you don't want a big family? If you aren't intending to fully live a godly life in Christ Jesus, then we should be *glad* that you're planning not to have a big family. The last thing we need is more marginal Christians. Those kinds of "Christians" are just going to bring more judgment on the church and make the battle tougher.

No, we're talking about *godly* Christians having more children. If you want to live a godly life and don't want children, how sad for you and your generation. We may not win this war for the culture in our generation. But if many of you will take this call seriously and raise godly seed, you *will* win.

Time — and arrows — are on your side.

The Upside-Down Kingdom

"There is a way that seems right to a man, but in the end it leads to death" (Proverbs 14:12).

What does it mean when it says that there is a way that "seems" right? Well, in every field of human endeavor, including parenting, there are two basic approaches — God's way and man's way. There are always two paths, two roads — even for the Christian.

But this verse is telling us even more than that. It is telling us that there is a way, a direction, that's going to sound good. You're going to hear about it or read about it, and it's going to click with your human nature.

And that's the problem. It clicks. It *seems* right. But it *isn't* right. It doesn't work, because you get the opposite results of what you had hoped for (see Acts 27:9–14). Few men would plan a way that would lead to death, but that's just what this road that seems so right leads to—death. You may not have ever applied this Scripture to parenting, but it applies directly and absolutely.

Our culture is chock-full of ideas on parenting. Many are very bad, some are weird, and a few are beyond incredible. Perhaps the worst of the lot is the idea that you as a parent don't have the right to "impose" your values on your child. When some people start telling us about the reasons behind this—the dignity of each child, the faultiness in our own character—it can start to sound logical, even right. But what's the end of it? You don't impose your values. The enemy imposes his. Your children die—spiritually, mentally, emotionally, even physically. You lose.

On the other hand, many of God's ideas—also called "truth"—sound strange. They just don't click. It's almost as though He's planned life in such a way that the things that seem good aren't and the things that sound strange are wonderful. It's as if He's turned things upside-down.

Amen! "Do not deceive yourselves. If any one of you thinks he is wise by the standards of this age, he should become a 'fool' so that he may become wise. For the wisdom of this world is foolishness in God's sight." (1 Corinthians 3:18–19). Occasionally, the godless hit upon a truth (see Proverbs 14:33), but if you're listening to the Benjamin Spocks and their progeny on a regular basis, you're in big trouble.

We need to train ourselves to listen closely to the things that sound strange, the upside-down truths that define the kingdom of God. And then we need to turn our children's lives upside-down with the power of this "foolishness"—that just happens to be absolute truth.

What are some of these truths?

- If you try to save your own life, you will lose it; if you "lose" your life to Christ you will save it. To put it another way, "God always gives his best to those who leave the choice with him." Does this have application to where and how you spend your time? Who do your children think is at the center of your life, you or God?

- If you exalt or promote yourself and your interests, you'll be humbled or even torn down; if you humble yourself, God will exalt you at just the right time. Does this have application to jockeying for position at work or church? Do your children hear you speak about humble service to your employer and church family?

- If you hoard your possessions for yourself, you'll lose them all; if you generously share with others, you will gain more and more. Does this have application to your family finances and how much (and how willingly) you give back to God? Do your children see you giving up personal pleasures for the benefit of others?

- If you try to live a good life in your own strength, you'll be wiped out; if you gladly acknowledge your own weakness, God's strength will be made perfect in you. Does this have application to how your children see you coping (or not coping) with stress? Do your children see you quietly under control when things seem to be falling apart?

When you hear an idea in the Word of God that sounds upside down, think about it hard. Maybe *you're* the one who's upside down.

The Work of a Champion

We all remember the old saying, "God helps those who help themselves." It's an interesting thought that sums up an entire religious philosophy. It implies that it is our job as Christians to try to live for the Lord, and the Lord's job to bless us in these righteous efforts. It says that "the Lord provides the fish, but we have to dig up the bait" and simply, that we had better work very hard if we expect to get any blessings. There's only one problem with this neat little idea.

It is totally wrong.

God does *not* help those who help themselves, and you shouldn't teach your children so. God doesn't even *like* those who help themselves, as evidenced by Scripture:

- Trying to worship God in your own strength doesn't work.

  > He said to Aaron, "What did these people do to you,
  > that you led them into such great sin?" . . . "They said
  > to me, 'Make us gods who will go before us.' . . . Then
  > they gave me the gold, and I threw it into the fire, and
  > out came this calf!" . . . And the LORD struck the peo-
  > ple with a plague because of what they did with the calf
  > Aaron had made. (Exodus 32:21–35)

- Trying to clear up sin in your own strength doesn't work.

> The LORD said to Moses and Aaron: "How long will
> this wicked community grumble against me? . . . Not
> one of you will enter the land." . . . When Moses re-
> ported this to all the Israelites, they mourned bitterly.
> "We have sinned," they said. "We will go up to the
> place the LORD promised." But Moses said, "Why are
> you disobeying the LORD's command? This will not suc-
> ceed!" . . . Nevertheless, in their presumption they went
> up . . . [and were beaten] down all the way to Hormah.
> (Numbers 14:26–45)

- Trying to fight spiritual battles in your own strength doesn't work.

> The LORD said to Gideon, "You have too many men for
> me to deliver Midian into their hands. In order that Is-
> rael may not boast against me that her own strength has
> saved her." (Judges 7:2)

- Trying to obey God's Word in your own strength doesn't work.

> Then the word of the LORD came to Samuel: "I am
> grieved that I have made Saul king, because he has
> turned away from me and has not carried out my in-
> structions." . . . "Tell me," Saul replied. Samuel said,
> "Although you were once small in your own eyes, did
> you not become the head of the tribes of Israel? The
> LORD anointed you king over Israel. . . . Because you
> have rejected the word of the LORD, he has rejected you
> as king." (1 Samuel 15:10–23)

- Trying to get God's blessing in your own strength doesn't work.

> "For the eyes of the LORD range throughout the earth to
> strengthen those whose hearts are fully committed to
> him." . . . Asa was afflicted with a disease in his feet.
> Though his disease was severe, even in his illness he
> did not seek help from the LORD, but only from the phy-
> sicians. Then . . . Asa died. (2 Chronicles 16:9–13)

- Trying to stand up for Jesus in your own strength doesn't work.

> Jesus began to explain to his disciples . . . that he must
> be killed. . . . Peter took him aside and began to rebuke
> him. "Never, Lord!" . . . Jesus turned and said to Peter,
> "Out of my sight, Satan! You are a stumbling block to

me; you do not have in mind the things of God, but the
things of men." (Matthew 16:21–23)

God wants His people to rely on Him, and Him alone, for strength
and power. He wants them to cease from self and the efforts of self.
Good actions not prompted by faith and strengthened by the Lord miss
the mark. It's true that I can do all things; but only because I have the
full power of God at my disposal. I *can* do all things—through my Lord
who strengthens my spirit.

Teach your children this truth. Don't let them get out on their own
without a good, solid sense of their own helplessness and inadequacy. If
they don't have this, their pride, along with Satan and the world system,
will tear them down to a level from which they might never recover.
They need to know that without God they are nothing, can become nothing, can do nothing, can have nothing. Hammer this home consistently
with your children, and teach them that those who help themselves have
a fool for an assistant.

This truth—our absolute dependence upon the Lord for true success—should even color our bragging about our kids. The only time we
should really brag is if and when our children step out from the ordinary
and do something because they are sensitive to the invisible realm—like
doing something around the house without being asked.

And as soon as we brag about it, we should pray for our children on
that very point, because Satan can't read our minds but he can hear our
words. Nothing could delight him more than to tear your children down
on that very point of success, whether by causing them to fall or by
turning it into a point of pride.

Even better than this kind of bragging is to teach your children (and
yourself) to boast about and delight in weaknesses just as Paul did. The
great result of this kind of bragging is that Christ's power will rest on
you (see 2 Corinthians 12:9–10). A believer who boasts about his helplessness is a Christian to be reckoned with.

Teach your children to "Taste and see that the LORD is good"
(Psalms 34:8). Let them know that absolutely *nothing* is impossible with
our God, and that absolutely *everything* is possible to the person—child
or otherwise—who believes. As the psalmist says:

Blessed is the man who takes refuge in him. Fear the LORD, you his
saints, for those who fear him lack nothing. The lions may grow weak

and hungry, but those who seek the LORD lack no good thing. (Psalms 34:8–10)

If you must teach the "old saying," at least teach it accurately. God *does* help those who help themselves — to Him.

Conclusion

If you will grasp the vision laid out in this chapter and the rest of this book, and apply it with your own children, you can achieve a great victory for God. No enemy, no corruption, nothing will be able to keep you from parenting a champion. You can do it.

You *must* do it.

Your great-grandchildren will thank you.

2

THE IMPORTANCE
OF HIGH EXPECTATIONS

Aim for perfection.

(2 Corinthians 13:11)

"Aim for *what? Perfection . . . ?* You must be kidding."

No, I'm not.

More important than that, *God* isn't kidding. He wants you to set your sights high, to the top of a lofty mountain. Our Father actually wants us to aim for perfection.

It sounds strange to our untrained ears. Aren't we still trapped by the flesh? Aren't we still just "full-time, full-fledged sinners," as a writer in one Christian magazine put it? Isn't it true that the only difference between Christians and non-Christians is that Christians are saved from their sins?

No. No. No.

The very fact that believers can ask such questions shows how far we've come from the goals of a God who says, without hesitation or qualification, "Be holy, because I am holy" (Leviticus 11:44–45; 19:2; 1 Peter 1:16). In 1 Peter it says right before that, "But just as he who called you is holy, so be holy in *all* you do . . ." (v. 15, emphasis added).

God is very serious about the fact that He wants you to aim for perfection. Do you think that He doesn't include parenting in this? Or that He doesn't really care whether or not you teach your children to aim for perfection? How can we settle for so little, when our Father offers — and requires — so much?

Too many parents in our day have been browbeaten and discouraged into believing that they cannot or should not set high standards or establish high expectations for themselves and their children. They're told that it isn't "fair," either to themselves or to their children, to expect too much. But, folks, there's one thing that's true about everything in life: You'll never get more than what you aim for.

At the high school I attended, I would practice on a large rifle range. I was told that if I wanted to have the highest possible score, I had to hit the center of the target. I knew, without being told, that in order to hit the center I had to *aim* for the center.

Really brilliant.

And yet many so-called experts on parenting don't even latch on to something this fundamental. If you want the highest possible score — "Well done, good and faithful servant" (Matthew 25:23) — you have to hit the center — "The father of a righteous man has great joy" (Proverbs 23:24). And if you want to hit this center, you have to aim for perfection.

I didn't always hit the center, of course. There were times when I was glad I wasn't hitting innocent bystanders. But if I hadn't been aiming for the center of the target, there's no telling *what* I would have hit.

You as a parent can aim for perfection: of yourself, of your parenting skills, and of your children. You *must* aim for perfection. You might make a mistake and get less, but you'll never get more than what you aim for. Aiming for perfection as a parent is not only acceptable — it's *crucial* if you want to raise a champion.

It's in your hands.

This is why God can absolutely insist that no man can be an overseer or elder in the church unless he has children who are believers, who obey him not just out of force but with proper respect, and who aren't able to be accused of disobedience (see 1 Timothy 3; Titus 1). How would this be a reasonable qualification if the results of parenting weren't under the man's control?

And if the church actually used this qualification, how many men would have to leave leadership positions? Make no bones about it: A man *must* resign from church leadership if his children don't have all the earmarks of being champions. If this requirement were taken seriously, seminaries would have extensive training in parenting, even for those who don't yet have wives or children. The idea of a pastor, elder, deacon, or missionary with out-of-control kids is foreign to Scripture and indicates strange priorities. God is saying: How can you let someone propose to help you manage your life, when he can't even manage his own flesh and blood?

Set your sights high. No matter how successful you are in every other area of your life, if you fail as a parent you will be judged by many as a failure. "He's a nice man," you can hear them saying, "but did you see those rotten, deceitful kids?" Is that what you want?

But if you succeed in parenting champions, you will be considered a success by those around you, no matter how insignificant your other accomplishments may seem, no matter how many enemies you might have. This is the meaning of the Scripture that says: "Be wise, my son, and bring joy to my heart; then I can answer anyone who treats me with contempt" (Proverbs 27:11).

Before we discuss further how you can develop high expectations and put them into practice, let's stop for a minute and look at some modern "wisdom" that can shred your vision to pieces.

Emperors Without Clothes

It's time that someone said it: The emperor has no clothes.

William Kirk Kilpatrick has said it, in several books discussing the attempted mixture of Christianity and psychology, the so-called study of the mind. But few people seem to be listening, compared to the thousands or millions who wait for the stale crumbs that slide off the tilting table of modern psychology.

The real question is: When are you going to turn off your radio and stop *listening* to this rubbish? When are you going to "turn away from godless chatter and the opposing ideas of what is falsely called knowledge, which some have professed *and in so doing have wandered from the faith*" (1 Timothy 6:20–21, emphasis added)?

There are a few really serious offenders, people who offer up jargon for Biblical substance, "scientists of the mind" who believe the hopeless presupposition that man can figure out who man is and what makes him the way he is. But beyond these few, you can hear the language almost any hour of any day, from a whole host of people, even on so-called Christian radio and television.

The basic problem with some of these ministries is that they're founded on the idea that it's possible to synthesize Biblical Christianity and secular psychology. It's not that some of these teachers aren't lovely people who really want to help you, but they have a flaw in their basic direction. Principles learned in psychology have been studied in depth; then the attempt is made to accommodate portions of the Bible to these principles. In essence, a Christian veneer can be put on secular psychology, with all of its incompatibility with the Word of God.

Am I mad?

Yes, but I'm not crazy. Take, for example, an idea that is trumpeted by some of these folks over and over — the idea of self-esteem. First of all, you see the focus on *self* rather than on God. Low self-esteem is focusing on self, which makes it a form of pride; high self-esteem is focusing on self, which makes it a form of pride. We can either focus on God, His values, and His people, or we can focus on ourselves. There's no way Biblically to do both.

Second, you see the substitution of non-Biblical phrases for Biblical terms, for example, "high self-esteem" for "pride." This doesn't, of course, mean that we can only use words that are in the Bible. But it does mean that if a concept or thing exists, that we should call it what the Bible calls it. If the Bible speaks on something, we should think about it first as the Bible describes it.

These two areas highlight the fundamental difference between the Bible and psychology: The Bible focuses on God and uses God's words to describe life; psychology focuses on self and creates its own vocabulary to make its teachings sound modern and scientific and worthwhile, when they are very often none of those things and only confuse our thinking.

When talking about people, the best and only completely accurate text is the Bible. Beware of those who use terms not used by God! The new terms are often used to reduce moral values to animal-like responses or to cover up sin with a pretty title.

Consider how they divide a person up into stages. God calls people infants, children, men, or women, and also calls them by their family positions — son, daughter, father, mother. But what about the psychologists? They have toddlers and "terrible twos" and pubescence and adolescents and pre-teens and teenagers and on and on. Then these various groups get afflicted with hormonal attacks and premenstrual syndrome and menopause and mid-life crisis, and if they're not careful, with manic depression and paranoia and schizophrenia. I mean, we're talking *science* here, right?

Wrong.

In a film series, parents of adolescents were told that the one thing that dominated their children's lives more than anything else in their transition from child to adult was their hormones. But what does the Word of God say?

> But I see another law at work in the members of my body, waging war against the law of my mind and making me a prisoner of the law of sin at work within my members. What a wretched man I am! Who will rescue me from this body of death? Thanks be to God—through Jesus Christ our Lord! (Romans 7:23–25)

God calls it "the law of sin" and "this body of death." The psychologist calls it "hormones." Once you've fallen for the rubbish that your child is totally driven by physical forces outside of his or your control, it absolves you and your child from any real responsibility. And so the "logical" and "profound" advice given to parents of adolescents becomes: "Get them through it."

Some vision, isn't it? Is surviving the flesh the ringing call to victory given in Romans 8? God talks about saving us and sanctifying us and working His victorious Son's life through us every minute of our lives, if we'll only listen to Him and believe Him. There's no "getting through it" anywhere in the Bible. But there's a lot about giving in to the flesh on the one hand, and a lot about conquering sin through the power of God on the other.

And then where do the psychologists take us? Since our child can't control himself, they say it's useless to set high standards. In spite of the Bible's call to aim for perfection, we are told to lower our standards so our children won't become frustrated. Try to find a Biblical basis for *that* teaching! You can search for the rest of your life, and you'll never see God willing to lower His standards, which are the ones *you* ought to be operating under and never lowering for your children.

God does say that we shouldn't "exasperate" our children (Ephesians 6:4). But He goes on to say "*instead,* bring them up in the training and instruction of the Lord" (emphasis added). Do you see what this is saying? We exasperate our children when we *don't* set standards high, when we *don't* ground them, in spirit and in actual practice, "in the training and instruction of the Lord." The best way not to exasperate your children is to set standards high.

Donald Barr, in *World* (May 19, 1986), said: "Adolescence appears to be a relatively modern invention, and the romantic wretchedness of it appears to be more modern still; and it could be argued that many of those wretched, stewing identity crises occur precisely because adolescents seek to build their identities as adolescents instead of reaching out confidently for adult identities." Amen.

But psychologists have a hard time accepting that and go on to a logical though erroneous conclusion: Since we don't even know what adolescence is, and it's all controlled by hormones anyway, we can't set standards too high. We will then have to deal with the almost inevitable guilt that we are going to have when our children turn out to be a lot less than we (and God) wanted them to be. But never fear! There is an answer for you: It's not your fault!

Psychologists get very serious as they prepare us to accept our freedom from blame, which of course would be very bad for our self-esteem. They go right to the Biblical heart of the matter: "Train a child in the way he should go, and when he is old he will not turn from it" (Proverbs 22:6). This should bother them, because it speaks so very clearly about parents' responsibility and children's certain success. But then they found a spokesman who shared the "insight" that Proverbs aren't promises — they're "probabilities"!

Funny, that verse *sounded* like a promise. It sounded like God's Word, flawless and unchangeable. But no, now we are told it's just a probability. What about the rest of Proverbs? Is it just a probability that God "takes the upright into his confidence" (3:32)? Or that there will be "joy for those who promote peace" (12:20)? Or that if you "commit to the Lord whatever you do . . . your plans will succeed" (16:3)? Or that "pride goes before destruction" (16:18)? Or that "better is open rebuke than hidden love" (27:5)? Or that "a man of lowly spirit gains honor" (29:23)? And is it even a probability that "Every word of God is flawless" (30:5)?

All of these verses are from Proverbs. Which ones are probabilities, and which ones can we count on? Where does the *Bible* ever call the proverb in question a probability?

Don't listen to people who focus attention on self and flesh and use different terms from God's to get us, even unintentionally, to think about life differently from God. Don't listen, no matter how decent their motives. Don't listen, because what they're selling is a lie.

The emperor — psychology — has no clothes.

Dare to Be Different

It may be that most of the people you know, including the Christians, get most of their information from the world and its gurus or the parachurch and its gurus. It may be that you've gotten most of your information in the same way. The language that they use — well, it all seems so familiar and comfortable. Can you really break free and begin to look at your parenting ministry as a way to put yourself and your family on the cutting edge of dramatic and positive change?

You can.

You don't have to stay in the "knowledge rut," but you can have a family that makes the world look more like the King who is, in fact, its Lord.

Now, if you're like me at all, you don't remember very much about your childhood. One thought, however, has not escaped me since my eighth-grade teacher spent so much time pounding it into my head. She had a motto for life, and she intended that we adopt it as our motto as well. I don't know if anyone else was listening, but I heard her motto loud and clear: Dare to be different.

This statement says so much. Most of us know in our hearts that we're supposed to be different, that God made us to be unique, that we have a special life to lead and a special contribution to make. But somehow this idea gets chipped away by others, and frittered away by ourselves, until it's so fuzzy and dim that even reading about it as you are right now only brings back a faint sense of longing and a sorrowful sense that you've missed something very important.

Now, I am not talking about being different for the sake of being different; this approach belongs to the fanatic or fool. I am talking about being different for the sake of Christ. What I mean is the living of a different kind of life, a different quality of life, a wonderfully eccentric and noteworthy life — a life that leaves a deep mark on a granite-hard world.

Many people are bored with their own lives; given the inexpressibly wondrous gift of life, they waste it by just "putting in time." Days blend into other days, weeks into months, months into years — and all the while no mark is left, no special loves are grown, no joyous victories are won, none of God's enemies are challenged and vanquished. Another year spent, just like the last one. What a waste!

Everyone is chasing the "American Dream" of a good education, which gets you a good job, which gets you a lot of money and debt, which gets you a house and a car and two televisions. Everyone is chasing . . . nothing.

God didn't make you or your children for such a tasteless existence.

"Dare to be different." It tells us that being different has a cost. There's a risk here, and your children need to understand this very early and very clearly. If you've taught them to "continue in what [they] have learned and have become convinced of" (2 Timothy 3:14), then you must also teach them that "everyone who wants to live a godly life in Christ Jesus will be persecuted" (2 Timothy 3:12). This doesn't just mean physical torture or imprisonment; in our society, at least at the moment, this is not the most likely possibility. This persecution will come more often in the form of ridicule, rejection, and hatred. Later, perhaps, the torture and imprisonment will come.

How can you and your children be different? Try speaking the truth, in love but without compromise, to your family and friends. Do something nice for someone because they *haven't* asked you to. Turn off the television and read the Word of God for four hours tonight instead. Proclaim the Word of God at school or at work or in your neighborhood, and do it without embarrassment. Stop to help a total stranger who needs help but isn't expecting to get any. Make a picket sign and protest the slaughter of unborn babies, or pornography, or the fact that they won't let your God into their "public" schools (these things are *really* different and move you quickly into being a "fool for Christ").

There is an unlimited number of ways to be different for Christ. Some of these ways may be knocking at your door right now. Stop, listen, and write them down. Then do them.

By your example and exhortation, you'll be able to teach your child not only to *be* different for Christ, but also to *value* being different and to rejoice in any suffering or rejection that might come as a result.

You must first *teach* your children the meaning of this "dare to be different" business. Look with them at the life of Jesus or Paul; these men were so different, and so daring, that they startled their world as they drew the line of decision down its middle. Teach them about risk and courage — and that God's wisdom and power are behind it all, making the apparent human risk seem insignificant or nonexistent by comparison. And, of course, you must teach them about the good kinds of "different" and the rebellious, evil varieties; the difference between Jesus' revolution of truth and love and man's revolution *against* truth and love.

Teach your children the words of Robert Ingersoll: "It is a blessed thing that in every age someone has had the individuality enough and courage enough to stand by his own convictions."

Then teach them to *dare* to be different. Daring includes actions as well as thoughts and words. Talk is truly cheap; teach them to do, as they do it with you.

You're the best and most available teacher of Christian derring-do to your own children. But none of your teaching or instruction will mean anything if they don't see you doing something. Nothing discussed here will work unless you dare to be different yourself. It's just too unlikely that your children will dare to be or do *anything* if you won't.

So dare to be different.

There's nothing like it.

Expectant Parents

How old should your child be before you begin to challenge him to deal in a godly and creative way with the issues facing him in the world in which he lives?

While we're at it, how old should *you* be before you start doing these things?

If you are old enough to read, you're old enough. In fact, you're several years past old enough. You should be finding yourself challenged by the Holy Spirit daily, and into the Word frequently enough

that you're finding godly and creative answers to the problems and opportunities that are finding their way into your life.

One of those opportunities is the child—already conceived and
shampooing himself with tuna fish or still a hoped-for blessing from
God—that prompted you to pick up this book. Do I mean that you're
supposed to challenge this child to use the prompting of the Spirit and
the guidance of the Word to find godly and creative answers for his life?

You bet I do. But first, we have to talk about a couple of viewpoint
problems.

The first mistaken belief when considering a question like this is that
you're the one who creates your child's inquisitiveness. The truth is, he
was born with more of it than you may now have because adults didn't
recognized this truth when *you* were a child. The main problem you will
have is how to avoid killing inquisitiveness in your child. You should try
to nurture it; you may be living proof that it's easily destroyed. But if
you can't keep from preaching spirit-crushing, un-Biblical rules and restrictions all the time, turn the reins over to someone else.

Wait a minute! There *isn't* anyone else. I guess that means you're
going to have to clean up your act.

The second unspoken, but persistent, belief is that children don't get
real spirits until puberty. We call children who are two, three, and even
four or five years of age "babies"; from then until they're twelve or
thirteen we dub them "youngsters"; and after this we christen them with
the nebulous title of "teenagers." The implication is always there that
they're somehow less than real people, that we need to do their thinking
for them, that their understanding can't help being immature.

Baloney.

I've heard a three-year-old girl give a better defense than many
adults for the existence of God. I've heard a five-year-old boy define the
virtue of peace in a way that would shame any world leader. It's not that
these children don't know enough, or that the world is too complex. The
fact is, they often have better answers to the important questions than all
of us "sophisticated" older people put together.

The amazing thing isn't that children can think and act in a godly
and creative way or see profound truths or ask piercing questions. The
amazing thing is that there are still some older people who can do these
things! Many of us were given pat, quasi-Biblical answers, or no answers at all to our questions. When the answers were Biblical, they were

all too often given without meaning and power. If you're stirred to have more for yourself, as an individual and as a parent, it's there. You just have to be enough of a child to want it.

And so I've drawn one major conclusion about involving children in deep discussions: Do it fast and do it early. The older they are before you start challenging them to believe, the harder it will be to get these potential powerhouses in the habit of thinking about why they believe these things. Whether they've already had part of their originality and inquisitiveness wiped out or you just haven't found the way to nurture it yet, they need encouragement. Someone's going to challenge your child — why not you?

I'll bet you know some adults who don't have any originality or inquisitiveness. God and His Word and His world have become boring to them — by their past training and by their own empty choices.

So what must you do? First, in your own spirit you should start questioning things early, keep at it relentlessly with God's strength, and finish strong. You need the determination of the tortoise more than the speed of the hare to aid you in your search for the truth, since a powerful champion for the Lord is built up daily, in the little things of life as well as the spectacular. Your children need you to run your race well. It's by watching you that they'll learn how and why to run, in what direction, for how long, and what to do if they fall down.

After you begin running a good race, you should challenge them to run the kind of race that you're running.

You don't have the right to challenge them to run any harder than that.

The Joneses

At any time, one of the easiest things for a parent to do is to compare his children with each other or with other people's kids. Satan would love for you to do this because it harms your goal of parenting champions.

As you begin to challenge your children, even at a young age, to be decently different and to choose wisdom over knowledge or popularity, you may be tempted to make comparisons with other families. These comparisons can be either positive ("our son isn't as godly as their son") or negative ("no one else's children are godly, so I guess we can't expect too much"). Don't make comparisons! According to Scripture, if you do this you are *not wise* (see 2 Corinthians 10:12).

When I speak of the importance of high expectations, I am not talking about a competition among Christians. I am talking about a competition that each Christian participates in alone: the running of his own race in order to get the prize (see 1 Corinthians 9:24–27). The higher the prize sought, the more strict training is required to win it. It doesn't matter if the runner beats everyone else but doesn't "run in such a way as to get the prize." You should want each of your children to run his or her own best race.

And it's not a race of knowledge and credentials; it's a race of godly wisdom and character. God's wisdom isn't a matter of what you know, although knowing true things about life is very important. It's a matter of what you're *like:* "Who is wise and understanding among you? Let him show it by his good life, by deeds done in the humility that comes from wisdom" (James 3:13).

Nothing is more plentiful in some churches today than children who have lots of Bible knowledge and "God words," and little or no character. In many of their lives, there simply aren't any "deeds done in the humility that comes from wisdom." If you fall for the veneer of knowledge and wholesomeness, and don't look for the character, you're a foolish parent who deserves the foolish children who will bring you grief.

This is the danger of the "Bible knowledge" competitions in all of their varied forms (e.g. Bible bowls, teams challenging teams, sword drills). It's an opportunity for one person or group to show how much they know as they try to outdo one another and show off their "vast" knowledge. Even at-home Bible games can degenerate into a board game mentality. When knowledge becomes a way to display how special you are, it's the wrong answer and must be abandoned forthwith.

God's wisdom is "first of all pure; then peace loving, considerate, submissive, full of mercy and good fruit, impartial and sincere" (James 3:17). Truly wise people don't try to amaze other believers with exhibitions of knowledge. Don't let your children become involved with these modern Christian aberrations.

Comparisons with others on the downward side can be devastating. If you only expect what you see in the majority of families around you, you're in for a big disappointment. Most families today are *drowning.* They don't have any answers, and they don't even know where to find them. To settle for the norm today is to settle for "getting by." It's like using the Mafia's organization as a pattern for your new business.

So pray for the Joneses.

But don't try to keep up with them.

Truth and Consequences

Your mission is to build godly wisdom and character into otherwise sinning lumps of rebelliousness known as *children*. It's absolutely crucial that you help your children see the stunning victory that awaits a life of faith, and the smashing defeat that awaits the life of self.

"Truth or Consequences" was a popular old television game show. We must not have watched too closely, however, because we don't seem to understand the consequences of missing the truth. And we also don't understand the consequences, the value, of having a clear picture of the truth.

It's costing us, and our descendants, a free and peaceful future.

We live in a day when there are so many horrible consequences to so many horrible ideas that the truth doesn't even seem to be an important factor anymore. We read and watch and believe almost totally worthless newspapers, magazines, radio and television programs, and "authoritative" studies. We swallow this junk every day while our Bibles collect dust. Folks, this stuff isn't wrong because it's secular or humanistic or any other fancy philosophy; it's wrong because it's *wrong*.

"Now," you might be saying, "that sounds pretty simplistic to me." Christian, you'd better *get* pretty simplistic fast. The lying juggernaut is wanting to roll over you and your children right now, and only a clear and simple understanding of the truth is going to keep you from pancake status. Paul said, "For we are not unaware of [Satan's] schemes" (2 Corinthians 2:11); but the way most Christians are acting, it would be more accurate to say that we are unaware of both Satan *and* his schemes.

You must learn — and then teach your children to recognize — the underlying principle in each situation that you and they encounter. The first thing you need to find is God's definition and description of the problem. You can't solve the problem — you can't even *understand* the problem — unless you're looking at it from God's perspective. And then you want to look for God's solution, outlined in His Word and in your heart, and begin to apply it in your family and church.

An example from the culture and age in which we live will illustrate the point. Everyone is now beginning to recognize the problem of teenage pregnancies. Cover stories in national magazines talk about the horrors of "children having children" and concern about the "social fabric" being torn to pieces. They come to you with an "obvious" statement of "truth": "Don't you agree that we have a devastating problem with all of these teenage pregnancies?"

And we are so dumb that we just sit back and nod our heads in mindless agreement. What's the *matter* with Christians in this society? Are we so far removed from God and His truth that we can't see the forest *or* the trees? If we agree with the world's definition of truth, will we be able to live with its consequences?

Don't we see the problem with their false definition of the problem? If the problem is teenage pregnancies — in other words, if the problem is *babies* — then the solution will involve preventing or getting rid of babies. If the root problem is the lack of knowledge about how to eliminate babies, then their solution will be more sex education, earlier sex education, contraceptives freely available and stashed in the desks, and more counseling to handle the "misses." Get rid of pregnancies — get rid of babies — they say, and you can eliminate the horrible results of the problem: child abuse, limits on career and economic status, poverty, and of course the staggering financial costs to the nation.

If they have the correct understanding of the problem and its solution, then it's only logical that they'll look at Christians who oppose sex education, birth control, and abortion as obstacles to the solution. Christians with moral absolutes will perhaps be viewed in the final analysis as the major cause of the whole problem. According to many articles and "letters to the editor," we already are.

But God looks at the problem quite a bit differently. In His Word He's relentlessly clear that the problem is sin, specifically in this case, the sin of fornication. Premarital sex. Promiscuity. There is a God and He does have absolutes, and His absolute with regard to sexual relations, outside of marriage, is chastity and holiness and self-control — not birth control and abortion and herpes tests. And babies are *never* a problem in the Word of God; it's we adults who are the problem when we violate His absolutes or allow our children to do so.

The root problem that's causing teenage pregnancies isn't too little sex education or availability of birth control and abortion; it's too *much* of these things and too little training in godliness and holiness. If we address the problem of teenage pregnancies with more of the same garbage that the world has been cramming down our throats, then the result will be more sin, more degenerate behavior earlier, and more teenage pregnancies. But if we address the real problem, the problem of sin, with more training in holiness, then the result will be less sin, less fornication, less disease, fewer broken lives, less child abuse, fewer abortions — and fewer teenage pregnancies, except for those teenagers who are married.

As for the limits on career and economic status, it's fair to say that God puts no value on these phony values. These things are more likely to be obstacles to godliness than they are a pathway to heaven. Contrary to the teaching of the overpopulation gurus, children in Scripture never cause poverty; in fact, children are wealth, a rich blessing from the Lord. Poverty is a result of the *Fall,* not of teenage pregnancies. And as for the costs to the nation, suffice it to say that the nation's increased expenditures on sex education, birth control, and abortion have been accompanied by a dramatic *increase* in promiscuity, fornication, teenage pregnancies, child abuse, and family collapse.

Someday, they'll develop a final solution to the problem that they themselves have caused, in order to save their precious money. Their solution may involve ideas and methods so horrible that to imagine them would make even the degenerate in our day shudder.

Get you and your children back into the basics of God's truth, so that together you'll be able to see the fundamental absolutes and principles that are *really* governing life and causing the consequences that we see and experience. Don't rely on your own common sense or on the world's common foolishness. Keep the lies out of your thinking, even the small lies, for as Paul said, "A little yeast works through the whole batch of dough" (1 Corinthians 5:6).

James Madison once reminded us of a great way to relate truth and consequences. In speaking of a group of men who went into action at the earliest opportunity, when they saw terrible results in the distance, he said that "They saw all the consequences in the principle, and they avoided the consequences by denying the principle."

We and our children must deny the principles of this evil age and focus all of our attention on the true principles of the Word of God. If we do, the positive consequences will reverberate through generation after generation and will bless countless people, including searching teenagers, for decades to come.

Quintessence: Is He the Best, or Isn't He?

As soon as we begin to set our sights on the glorious goal of parenting a champion and begin to understand the critical need for high expectations, an important question begins to crowd into our minds: Can he really be the very best that God intended him to be?

Yes, he can. Your child can be the quintessential Christian champion. And here's more. *You* can be, too.

What on earth is that? *Quintessence* is "the essence of a thing in its most concentrated form . . . The most typical example; the consummate instance of a quality." People should be able to look at each one of us and our children and say, "Yeah . . . so *that's* a Christian! Christ just shines through him. What joy and courage!" Christ fully reflected the Father. We are supposed to fully reflect Christ. If Jesus was a champion, and we are supposed to walk as Jesus did, how can we settle for anything less?

Some may think I'm talking about lifting ourselves up, about things that could lead to pride. Nothing could be further from the truth. I'm talking about living a life that embodies Christian character in its most concentrated form. I'm talking about living a life in such a way that people sit up and take notice — of our Father and our family and the principles that undergird our lives.

In fact, we aren't being honest if we won't admit that we want our children to live special lives. It's the most natural thing in the world to want our children to be one of the best at what they are and do. We want them to have a tremendous impact on their world, and we desire that they live out their lives in an excellent way.

In fact, this desire is more than natural for the godly Christian; it's *super*natural. God desires godly offspring, and we, because we are made in His image, desire the same thing. We want godly offspring. We want the very best. Pride could get in here, but there's a desire that's right, a hope for children who "shine like stars in the universe" (Philippians 2:15).

Paul goes on to say that he wants his readers to be this kind of believer so that he can "boast on the day of Christ that [he] did not run or labor for nothing" (v. 16). Paul didn't boast about himself, but he *did* boast about the fruits of his labors, about the Christians who were becoming Christian champions. We have got to get past this false humility that denies some basic scriptural truths: that we're in a race to win the prize, and that this reward comes as a result of our work in Christ's strength for others.

Listen to Paul: "For what is our hope, our joy, or the crown in which we will glory in the presence of our Lord Jesus when he comes? Is it not you? Indeed, you are our glory and joy" (1 Thessalonians 2:19–20). If it was good enough for Paul, it should be good enough for us, especially when we are talking about our own flesh and blood. We should want our children to be the very best that they can be and should look forward to the day when we can glory in them in the very presence of the Lord Jesus when He comes. What an exciting thought!

This joy of glorying in the success of another was brought home to me by my sister Patty when she was a little girl and I had gone off to college. I didn't think about her relating to what I was doing at all, until one day I received a note from her. "I told my friends that my big brother went to college," she wrote, "and I was acting big about you to them." Some of her feelings might have been childish, of course, but the idea was pretty basic: This person belongs to me — and isn't he special!

Don't deny the excitement of this glorious future. Look forward to it. *Plan* for it.

Often, though, when we tell ourselves and others that we want children who'll reach the pinnacle of Christian joy, peace, satisfaction, wisdom, and power, we start focusing on things. We think of picking the right schools, the right friends, the right career or vocation, the right marriage partner, the right church. Of course these things are important, even crucial; but our children will never reach the epitome of excellence unless we give them the one thing that is guaranteed to bring them honor in all of these areas for the rest of their lives, right up to the time that we get to show them off to Jesus.

And what is that one thing? For your child to be a quintessential Christian — one whose life represents the life of Christ in an undeniable manner, one that changes those around it by its very presence — you must work to give your child a lowly spirit.

What? A lowly spirit? Am I kidding? No, I'm not kidding. More importantly, God isn't kidding. He says, "A man's pride brings him low, but a man of lowly spirit gains honor" (Proverbs 29:23). The way to honor — so much deeper and longer lasting than fame — is to cultivate and cherish a lowly spirit.

The first thing that's pretty easy to see here is that this is the opposite of what most parents try to do to get their children ahead. We want to have children who are A+ students at one of the "name" schools (Christian or otherwise); whose friends all make Mother Teresa look nasty and stingy by comparison; who have multiple degrees in law, medicine, engineering, and Bible and who will head a worldwide missionary organization while running a Christian school and sitting on the boards of several major corporations; whose marriage partners do everything perfectly but always seek and follow our counsel; and who are active in twenty activities in a church that is totally uncompromising and fast-growing (two ideas that today might be mutually exclusive).

All of these things may be just as good as they are unlikely. But the point is, this isn't the pathway to honor. This *looks* like the pathway to honor, but it isn't. The pathway to honor — to God joyfully lifting you and your children up — is a lowly spirit.

One of the reasons that this can sound like such a strange idea is that we parents don't even know what a lowly spirit is. We can, perhaps, almost picture Jesus as a person of lowly spirit, but we have a hard time escaping the idea that that was His *job*. Being lowly was part of being the Savior, and now that's done and we can all get on with our lives. We too easily equate being lowly in spirit with being a doormat.

But God says that we are all to be like Jesus, which means, among other things, to be lowly in spirit.

There are two things that a lowly spirit is not. The first is that a lowly spirit isn't proud. The way you work on this with your children is to let them know that pride is disgusting to God and disgusting to you. You need to make them understand that pride in word or action will not be tolerated by God or by you. You must listen and watch closely for any signs of pride, and when they come up, you must move into action.

But being without overt pride isn't necessarily the same as being lowly in spirit. We can pound overt pride out of their lives, but leave the pride itself within, waiting to come out in self-glorification or self-gratification later. We need to give our children a full understanding of what it means to "have the mind of Christ" (1 Corinthians 2:16). We need them to realize how great God is, how small they are, and how much God will bless them and use them if they will only get themselves out of the way. We need to drill into them how horrible their lives will be if they try to do anything in their own strength. We need to convince them that they must only move in the light of His presence.

Secondly, a lowly spirit isn't a *beaten* spirit. We want to work the pride out while we work godly humility and gentleness in, but we never want to beat the pride out while we leave only worthlessness and bitterness in. There are already too many beaten Christians and way too many proud Christians. Neither is going to be blessed, and neither is going to gain honor.

So how do we learn to have a lowly spirit? Many Christians have lived a long time without one, and hidden pride can be so very hard to detect. Here are some suggestions: First, have a quiet time with your Lord and ask Him to help you; second, have a quiet time with your spouse and ask him or her to help you; and third, have a quiet time with your spiritual shepherd and ask him to help you. The part of you that doesn't want to do these things is the pride part.

One final thought: Let your children be the godliest "them" that they can possibly be, not the godliest "you" that they can possibly mimic. Let them use you as an example of a developing lowly spirit, but even in that, let *you* only be an arrow pointing toward the Master.

Is your child the best, or isn't he? That's really the wrong question.

The right question is: Is he lowly enough in spirit to be called great by Almighty God (see Isaiah 66:2)?

Crowns of Splendor

We all give our children gifts, but we should note this: A child can't receive anything greater than wisdom. It's a simple fact and one which should lead us to make their getting of wisdom a major priority. You should want nothing less than a little Solomon.

Now, you can't *make* a child be wise. Children's hearts must deal with or avoid God directly; the ultimate responsibility for this is out of your hands. You aren't a mediator between God and your children, because Christ already has that job. All you can do is make the choice for them as simple as possible. You want to deal with them in such a way that each one of them can say with Solomon: "When I was a boy in my father's house . . . he taught me and said, 'Lay hold of my words with all your heart. . . . Wisdom is supreme, therefore get wisdom. Though it cost all you have, get understanding'" (Proverbs 4:3–7).

The cost, to you as a parent, of getting wisdom is your time. You must talk and live these words *constantly,* so that your children will accept this manner of life as *normal.* Sunday school won't give them wisdom without a lot of real-world supplement. They must be immersed in wisdom, so that their manner of thinking and speaking flows in these deep channels.

In short, they must stop speaking English and start speaking wisdom.

Obviously they'll have a hard time speaking wisdom with you if wisdom is only in *your* heart and head and not in theirs. This special language has to be part of their nature, too; but you must understand that it'll take their time to learn it, and Satan will oppose their education in every possible way. This evil creature who speaks only in lies hates wisdom — not the least reason being that he will never again understand your child once this little one begins speaking it.

This process of learning wisdom must certainly start with learning the words. The vocabulary of wisdom is Scripture, and every child should be encouraged to read or listen to massive chunks of real Scripture, as opposed to the abridged and remedial versions that are written for children, as though their spirits were handicapped. They should be taught to memorize, particularly passages that have special meaning to them. Don't fall for the trap that general memorization alone is sufficient. All Scripture doesn't have the same impact on you at any given point in time. It doesn't for your children either.

The book of Proverbs is especially useful for promoting this wisdom. We have established wisdom charts in our home to encourage this. These can be homemade or store-bought, monthly calendars that contain a verse or two of Scripture, some personal thoughts of the child, and some interesting art work. Each day of wisdom reading or listening earns a sticker; a whole month earns dinner out for the family (which gives all of us incentive for the child to get wisdom) or some other tangible reward. These charts are posted in the kitchen and explained to any visitors, preferably within earshot of the child.

It's crucial that you get this wisdom into their heads when they're *little*. These little ones can learn English, which can take an immigrant adult years to master. Better that your children learn the language of wisdom even more than English.

It's important even for little children to meditate on God's Word in private. I recorded Proverbs for our children and explained the verses as I went (I think it's best if you dads do at least some of the recording, since you're the spiritual head of your family). My wife recorded the Psalms. Store-bought tapes are okay, too, but there's value in it being your voice with your instruction. It's really exciting to see a little one huddled up next to his tape recorder and soaking up God's Word.

More is needed. This wisdom must be related to the child's world — to school, peers, world events, sorrows, joys, or anything that's covered by their wisdom vocabulary. They must see how wisdom works and how foolishness works. They must learn to differentiate between short-term and long-term effects and to know that ultimately, wisdom is rewarded and foolishness brings on its own built-in destruction. You must teach them this, quickly but surely.

Still more is needed. True wisdom goes beyond the head and into the heart, and starts with a holy fear of the Lord God Almighty. Too many of us miss teaching this. We talk a lot about God's love and don't stress the importance, the *practical* importance, of His justice. We have to give our children an honest, realistic, down-to-earth appreciation of the fact that they're in the constant and unavoidable presence of a God who will judge them with perfect and inarguable justice.

In Biblical times, Jewish families had a scroll containing Scripture placed in an insert (called a *mezuzah*) that was seen every time anyone entered the house. Only one word could be seen through a cutout in the insert: *Shaddai*. Almighty. The One who is without equal. The sovereign and unchallengeable God.

It's too easy for us to teach our children about a soft, puny, milk-toast God who really isn't paying close attention to what's going on down here. A God who loves us "just the way we are," even if the way we are is spitting in His face and bringing disgrace to His name. The real God isn't like that. A little reverent awe around your house is a must. A lot of it will produce champions. Scripture tells us that true and godly wisdom begins with this basic attitude toward God.

This respect and reverence makes way for a deep and genuine love of God. Only when your child appreciates what God expects and what God hates, and understands God's perfect justice that grinds so very fine, can he really begin to appreciate God for not pouring out heavenly wrath and displeasure right on his head. Jesus reminded us that he who is forgiven of much will be more grateful and loving than he who is forgiven of little (see Luke 7:47).

The child who understands God's close monitoring and pure standards will have a much better chance of knowing how much he's been forgiven. He'll know that "to fear the LORD is to hate evil" (Proverbs 8:13); and he'll have the valuable possession of the truth that "the fear of the LORD is a fountain of life, turning a man from the snares of death" (Proverbs 14:27).

When a child has this deeper beginning to his relationship with the Lord, then he can truly love God with a devotion that involves the child's whole being, not the phony-baloney head love that they learn from slick Christian books and messages. Your child has to know that God's wisdom is good stuff, and he has to be able to say to God, "I rejoice in your promise like one who finds great spoil" (Psalms 119:162).

They can learn about this from your spirit as you are controlled by the Holy Spirit. They will only learn this, of course, if they choose to know, but you have to help them by talking and living the holy language of Wisdom. The payoff is a big one for your children, if they get wisdom: "Esteem her, and she will exalt you; embrace her, and she will honor you. She will set a garland of grace on your head and present you with a crown of splendor" (Proverbs 4:8–9).

I don't know exactly what this crown is, but it sounds mighty fine.

I've got an order in for four.

Conclusion

Aim for perfection in your own life and in your parenting. Don't let anyone talk you into lowering your sights. Be a family that dares to be different and that expects new and great things from God. Teach your children to make the choice of godliness and to run their own race for God and not in competition with others. Show them that every decision has consequences that relate directly to God's truth. Finally, teach your child to be like Jesus and walk with a lowly spirit and with wisdom. If you do these things, you will put your own order in for "crowns of splendor."

3

EXCELLENT COMMUNICATION: CRAWL INTO A HEART

Do not let any unwholesome talk come out of your mouths, but only what is helpful for building others up according to their needs, that it may benefit those who listen.

(Ephesians 4:29)

You've got to crawl inside your children's hearts. And it can be a very challenging journey.

In the first place, God reminds us how deep and potentially impenetrable a heart can be: "Each heart knows its own bitterness, and no one else can share its joy" (Proverbs 14:10). Without a balance, this could be pretty discouraging. But God also says, "Rejoice with those who rejoice; mourn with those who mourn" (Romans 12:15).

In the second place, it's too easy to miss the golden opportunities our children present. One way is by just not being there. My own father had much to share with his five children, but he couldn't because he was working two jobs, seven days a week. Too many fathers—and now mothers—are just not there most of the time. They would be better off living in a shack and eating bread and water, if that would only allow them the time to crawl inside a heart.

In the third place, the time you do have together can be swallowed up by activities and idle chit-chat about the miscellaneous details of everyday life. Now, we do have to talk about the details — meals, clothes, cleaning up, baths, chores — but we can't allow these things to keep us on the outside of a heart. And as soon as activities start eliminating family meals and sharing times, it's time to eliminate the intruders.

Finally, we can miss the boat if we aren't prepared to take advantage of the opportunities that God provides. God is interested in deep relationships, but we have to pay attention.

The purpose of this chapter is to provide some help for you in your effort to crawl inside your children's hearts. If you understand that it's a tough assignment, and are willing to put in the time and take out the chit-chat and intrusions, perhaps together we can find some ways to get you on the inside.

Where you belong.

Communicate the Vision

If you want a champion, the words you use must constantly elevate your child's mind and heart. Your child needs to be on the high ground, and you can either help him get there or keep him away, build him up or tear him down. Your words can be an encouragement to be victorious or reckless weapons that "pierce like a sword" (Proverbs 12:18).

Where are your words taking your children?

Start thinking and talking like a godly poet. Think big thoughts about your children — where they are, where they can be — and then find a memorable way to say them. I've given you a small example in the front of this book on the Dedication page. You can probably do better than that with your loved ones, if you'll only try.

Most of us can remember a special comment that someone important to us made, a comment that gave us an exciting new idea about ourselves, an insight or encouragement that seems as crystal clear as it did the day we first heard it. Sometimes, if he or she wasn't important *before* the comment was made, that changed *after* we heard what they had to say! This ought to prove to us how crucial words are. Wouldn't it be something if your children had a long list of special things you said to think back on, even after you've gone?

I can remember a grade-school teacher who told me that I was going to accomplish something special; it helped me to believe my life was actually worth something. I recall a comment that a stranger made to me in a restaurant, when he came over to tell me I had a gift for speaking; whether true or not, it encouraged me that I could actually do something worthwhile from a pulpit or platform. And I am still writing music and have a long-term vision about it, even though I've never had any of it published or professionally recorded, in part because many years ago a woman told me that she thought people would still be singing some of it in fifty years.

Your comments *can* plant or nurture a vision.

And on the other hand, how many of us are carrying around a *crusher* — a brutal, devastating comment that made us rethink our whole value as a person? I have some of those; my guess is that you do, too. Too many people have been told that they're stupid or worthless or undesirable. Sometimes it's done under the guise of being "honest."

God save us from that kind of "honesty"!

Whether the memorable comment was positive or negative, the person may not have even known what effect their statement was having. This tells us two things: First, how closely we have to guard every word; and second, how much better we should be able to do if we actually *plan* to make memorable comments of the positive variety.

Guarding and Planning Your Words

It's a very good thing for parents to involve their children in discussions about family budgeting and finances — it helps to train them in an important area; it teaches them that money doesn't grow on trees; it can give them a way to be responsible in helping to trim one budget area (e.g., the light bill) so more can be spent elsewhere (e.g., the poor). If you're not already doing this, I encourage you to plan with your spouse and make it a part of the menu at dinner from time to time.

But there are so many ways for you to say something that will make your children feel that they're a burden: "I can't believe those doctor and dentist bills!"; "Can you believe the school is raising tuition again?"; "We'll never get ahead with all these expenses!"; "I think I'm going to have to get a second job to support this bunch." Or how about this one, made kiddingly at dinner to a guest: "Just look at the way our little guy eats! I'm going to have to get a loan to pay for his food when he's a teenager!"

Picture yourself at age eighty. And picture this comment: "I don't know how we'll ever get ahead with having to take care of Dad."

Doesn't sound so hot, does it?

And what about the planning of memorable words? The first one you should start with is the communication of your vision of parenting a champion to your child. You don't want to keep that to yourself, as if it's some kind of big secret. Let him know where you want him to be, *who* you want him to be.

This *doesn't* mean you put a lot of pressure on your child to be something that he isn't able to be. You want him to be the best that he can be in everything, but you don't want to push for more. That can and will discourage him. If math and science don't register, don't push him to be a nuclear physicist. If he's done as well as he can and gets a B, remember that B stands for "Bully for you!"

But all children can and should be pushed to be godly, spiritual champions. Nobody who has the Holy Spirit is unqualified here. Nobody needs to get a B in making Jesus known as the Lord of life, one's own as well as all of life. Let your children know that God and you are negotiable on the details of life, but not on the vision "that you may be filled to the measure of all the fullness of God" (Ephesians 3:19).

This may seem beyond your own abilities. That's because it is. Certainly, attempting to parent a champion is no place for the faint of heart. But remember, you're not going to do this in your own strength. Without God's wisdom and power, you're in deep trouble. But with His wisdom and power, which He has promised over and over to give us in abundance, you can accomplish this.

God *wants* you to parent champions. He's your Papa. He'll help you.

Use Your Own Life

Anyone who speaks, teaches, or preaches knows the value of illustrations and examples to highlight the point he's trying to make.

You can spend a lot of time searching other people's lives to find examples to use in your communication with others. This is true with your children as well. They need to know the rock-solid reality of the Word of God and how it always proves itself out in practice. Biographies, news items, articles can all be used in your effort to communicate truth to your children.

But you want to do more than communicate truth.

You want to crawl inside a heart.

The place to start is not out there. It's right inside your own heart. Nothing will be more powerful in reaching inside the citadel of another heart than using your own experiences, feelings, and memories to reach inside and touch those same things inside your child's heart. It's so personal and rich and deep — it's almost guaranteed to be effective.

It sounds easier than it is, however, because most of us are so reluctant to be transparent. We are afraid that somehow being vulnerable will allow our children to see that we are not a bastion of perfection. Well, we usually *haven't* been a bastion of perfection, so we might as well give up the charade and get it out in the open. Be transparent. Be vulnerable.

Crawl inside a heart.

The Good and the Bad

Tell them about mistakes you've made, and what you've learned, and how God brought you through onto higher ground. Tell them what things hurt you and what things make you laugh and cry, and why you think it's so. Share the good memories of days gone by, the things that God has done for you, the distinct recollections of when God unmistakably laid His hand on your life. Let them see that you have a heart of flesh and not a heart of stone (see Ezekiel 11:19).

Why is this so effective? For one thing, it's so deep and intimate it has to have impact. For another, "parents are the pride of their children" (Proverbs 17:6), so what you were and are is important to them — it really is! And finally, you have to understand that your children are yours by *design.* Your life and experiences and feelings and memories are going to impact your children in ways that may reach very few others. Your life is, in some grand and glorious way, bound up with your children's, with an unseen, but eternal, bond.

Some cautions are in order. First, don't wallow around in the past (see Ecclesiastes 5:20). That won't do you or your children any good.

Second, don't share certain things at all (see 1 Corinthians 14:20). You know in your own heart what I mean; some things just need to be forgotten, washed away forever by the blood of the Lamb. Third, don't share all of the details about things that you do share, and be careful how you present the details that you do bring into the open (see Ecclesiastes 8:5). Finally, don't glorify or "puff up" your past—"Do not say, 'Why were the old days better than these?' For it is not wise to ask such questions" (Ecclesiastes 7:10).

Three-Minute Truths

One thing that can keep you from being effective in this area is the feeling that you've got to have a long conversation in order to get your hearts to touch. Don't let Satan lay that one on you, not even when you're out on an extended time together. This feeling of "lots or nothing at all" can devastate you in your spiritual life in many areas—Bible study, prayer, or writing a note to a friend. Parent-child communication is no exception. It doesn't have to be a big deal in order to be effective. Just three minutes can be plenty, if it's the right three minutes.

One of the worst things we can give our children is a sense that their early lives are disposable, that those years are to just be enjoyed and spent on themselves. Nothing can seem further away to our children than old age and death, and our culture does everything it can to deny those twin realities. Too many Christian parents fall into this trap and let their children exist in a kind of irresponsible fantasyland, which, among other things, can be a playground for the devil.

But I want my children to understand the brevity of life, the urgency of running a good race all the way through, and how things come full circle, with the weak becoming strong and then becoming weak again (see Proverbs 20:29). I want them to have a sense of passing time, of generations coming and then fading away, of the intimate connection they have with their own older years.

I could say all of those things to my children in so many words. But there's no better way than to look down the road with them with just a simple comment. Here's a few examples:

- "You know, honey, I got to carry you in from the car last night and tuck you into bed. When I'm older and fall asleep in the car, will you carry me in and tuck me into bed?"

- "Sweetheart, I really enjoy cutting your meat for you. I think a day might come when you'll have to cut mine. Will you do that?"

- "Do you enjoy it when I read you a bedtime story? You know, some day many years from now we may trade places, and I might be looking forward to your reading me a story at bedtime."

These are pretty humbling thoughts and there's more truth to them than many of us are willing to admit. Wait until you see the looks you get from your children when you share thoughts like these. They won't laugh at you—they'll esteem you all the more, just like God does: "This is the one I esteem: he who is humble and contrite in spirit, and trembles at my word" (Isaiah 66:2).

Spend Time Together

Being successful in crawling inside a heart means that you're going to have to be there for the little times, the everyday happenings and comments. The most important thing about quantity time is not that you fill up the whole thing with conversation; the most important thing is that you're there to listen and observe and share life together. And then, as God and circumstances lead, spend a few minutes crawling into a heart. You may need four hours of quantity time to get the three minutes of quality. If you're only there for an hour of quantity time, you may not get any quality time at all.

Try to have some comments or questions ready for when these quality times occur. These can come from your own reading and learning—"We only see one side of that pretty moon; I wonder why God designed it that way?"—to observing his or her interests—"I think it's neat how you like to work with wood; I wonder why Jesus was a carpenter instead of something else?" Simple thoughts and simple questions.

Be there to ask them.

Datings and Outings

No matter how much other quantity and quality time you try to have with your children at home, you need to consider establishing a practice with each of your children that will allow your relationship to grow deeper.

Having a regular date or outing with each of your children separately is one of the most effective methods of discipling available to parents, and yet I personally know of few other parents who are doing it. Team, this is the easiest thing that you will ever do. It's even *fun*, as long as you don't trip over your own seriousness.

People have asked me at what age this activity should be started. I was twenty-seven, so that certainly isn't too young. (Oh, and my oldest daughter was two and a half.) We talked about it for several days ahead of time, but I wasn't sure if she knew what we were going to do, or even what we were talking about (in fact, *I* wasn't real sure about any of this either). I came home to find that she'd insisted on dressing up in her Sunday finest "for Daddy," and we went out and had the time of our lives.

We have "suffered" through this fun and growing together on a monthly basis ever since. We have missed a few, but we are sorry when we have missed one and always try to make it a priority. After all these years, this daughter has developed a very interesting philosophy: Since it's natural to talk about problems and challenges with me, she thinks that only a fool wouldn't ask her own dad for advice or help.

You know what? She's right.

This whole thing has worked so well that I also do it with my oldest son, who was about the same age that my daughter was when we started (I was over thirty by then). He insists that we call these times *outings* instead of dates, but the procedure — and the payoff — is the same. My wife used to have a regular date with one while I had an outing with the other. Now that we have a second son on the program and another daughter getting ready, the details have gotten a little stickier, but we'll always try to find a way. It's just too important.

These times are ready-made treasures to stuff in *both* of your pockets. This idea will work for you with other people as well; I've used it as my primary means of discipling high-school aged guys and girls for many years.

What you do isn't as important as the fact that you're doing it together, but here are some ideas:

- Go for a walk (preferably a long one).

- Go to dinner (hot dogs are fine — it doesn't have to be expensive).

- Go to the movies or theater or ballet or concert or ball game or museum, and scan the papers to see about other activities — many of them free (and make sure you allow time over dessert afterward to have that important thing known as *discussion*).

- Go window shopping.

- Go shopping for something for someone whom you both love.

- Make or buy a dinner for an older person or shut-in.

- Go on a picnic.

- Build or make a project together.

Don't think about this dating idea. Don't talk about it, either. Just do it. Tonight wouldn't be too soon to start. Surprise your child with a date now, and maybe on some far-off day she or he won't surprise *you* with one. You'll know about it well in advance, and it will only be with your advance approval.

It may be so natural that they might even invite *you* along.

Send Notes

One final thought that could help: Send your own children notes in the mail — not only when you're on trips, Dad, but just when you're at work. Write these notes when things are quiet and you can say something tender and vulnerable and memorable. Everybody likes to get personal notes. They can be read over and over and saved and treasured.

You don't need to discuss the letters when you get home, either. Let the letters do their own work. Unlike conversations, letters can be read many times without an argument cropping up. Some things need to be talked through. Other things just need to stand alone, beautiful and memorable.

And don't just put these notes on your child's dresser. Be a big spender and put stamps on them and really mail them.

It could be the best work the post office has done for you in years.

"Talk About Them"

"Impress them on your children. Talk about them when you sit at home and when you walk along the road, when you lie down and when you get up" (Deuteronomy 6:7). This suggestion is pretty radical, but if used wisely will boost your child's spiritual wisdom and strength dramatically as a byproduct of doing an enjoyable thing.

Do you remember the story about the children trying to hang around Jesus? The apostles, operating under the "children shouldn't be seen *or* heard" school of child management, tried their best to get the little buggers out of the conversation. They obviously felt that Jesus had more and better things to do with His time than to play with children. They might also have believed that there wasn't anything for children to get out of the important teaching of Jesus anyway.

How often do we react to children in the same way? Much too much, I'm afraid. We sit them at separate tables when families get together, we let them miss or sleep through meetings, and we hurry them out of the room so that we can have some undoubtedly weighty and crucial adult conversations. We, in effect, deny them access to truly meaningful dialogue.

We shouldn't send children out of the room too quickly; in fact, we should be indignant, as Jesus was, if anyone else tries to do it either.

Children, amongst themselves, rarely have life-changing discussions of eternal value. Even if they wanted to, most of them aren't old enough or experienced enough or wise enough to make such conversation possible. So what do we do? We send them along on their merry little ways to play in the sand and stick gum in each other's hair and talk about Joey's big ears instead of letting them grow — *insisting* that they grow — by listening to the conversations of some Christian adults.

Some of the best of these conversations can occur after some meetings at your church. You've just been stimulated spiritually, and if you can refrain from the standard claptrap about the weather and sports, you might even be able to ask a good question or make an incisive comment that might get a valuable conversation going. We and our children call these the "meetings after the meetings." The same thing can and should happen any time Christians come together. When it does, you've created the perfect environment in which your children can grow.

One serious difficulty with this approach is that many adult conversations are trivial. Another difficulty is that many of them are boring. Change this for your children's sake as well as yours.

Guiding Conversations

We have to learn how to think about something worthwhile, and then learn how to ask questions and start and continue conversations in such a way that growth results in all of the listeners. How much of your talk is really significant? I have to wonder if children are invited out of many conversations because the objectives and words are really worthless — or worse, shameful and embarrassing gossip, rumor, slander, and foolish talk.

Here are some quick ideas for conversation starters that you can use:

- "Tell me what you think about the loss of ethics in America."

- "Tell me what you think about the sanctity of life issue, and how you think that relates to capital punishment."

- "Tell me what you think about the different kinds of schooling."

- "Tell me what you think about God's law, and whether or not it applies to nonbelievers or believers."

It isn't necessary that children actually participate in these discussions, except by their active listening. If they're allowed to speak, they certainly should not be allowed to dominate the time, as children can be prone to do. Children, especially younger ones, can be masterful at distracting conversations by off-the-cuff comments or questions.

Another diversion that they specialize in is in distracting their parents, especially their mothers, with such important items as stating that their sock is dirty or they're hungry or they don't like brussel sprouts or that little Billy says he likes to sleep with frogs. Respond if it's a sin or a real problem, but *don't* let children control the time and flow of conversation when you're together with other adults. Everyone involved, in this case, ends up a loser.

Living Examples

So why are children often so interested in joining interesting adult conversations? When something is important enough to command the attention, even excitement, of a group of people that they know and love and respect, the subject will generally grab their attention. It can be irresistible to them, especially if it sounds like a real adult conversation. I don't believe that children should be in all conversations, of course; but I do believe that our orientation ought to change from "What are these kids doing here?" to "Is there any legitimate reason why the kids shouldn't be listening to this?"

And what do you do if your kids aren't *interested* in listening? If you've either never had these kinds of conversations, or have never let the children join you, you shouldn't be too surprised if they think at first that this is for the birds. Ask them questions, both during and after the conversation. Get them ready for some of the subjects that you intend to discuss with a certain individual or group. Build on it with follow-up discussions. But get them involved. This isn't a minor exercise; this is *very important for their development.*

Whether your children are interested initially or not, if you can get this going, you'll find this to be an excellent vehicle for teaching them about important things in an indirect and non-challenging way.

Suppose your child likes to wander off from where you told him to be. Lecturing and disciplining the child are vital and must be done. But look at the possible effectiveness in bringing up, with some Christian friends, the subject of the dangers of being in the wrong place. Have your friends share some of their bad experiences from childhood or adulthood, and you share yours. Share with each other what you learned from God about these things.

My experience says that real flesh-and-blood people talking about real flesh-and-blood learning experiences can outweigh the effectiveness of a good lecture or spanking, in many cases, by a five-to-one ratio. It's powerful teaching because it's *real* to the children.

This form of teaching and developing your children reaches its pinnacle when the conversation is intense. When your children see you defending the faith, presenting God's principles, and standing up for what you believe in, you can get the equivalent of 892 lectures in the space of an hour. Don't shield them from this, if you have any confidence in your God and commitment to His absolutes. Your children will not only *learn* the truth in these situations — they'll also be encouraged to live that truth out and to *fight* for it.

So go out tonight and talk a little with your family and friends. *And take the kids.*

Enough's Enough

"Having a good conversation is like taking a good vacation; it helps to know where to stop."

I don't remember who said it, but it's certainly true. As parents, how can we know when we have said enough? I think that the more serious problem is not in saying too much, but rather in saying too little. More to the point, the problem is that we talk about some fairly unimportant things endlessly, not having the good sense to know when we have said enough. And we don't talk about some fairly important things at all.

This omitting of the important starts with our general apathy and unwillingness to talk about the Word of God. "These commandments that I give you today are to be upon your hearts. Impress them on your children. Talk about them when you sit at home and when you walk along the road, when you lie down and when you get up" (Deuteronomy 6:6–7).

Although many of us know these verses, we don't really put them into practice. We figure that Sunday school, an occasional Bible story at home, and a few religious cartoons will be enough to produce strong believers.

No way.

We are supposed to be talking about life and faith all the time. Sitting, walking, resting, and getting up pretty well cover the better part of your day. You get the picture that God wants this particular family activity pretty high on your priority list as parents.

You shouldn't have to force discussions about what God has said. Every subject is part of God's creation and life. Every subject can be made eternally valuable by discussing its Biblical background, and every subject has value because it makes a Biblical point. If you find yourself having to force these discussions, you're probably having to force the rest of your Christian life as well.

Just talking about the Word of God won't cut the mustard either. You're supposed to *impress* these things on your children, and you can't do this by hollering the words into their hearts. The purpose of this talking is to get your children to love the Lord their God with all their hearts and all their souls and all their strength. God is quite clear that this is made easier if *you* love the Lord your God with all your heart and with all your soul and with all your strength. And act like you do.

Not talking enough includes areas other than Scripture. We don't talk enough about our:

- Experiences. Your kids really take pride in you. They'll delight in hearing about the many ways that God has worked in your life.

- Mistakes. Your children don't have enough time to make all of the mistakes that they are capable of. Hearing about yours can save them a lot of grief, in addition to giving you both (if you're big enough) a big laugh. It will also show them that you're human, which they're going to figure out anyway. You might as well tell them now and save the suspense.

- Values. We usually have some, but we don't describe them very well. We also don't take the time to give our kids the details of these values, including some practical applications. For example, if you think that thriftiness is important, tell them *why* you think it's important, tell them some ways in which you are thrifty, and give them some ways that they can try it out. Let them see the results of being thrifty. If they've been turning off the lights and lowered your bill, take them out for an ice cream that they wouldn't have gotten otherwise. Make a list of your top ten values in order of their importance, and present one a week for ten weeks. You may never have more fun.

- Friends. Your kids can already tell much about you by the company you keep. Tell them why you spend time with each of your friends. If you're helping someone who has a lot of problems and is not a close friend, tell your children about that, too. Jesus spent time with sinners, but everyone knew where He stood on their actions.

- Work, school, and other activities. Most of us are silent about how we spend the better, or at least longer, part of our time. Many will advise you not to bring work home, and this is a good practice; but this should not mean that you don't even talk about it. If it's at all possible, you should try to get your children to your places of work and action. Joseph must have been a very special person to be chosen to raise the boy Jesus. Think about the excellent education that must have taken place in that carpenter shop!

- Pleasant things. Most of us have a thousand details of God's creation that we love, and we just don't share these happy things with our children enough. Whether it's certain kinds of days, weather, scenery, food, music, books, or whatever, share this with your children. A good way to say it is: "You know, I really enjoy . . ." It will teach them how to enjoy what God has so generously given.

Do these things and you'll become more than parent and child. You'll become rich, deep, exquisite, and delightful friends, and this friendship will be passed by your young friend to his young friends to the third and fourth generations.

Of course, there is such a thing as talking too much. Most of us like to babble, and we are much too prone to nag our children long after we have made our point and good sense has disappeared from the conversation. Sometimes, we try to cram the whole nag in — mane, tail, whinny, and all. Most of what kids need to hear they never hear, and the rest they hear and hear and hear.

Scripture has a memorable verse that isn't addressed specifically to parents, but it seems to have some of them in mind: "Even a fool is thought wise if he keeps silent, and discerning if he holds his tongue" (Proverbs 17:28).

Conclusion

Your vision for your children must be communicated to them by guarding your words and planning memorable things to say. You can use your own experiences, feelings, memories, "three-minute" truths, special notes, and delightful outings, in your efforts to crawl into your children's hearts. You should involve them in your conversations with other adults. And you must train yourself to say enough about the important things of God's Word and life, even as you know when you've talked enough about the passing things. If you do these things, you can crawl into your children's hearts — deep inside. Do it!

4

EXCELLENT COMMUNICATION: COUNSEL IN LOVE

Perfume and incense
bring joy to the heart,
And the pleasantness of one's friend
springs from his earnest counsel.
(Proverbs 27:9)

E arnest counsel"—what a special, pleasant thing, and how rare it can be between those who love each other!

In this chapter, we will be talking about some deeper, even tougher, areas of communication. We will be taking a look at some of the things that can kill, rather than nurture, excellent communication. Together we'll try to "prune" our communication and to "trim the edges" of our relationships with our children. And please remember: These things are not an addition to loving communication—they are part of it.

Leading Questions

Once you've come upon one of those special quality times with your children, you'll want to do everything in your power not to waste it, and one sure way to waste it is to ask leading questions. It's absolutely essential that you learn the skill discussed in this section, if you want to have children who are truly grounded in the Word and life of God and who don't simply have the "right" answers—while living few or none of them.

The problem is that some of us are frustrated Perry Masons. We envision ourselves leading our children through a complex maze of questions that have only one correct answer, until after a brilliant cross examination the children gasp, "I see, I see," and collapse in an exhausted, but enlightened, heap. You feel very good, have a nice victory under your belt, and plan on being back at the same time next week.

But your children might not tune in.

When we are discussing the questioning of children, I am not talking about a game of twenty questions. Children are smarter than you might think and will always tend to minimize pain, or at least put it off as long as they can. They'll know if you're asking leading questions, and they'll learn how to answer them to satisfy you.

A leading question is a question that leads to a single, expected answer. It's almost a rhetorical question, except that it calls for a catechetical answer drawn from a well-trained memory bank. It's the right approach if you're trying to produce a "quiz kid" who knows the answers, but it can be a disaster if you care about *why* he knows them.

Questions that produce a single word answer—yes, no, true, false—are very often ineffective when you're trying to grow a deep spirit in your children. In fact, there are very few good questions that are longer than their good answers.

Instead of asking, "Did Christ die for your sins?" how about, "How do you know that Christ died for your sins?" or "Why do you think some believe that Christ died for their sins and others don't?" In place of the quick and predictable answer to the question "Is evolution true?" imagine the possible dialogue created by "Will you explain why *you* believe either creation or evolution to be true?" or "Can you contrast for me the strong points and weak points of both creation and evolution?"

Wording is *critical.* Never, ever, build the answer into your questions. The best answers will come when your children aren't completely sure which answer will please you. Even wrong answers can be an excellent base for future learning. If you never get a wrong answer or one that shows some uncertainty or confusion on the part of your children, then you've either got another Paul (*after* the conversion), or you're just not asking very good questions.

Even very young children shouldn't be treated like simpletons. As soon as they're able to speak with any fluidity, they should be able to answer thought-provoking questions based on what they've picked up from God's Word and God's people who surround them. If they don't know how to answer, perhaps the problem is that you really don't know how to answer either.

Watch the tone of your questions. Very often we get more from the tone of questions than the questions themselves, and children are no different. If you ask even a very good question with different intonations and emphases, you can cue your children on the "right" answer.

Also, try to avoid leading the answer with nods, interruptions, grunts, groans, and grimaces. This stuff can kill a good answer to a good question nine times out of ten. Just ask the question as well and as balanced as you can, and then try not to run over the answer.

Goethe's advice is appropriate: "What you have inherited from your fathers, earn over again for yourselves, or it will not be yours." This is serious business. Your children need to own these truths for themselves. You can be an indispensable help in their development of wisdom and godliness, or you can be the steamroller that crushes them by the weight of your relentless, sure-fire questions.

I hope by now that I've got you where I want you. I'm tempted at this point to ask you a leading question, such as "Don't you agree that it would be incredibly stupid of you to keep asking your children leading questions?" but you would probably object, and my question would be thrown out of court. So I'll just ask that you carefully consider your future line of questioning with your children.

Don't Lecture; Listen

Not too long ago, I saw a great line in a Father's Day card: "If I didn't have you, Dad . . . I'd have to lecture myself."

Why do most of us lecture, when instead we could help our children to teach themselves? This would be much more effective and easier on our relationship with them.

When a child brings you an idea or request that you think he hasn't thought through, or that you simply disagree with, or that really may be the dumbest thing you ever heard, don't jump into a *no* or a lecture.

This knee-jerk response will teach him not to ask you any questions at all, even when you really want him to. Besides that, it's a simple fact that he'll understand more certainly if he lets God's Spirit tell his spirit, rather than if you just impose an answer on him.

This shouldn't be a big surprise to you. Your own prejudices are usually stiffened when they're attacked but can be modified or discarded when they're moved along slowly under someone's patient hand. Think about your reaction if someone would say to your idea, "Ho, ho, ho. That's the dumbest idea I've heard from anyone." Think about how different your reaction would be if the same person said, "That idea may have some truth to it, but have you thought about. . . ." It's the same idea, but how different it sounds!

Listen to the Strong Points

Start by asking your child to explain the strong points of his idea or position. Probe with questions that are honestly seeking to know. He'll have to do some more thinking, and it might even be that *you'll* learn something. In fact, if you give yourself and him a chance, you might even change your *own* opinion on the subject.

As a minimum, this approach could land you in the Parental Hall of Fame, alongside the other five parents in history who actually had the humility to believe that they could learn something from their own kids. Most children can identify all too well with the Lord's sad statement that "only in his home town, among his relatives and in his own house is a prophet without honor" (Mark 6:4).

Listen to the Weak Points

Next, move on to the weak points of his argument. Now, this can be the clincher, but it'll be hard to get yourself out of the way and stay there. After all, you might think, *I'm so smart and he's so dumb . . . er, little. Wouldn't it be better just to point out the weak points myself, and nail him . . . er, it to the wall?*

No.

Ask *him* to point out the weak points himself. Help him do this, but don't do it for him. As he works his way through it, you might be absolutely *amazed* at how smart he is, how thorough, how delightfully excited to be allowed the courtesy of thinking. You might even start a whole habit of thoughtfulness in your child.

For example, your sixteen-year-old son has asked if he can hitchhike to New Orleans and catch a tramp steamer to the Bahamas, where he intends to spend a year working odd jobs on the beach. If you say, "That's the dumbest idea I've heard since my high school science teacher told me that whales evolved from cows," you've blown it. Even if you win and he doesn't actually go, you've blown it, whether you order him not to go or humiliate him and pound him with your logical arguments (which might sound like a lot of old-fashioned "hooey" to him).

Here he's given you a marvelous opportunity to help him learn how to *think*, and you've used it as an opportunity to exhibit your power and win. What happens in eight years when he has another fabulously ridiculous idea, and he isn't asking for your advice or taking your orders anymore?

But you could do it totally differently. You could ask him for the strong points of his idea. He might tell you that he could learn how to take care of himself, he'll learn some things about the world, the beaches and surf will be like heaven on earth to him, and he'll be able to learn a lot about sand. He might even shuffle his feet and suggest that he could do some real missionary work while he's surfing. You could stop him here and attack all of these "strong" points in merciless fashion—and you'd probably be right—but don't do it. Keep going; ask him for the weak points, and listen.

He might tell you that he could be placing himself in danger by hitchhiking or catching the tramp steamer. He might tell you that he'll miss the family and church and friends that he has back home. He might think that missing the big church retreat could be a real downer. He might even suggest that taking a break in his education could ruin his college or career plans. With a little gentle prodding, he might even confess that his real intention was to do more surfing than sharing. If you've done anything right as a parent, and you ask something like "Are you absolutely sure that this is God's will for you?" he'll possibly end the idea on that score alone. If he's resistant to answering or yielding to his own weak points, keep up the probing for days or weeks if necessary.

If you've done most everything else wrong as a parent, this approach might not work, and you might have to resort to a lecture or just a firm no. Those who have waded into quicksand need to grab whatever line is thrown to them. But if you've trained him to be a godly young man, this process can help him cut through bogus ideas and satanic distractions.

Cautions

Two cautions are in order. First, don't pounce on your child's weak points with mindless and heartless gusto. If you do, you'll eliminate this wonderful tool from your workbench. Have an honest discussion, seasoned with a generous amount of humility, and this can be one of his and your most rewarding disciplines. If you need help on your humility, just remember some of the strange things that you thought about when *you* were younger.

Second, always make sure that you let this young soul save face. Don't play sportscaster and insist on being concerned with who wins. Jesus wasn't concerned about winning *arguments;* unlike us, He was concerned about winning *hearts.* Allow your child the opportunity to go on from your conversation free to withdraw his request or idea and free to believe that he learned to withdraw it on his own.

One great benefit for you is that you won't have to defend your own position. This can be very hard to do well, especially if your child isn't listening because it sounds like a lecture, and very confusing if you haven't thought through all the fine points. If you're like many parents, it's safe to say that not having to continually defend your position is a definite plus.

Your kids will think so, too.

Don't Ignore Evil

Many adults try to teach life as though it's a coin with the same image on both sides. No matter which way things are flipped, we always get the same answer. If we are honest, we'll admit that the reason for this is that we would prefer not to have to distinguish between side A and side B ourselves. Or we might be afraid that our faith isn't strong enough to deal with challenges to it.

Whatever the reason, our purpose is often simply to teach that side A is not only right, but that it's the only choice. But if side A is so obviously right, why are we so obviously afraid to show our children the other side of the coin? It has one, you know, and someone will be glad to show it to them. Why not you?

The odds of true gray areas appearing are about the same as the odds of a coin landing on its side. The Bible talks about "one Lord, one faith, one baptism; one God and Father of all, who is over all and through all and in all" (Ephesians 4:5–6). There's only one truth, and everything not true is a lie. There's no middle ground, at least not for any believer who remembers what the Bible says about lukewarm things (Revelation 3:15–16).

Caution, of course, must be exercised when you begin to show your children the other side of the coin. One way to arouse the wrong kind of curiosity is to shower children with too much detail about the other side of the coin. Some leaders and organizations spend vast amounts of time and money to give us vast amounts of details about sexual and other degeneracy. They go too far. We don't need to have our heads in the sewer to know that sewage stinks.

Another way to arouse the wrong kind of curiosity is to tell your children too much too soon. We need to be especially careful not to lay things that have been problems for us on our children before they're ready to use the information properly. Protect their spirits, and wait until "all systems are go" before you launch your effort. Too much information given too soon is too much visibility for the other side of the coin. Wrong curiosity can be a likely result.

But another way that is at least fairly certain to arouse this curiosity eventually is for you to try to convince your children that the other side of the coin doesn't exist at all.

Be Prepared

I've been told that the way some U.S. agents become expert at picking out counterfeit bills is by studying only the real thing. These agents also know that there *are* counterfeit bills, why people make them, and what they're used for. These agents also know the dangers of counterfeiting. Your children must learn from you about the counterfeits and their dangers. Not the gory details, of course, and not too soon, but they need to know who believes the lie, why they believe it, and the results of such misplaced belief.

Jesus warned His people to be ready, to be prepared to deal with the great lies that are inevitable in an evil world. He said:

> Watch out that no one deceives you. For many will come in my name, claiming 'I am the Christ,' and will deceive many. . . . many false prophets will appear and deceive many people. . . . if anyone says to you, 'Look, here is the Christ!' or, 'There he is!' do not believe it. For false Christs and false prophets will appear and perform great signs and miracles to deceive even the elect—if that were possible. (Matthew 24:4–5, 11, 23–24)

Jesus was obviously concerned about His people being unprepared and gullible, having no understanding of who and what evil is or how to deal with it. He taught us about the other side of the coin, not as an exercise or just to show He was wise, but *because He loved us and wanted us to be ready*. We should do no less for our children.

Confront Evil

As you begin to teach your children about both sides of the coin, you might learn something, too. You might learn how really evil the world is, and how close your walk with the Lord needs to be just to survive it, much less stand against it and be victorious. If you gain a true understanding of the nature of the enemy and of the war that he's waging, it can only drive you more and more into the powerful arms of your Father God.

A perfect example is the incredibly rapid collapse of Western civilization, as exemplified in the almost total disregard for human life in our supposedly compassionate society. Millions upon millions of beautiful little babies have been killed in the death chambers that their mothers' wombs have become. Handicapped babies are being starved to death because they're "defective," and the Supreme Court says the government can't interfere. Elderly people are on the verge of becoming as expendable as the unborn. And the terminally ill are about to lose all of their rights except the "right" to die.

And the church—God's own people, who have been *warned*—barbecue in the backyard and putter in the garden and choose to pretend that it isn't happening. But it *is* happening, and your children and you need to know about it, understand it, and prepare to fight it by the power of God. You need to know about the results of murderous sin, without knowing all the details of the sin itself. The only alternative is ignorance, which will lead to more and more murder—perhaps including eventually your own children and grandchildren and great-grandchildren.

It's all too easy to say, "I just don't know if this is all that bad." If you can say that, your willful ignorance of the other side of the quality-of-life versus the sanctity-of-life coin will bring God's condemnation down on your own head. And if you do think it's bad, but don't want your children to think about or be aware of the ugly side of life, your willful allowance of such ignorance will bring God's condemnation down on your deficient teaching and the culture that your children will inherit.

Teach the Truth

You must teach what the Bible and history teach about life, but also what they teach about death. Without both sides of the coin, your children will be ignorant, unprepared, gullible, and caught off guard by something that has no power except its power to deceive.

Teaching your children the truth includes teaching them that certain things are lies, because *it's true that these things are lies!* Don't be afraid to grab hold of the lies by the neck, to expose them by the light of God and His Word, and to show your children how rotten and sickly and worthless these satanic deceptions really are.

The church in the nineteenth century tried to ridicule the new "science" of Darwin and others without even trying to understand it or develop scientific arguments against it. The church was steamrolled. You will be too, if you can't make an intelligent defense of your faith after you've done an intelligent and honest job of analyzing and explaining the other side.

It can't just be a "heads I win, tails they lose" type of argument, where you set up and knock down straw man after straw man. If there are some problems raised about your beliefs, let your children see them and work with you to resolve them. Let them see that you're open to truth no matter what the source or where you find it. Let them know that you are both discoverers of God's mighty truth and life. Look together at the strong points and weak points of both sides of the coin. And never stop before you both commit your hearts to the side of truth, even if all the details aren't clear or can't yet be fully explained.

This is the approach, for example, that many Christians are using today to explain the creation model of origins versus the evolution model. Looking at the other side — the evolution side — as well as the creation side strengthens the power of the creation viewpoint, even as it shows evolution to be one of the great lies of modern times.

And guess who has been caught this time, stuttering and stammering, teaching that, in this case, the coin has only one side? You guessed it.

It's not us.

We Interrupt This Broadcast . . .

"He who answers before listening — that is his folly and his shame" (Proverbs 18:13).

If someone wants to drive us up the wall, one of the surest ways to do it is to interrupt us when we are talking. It says to us that what we're saying isn't even important enough to allow us to finish. Interrupting consigns our conversation to the ash heap of forgotten dialogue. If it's done to us often enough, we can even develop a complex about the whole thing, start questioning the worth of what we are saying, and resent the one who obviously thinks so little of us.

I'm amazed at how many parents will allow their children to interrupt them while the parents are talking directly to them. We excuse it in younger children because of their short attention span, or because they're hyperactive, or because they're insecure or curious or have a lot of questions. Most of these modern excuses have their origins in some "expert" and have no basis in Scripture. Ignoring and interrupting others is just the same old rudeness that it has always been. Shut it down.

Worse for most families is the constant interruption of adult conversations by these small human beings, who may be operating under the egomaniacal delusion that they are the center of the universe. Although both parents can fall for this, moms are often the biggest suckers, and the children can play them for all they're worth.

But, a mom might be asking: Aren't my children my number one priority? This is the wrong question. The right question is: Do I really want my little white rose to be à toad?

I dare say that all of us have been talking to a parent when their little Gustav or Myrtle comes running up to announce to the parent the news that he or she has just stepped on a slug. There goes the parent's attention, no matter how important the subject you were discussing. This nonsense can destroy the spirit and effectiveness of a conversation eight times out of ten, and there's nothing in God's Word to allow for it.

To be fair, I must admit that accidental slug-squashing can be an important subject (especially if the child was in bare or stocking feet), but the point is that it's *not* an emergency and should not be allowed to interrupt even lightweight conversations. Dead slugs tell no tales, and neither should your child — until the time is right.

Some parents have attempted to soften the interruptions by having the child come up quietly and interrupt the parent in his or her ear. This has some of the appearance of not interrupting, but appearances, as we all know, can be deceiving. This still *is* interrupting. The parent's conversation with you and others comes to an end, tempting those other than the parent to think nasty thoughts about the rude child.

From lengthy studies done by the writer while driving on the interstate highways, it can be shown empirically that the world is full of rude people. Don't let your child add to that obnoxious statistic. *Never* let him interrupt you or anyone else, unless it's an absolute emergency. When he comes up to interrupt, hold up your finger in front of his face, and make eye contact and shake your head if necessary. (If he's having trouble letting you know he's there — usually unlikely — you can allow him to tap you on the arm, *once.*) Always make him wait until the conversation is at a stopping point or finished, and then allow him to make his announcement.

Consistency is absolutely crucial for success. This area will be a constant frustration for you if you're not consistent. You might be tempted to restrain him if the conversation is important, but let him interrupt if it's trivial. But you'll only confuse him, since he might not know whether your conversation is important or not. It's *always* important, though, that he knows that interruptions are *never* trivial.

Your child must learn the finer points of not interrupting the *conversation* as well as not interrupting any individual *in* the conversation. At first, he might simply wait until someone stops to take a breath and then thrust a verbal javelin into the air. It will take some real effort and training to help your child to learn when the right time for the comment has arrived.

Then you might discover that he has "forgotten" his comments, a gambit used to make you feel bad for having the unmitigated gall of not treating him like Caesar. While it's possible (and given the nature of many of a child's comments, perhaps even probable) that he *has* forgotten his thoughts, you should coax and pressure and demand that he get the comment or question out and learn how to get over his foolish hurt over being temporarily silenced. Tell your children to practice remembering. If you do this, it will become easier and easier for him to wait, knowing that you really are interested in him — and harder and harder for him to angrily "clam up," knowing that you'll persist in hearing him until he speaks.

As with other things, you'll have to set the pace in this area by not interrupting others. This includes other adults in conversations that your child might be watching. Even harder, it includes not interrupting your child or other children in their *own* conversations. It's all too easy for us to assume that their dialogue isn't very important and to barge into a room and interrupt it. Shame on us.

Just as important as teaching your child not to interrupt is teaching him to listen to what others are saying, and not just to wait selfishly to get his own thoughts on the table. "A fool finds no pleasure in understanding," says Scripture, "but delights in airing his own opinions" (Proverbs 18:2). You don't want a fool for a child, and he doesn't need to carry around his folly and his shame by interrupting before the others are finished.

If you're doing something and he interrupts your activity, and what he has for you is important (or you want him to know that he is important), then by all means stop what you're doing and devote yourself to him. But never let him interrupt your conversations with anyone, unless it's an emergency — and make sure it's a *real* emergency.

Token Interest

There's another side to this idea of interruptions. It's when we are so uninterested in a conversation with someone that we are distracted by anything and everything around us. It can get to the point where we *want* someone or something to interrupt our conversation.

And is there anything more maddening than talking to someone who isn't really listening to what you're saying?

If you're like me, you hate it when people are acting like they're listening to you, but they are really partly or completely unfocused on your thoughts. It's especially horrible when you feel that what you're saying is very important for the other person to *comprehend.*

You know the signs: people not really looking into your eyes or even at you at all; people doing something else while you're talking; people straining their ears to listen to other conversations in the room; people making comments or asking questions that show they haven't heard a word you've said; people asking you to repeat things, perhaps over and over, that were really very simple and clear; people easily taken away from your conversation by the flimsiest excuse. It all says, "You're not very important, but I guess I'll put up with the inconvenience — for a while."

This isn't real Christian behavior. We hate it, and rightly so. When we see a brother or sister in Christ doing this, we have an obligation to go to them privately and rebuke them. They need to know that this misses the gist of a very important Scripture: "Do nothing out of selfish ambition or vain conceit, but in humility consider others better than yourselves. Each of you should look not only to your own interests, but also to the interests of others" (Philippians 2:3). Not following this one command could, all by itself, bring a family or church or country to ruin.

So let's agree that we hate this token interest. We just think it's about as poor a treatment as anyone can give to us. And so we pay special attention to not doing this to anyone. Right?

Wrong.

Many of us don't even get out of our own homes intact on this one. By our inattention to our spouse's comments and questions, we show our children, not to mention our wives or husbands, that their mothers or fathers aren't really very important to us. Don't miss how powerful this negative lesson can be. If you show token interest consistently, no volume of miscellaneous compliments will cancel out the black impressions you will have made on your children's minds and hearts.

Take Time to Listen

And then there's our children.

We can be so tired or so busy or so not wanting to be bothered, that we can turn almost our entire relationship with our children into one big "token." It's particularly easy when they're little, and the things that are so important to them are so truly trivial to us — "Mommy, look at this wonderful doll I made out of this disposable diaper"; "Daddy, look at this leaf I found squashed under your snow tires." To be honest, these things really *aren't* important — not to us, not to others, not at all. They're only important to our children.

But that's enough. These things are important because your *child* is important, and these things are important to him. They're part of his life and growth, and he has a God-given desire to share these discoveries and inventions and joys with you. If you listen when they're little, they'll still be talking when the subjects *are* important. If you don't listen now, you may never know when the truly important things aren't being shared with you.

No more token interest. Get rid of all this half-listening, half-paying attention while your child or spouse is talking. Eliminate the "uh huh" while you continue washing dishes or reading the newspaper. Cut out this not expressing any real interest or enthusiasm when your child is interested in sharing with you. You might not think that these things are discourteous, but they are. When you listen with token interest, you've given your child part of your ear and none of your heart.

When your child comes up to you, you should either say, "Okay, let's talk about it" or "I can't give you my full attention right now, but you deserve it, so let's talk in an hour." The time delay can probably be longer for older children than younger ones, to whom an hour might seem like a month. You must be careful not to let them interrupt. But don't sit in the middle between listening and delaying. Back where I grew up, we used to call that *rude.*

Go beyond just listening when they come to you, and look for areas in which you can express more interest. One thing that we do is have our school-age children put all of their projects and papers under my plate each day. We review them together before or after dinner.

One important caution. When you actually start listening, you're going to hear some things that you disagree with or that don't sound proper. But don't sail into their words. Don't interrupt to make your own points. Scripture says, "He who answers before listening — that is his folly and his shame" (Proverbs 18:13). Too many of us can produce about two hundred cases of folly and shame in a twenty-minute conversation.

And when the time comes to respond, don't jump into their comments harshly or unthinkingly. We have all heard the expression, "If you can't say anything nice, don't say anything at all"; but the real truth is, "If you can't say anything *loving*—including rebuke as well as exhortation—then don't say anything at all."

We should at least listen to our own flesh and blood as we would listen to an interesting dinner guest. And if you do this, when your child is old, he may still be one of your interesting dinner guests.

Make Yourself Available

As I said earlier, delaying a conversation until a later time when you can give it more attention can be a good idea. But you want to avoid having to delay conversations as much as possible, especially when what you're doing isn't very important to the kingdom of God. Availability is so important, and so much of your success will depend on being able to strike while the iron is hot.

All of the tips in the world won't make you a better parent or your child a better person if you don't spend a lot of raw time on the effort. One of the popular ideas to be expected in a society that's abandoning its children on its own doorstep is that "it's the quality of time, not the quantity of time, that matters."

Sounds good, doesn't it?

Now, I can have no argument with the fact that time spent with children should be of very high quality. Time spent abusing or humiliating or wrongly instructing a child certainly has a value, but it is a negative one—and is not thought of highly by our child-oriented God. Nothing is of higher quality than teaching your child about God and His Word, and Scripture tells us that we should be doing this all day long (see Deuteronomy 6:7–9).

If you're trying to be a parent who works his craft with any kind of skill at all, you must spend a lot of quality time with your children. Just as a person can leave a more lasting mark on a company or profession or school by his intensity and length of service, so can a parent leave a more lasting mark on his child. There is, as a matter of fact, no substitute for just being available.

How many children—how many of *us*—have been stifled in a potentially exquisite relationship with parents who ended too many conversations with a hard, cold "not now"? Or "Can't you see I'm busy?" Or "Don't you have anything else to do?" Too many of us. And when we and they are older, how many of us will hear, from those rebuffed so many years before, another hard, cold "not now"?

And how soon will we be wondering about where all of our time with them went?

Next time your child asks you to do something with him (if he's still asking), do one thing before you tell him "not now." Just look into his eyes for fifteen seconds. Look deep and look hard. Force yourself to realize that this time, this request, this need will never come again. This alone will get you to spend more time with your child, unless you're a pretty cold and unfeeling person.

William Gladstone coined the phrase "Time is on our side." It isn't true in everything. Although in the matter of raising powerful people, it's certainly true that time *is* on your side.

But only if you take it.

The Art of Rebuking

"Better is open rebuke than hidden love" (Proverbs 27:5).

Okay, Lord, I hear You—I think. Are You really serious, Lord? I'm sure You realize that this rebuke business can really hurt the old ego, don't You, Lord? Do You really mean it?

You bet He does.

God has a straightforward list of priorities:

1. Open Love

2. Open Rebuke

3. Secret Love

4. Secret Rebuke

God wants us to be transparent in our relationships with all people: men, women, children, believers, unbelievers. He wants us to love openly, and hard as it may be, to rebuke those who need it for *their* benefit, *because* we love them.

Rebuke vs. Criticism

Bernard Baruch said that we should never answer a critic, unless he's right. The first thing to teach your children is the difference between *rebuke* and *criticism*. *Criticism* is the highlighting of either good or bad points about a person or thing. Theoretically, it can be used to make someone or something better, as in the term *constructive criticism*; in practice, however, it's most often used to tear someone or something down. Webster's defines it as "the act of criticism, especially unfavorably." Your children need to learn to reject criticism — unless, of course, it's true.

What is *rebuke*? According to Webster's, *to rebuke* is "to reprehend sharply." But in God's scheme of things, rebuke of another human being is the loving, caring attempt to restore him to solid footing on God's path. Your children must learn to accept your rebuke. Nothing less will move them toward their potential, nothing less will teach them how to accept rebuke from others, and nothing less will teach them how to rebuke others — not just someday, but right now, for youth is no excuse not to love and rebuke.

Your rebuke of your children must be wise to be effective. Scripture says, "Like an earring of gold or an ornament of fine gold is a *wise* man's rebuke to a listening ear" (Proverbs 25:12, emphasis added). You must ask yourself: *Is this rebuke? Or is this just nagging?*

Next, your rebuke must be *faithful*. Scripture says, "faithful are the wounds of a friend" (Proverbs 27:6). How can wounds be faithful? This certainly implies that your wounds, your rebuke, must be consistent. But there's more to it than that. It's also telling us that the rebuke must be full of faith; it must be prompted by your faith and centered around the idea of encouraging faithfulness in your child. Your rebuke must be based upon your own walk of faith if it's to be effective.

Your rebuke must be given in love, following Jesus' example. "Those whom I love I rebuke" (Revelation 3:19). Remember that only a friend's wounds are faithful — the rest just hurt. Jesus rebuked His apostles and followers *because* He loved them.

There comes a time when adults and children won't listen to godly rebuke and need to be dealt with more strongly, as when the Pharisees ignored and rejected Jesus and He warned them severely (see Matthew

23). But you should do this only at the leading of the Spirit, and only after all attempts at gentle rebuke have been exhausted.

Your rebuke should only relate to a sin on the part of your child. Jesus said, "If your brother sins, rebuke him" (Luke 17:3). Don't take on such an awesome duty lightly or for trivial things. Make your rebuke count by making it appropriate. Learn the difference between rebuking and nit-picking.

Finally, your rebuke of your child should go right along with correction and encouragement, "with great patience and careful instruction" (2 Timothy 4:2). You want to let the child know that he's out of line, but you also want to show him the correct way and encourage him to run on that path. Rebuke without these related actions can easily become harsh and unrelenting. The call for great patience eliminates the idea of rebuking in a rage, and the call for careful instruction means you should actually *plan* the rebuke!

Paul reminds us, "The Lord's servant must not quarrel; instead, he must be kind to everyone [even children!], able to teach, not resentful. Those who oppose him [even children!] he must gently instruct, in the hope that God will grant them repentance leading them to a knowledge of the truth, and that they will come to their senses and escape from the trap of the devil" (2 Timothy 2:24–26).

If your rebuke of your children follows this pattern, you can test your child's level of wisdom by his reaction to your rebuke. If your rebuke gets you hate, then he's a mocker; if it gets you love, then he's wise (see Proverbs 9:8). In fact, how he listens to your rebuke is really all the test that you need, since "a mocker does not listen to rebuke" (Proverbs 13:1), but "a rebuke impresses a man of discernment" (Proverbs 17:10).

Keep current with rebuke, even as you keep your criticism and nagging in the closet. Teach your children by word and example how to rebuke their friends. You really can and should expect your children, even little children, to confess their own sins to one another, to go to another child when there is a sin or an offense in the other child's life, and to lovingly rebuke the other child so that he or she might better live for Jesus.

Don't look at problems between your children and other children, or sins in other children's lives, as confounded nuisances. Look at them as opportunities to restore the other child, even as you train your own child how to live some supernatural principles.

Rebuke and Church Authority

"If your brother sins against you, go and show him his fault, just between the two of you. If he listens to you, you have won your brother over. But if he will not listen, take one or two others along, so that 'every matter may be established by the testimony of two or three witnesses.' If he refuses to listen to them, tell it to the church" (Matthew 18:15–17).

Too few Christians apply this passage to their lives in any way. The violation of this command has to be one of the greatest destroyers of body life in church after church. Too many Christians tell everyone *but* the one who needs to hear. They've got lots of gall but no guts. Others are brought in, not as witnesses but as connoisseurs of slander. Church leaders may not be brought in at all, at least not until the people in question — if not the church itself — are at the verge of ruin.

Even fewer people apply this straightforward passage to their own children. Mom, if you have a problem with your children, try to work it out there and leave Dad out of it. Your children deserve to be beneficiaries of this Scripture. If you get results, stop there. If you don't, then bring Dad in. Your spouse will usually be delighted not to hear about problems that are already solved.

And what if you both fail to get a response from your child? What if your child is hardening his heart against your authority? Then "tell it to the church." What? The *church?* Yes. Contrary to popular belief, the church isn't there just to entertain you. Your pastors and elders are there to help you with the nuts and bolts of your family life.

What's the basis for this? "If a man has a stubborn and rebellious son who does not obey his father and mother and will not listen to them when they discipline him, his father and mother shall take hold of him and bring him to the elders at the gate. . . . Then all the men of his town shall stone him to death. You must purge the evil from among you" (Deuteronomy 21:18–21).

The "stoning" can involve rebuke by the elders, assistance to the family in the area of rules and discipline, and in extreme cases, discipline by the elders and even excommunication from the church. The family is to accept this and choose to honor God and His Word over their sentimental attachment to their children. If you have a problem with this because it's an Old Testament passage, please note that Jesus, in Matthew 18, also uses an Old Testament passage. Do you think that God no longer considers rebellion against parents an evil to be purged?

This is pretty tough. But holiness is tough. Parenting is tough. Parenting without the help of your church's shepherds is very tough. Involve your leaders when you need them, even if you have to drag them in, kicking and screaming.

Conclusion

You owe your children earnest counsel. You can use godly principles to ask digging questions, help your children see the weak points of their arguments, and discover together all sides of an issue — even as you lead them to God's conclusions.

You can and must guard against the communication killers: impertinent and inappropriate questions from your children; center-of-the-universe interruptions; token interest as opposed to intense listening; and never having the time to listen to your children but always having the time to say, "not now."

You must lovingly rebuke your children *because* you love them, and follow God's principles of restoration.

If you do these things, your children, sooner than later, will count you as a pleasant friend.

5

THE POWER
OF AN EXCELLENT
EXAMPLE

Everyone who is fully trained will be like his teacher.

(Luke 6:40)

T his is where the rubber meets the road.

My dad used to tell me, "Don't do as I do, do as I say." Maybe some of you heard this from your parents as well. Even when parents don't say this, it is the implication of the way many parents live out their lives.

You might just as well try to convince your children that they hate getting presents or going on vacation. The Scripture says that "parents are the pride of their children" (Proverbs 17:6); for better or worse, this means that your children are going to be like you *are,* not like you *say.* The ideal, of course, is that what you are and what you say match up with each other and that both are godly. In fact, when they don't match up, the Bible calls it *hypocrisy.* Most people call it the same thing.

But beyond the simple fact that your children are going to imitate you — good and bad, decent and indecent, worthwhile and trivial — is another simple fact: Jesus says that a fully trained disciple is one who is just like his teacher.

This "being just like" can be unpredictable. You can let your children see the parts of you that you want them to imitate and try to hide all the ugly stuff. Maybe they'll pick up the good parts, and maybe if you're really shrewd, they won't pick up many of the bad parts.

But you're deluding yourself if you think that your life isn't an open book before your children. You can hide some of the actions, but they'll pick up your responses, your looks, the way you spend and prioritize your time, the edges of your sloppy ways. According to Scripture, the way you think is the way you are (Proverbs 23:7 KJV). If the junk is in there, sooner or later it's going to come out. And your kids will be there to see it.

Since you didn't really plan the good parts, they probably won't be as strong in your children as they are in you. And since you can't keep all the bad parts out, they will probably be stronger in your children than they are in you. Sin always gets worse as it gets passed down.

The alternative to this loose parenting is for you to actually *plan* to train your children to be just like you when you're done with their training.

Kind of a scary thought, isn't it?

But that's the way you're going to get the result — parenting a champion — that you're looking for. That's the way Jesus trained His disciples — every day showing them how to walk as He did. If you don't plan it, you won't get it. It's just as simple as that.

Now it really gets scary.

Planning to have your child be just like you in spiritual values and understanding, not in all the details of life, is the teaching/discipling method used by Jesus. It's the one He laid out as the pattern for discipleship. But making the decision to train your children that way is the easy part. The hard part is making the decision to *be* a champion for Christ so that when you're all through training your children to be like you, it'll be worth writing home about.

It's absolutely futile to try to develop a spiritual champion if you yourself aren't a champion. It just won't work. Nobody has ever been able to make it work, and you won't be the first. Your child may still become a champion, but it won't be because of you — it'll be in spite of you. If your child still achieves great things in the kingdom of God, people will look at you and look at him and say, "Wow, I wonder how he overcame *his* upbringing?"

That's not very encouraging, is it?

So you're just going to have to give up the idea that you can lecture your children to greatness, while all the while you're just floating through life and cruising toward the Rapture. Everyone learns by example. You did and do. Your children do and will. God hasn't made the person that doesn't learn by example, whether good or bad.

Even passionate lectures won't make up an example gap. Alfred Adler reminded us that "It is easier to fight for one's principles than to live up to them." It's shamefully easy for us to put an exuberant mask in front of an empty life, to fight for something that we aren't even putting into practice. We can fool some people for a while. You won't fool your kids. They live too close.

But if you'll apply God's principles, and let your children see the life and then hear the words, your children "will be mighty in the land" (Psalms 112:2).

God guarantees it.

The Unspoken Law

You've got to choose to be spiritually inquisitive.

All champions for Christ have been spiritually inquisitive — wanting to know more about God, His Word, and the life and world that He created. They're "on fire" to find God's best and incorporate it into their lives. They want to "receive the full rights of sons" (Galatians 4:5) and study to know what these rights are. They're careful to learn about God's boundaries and conditions. They want to see God lifted up and honored, and so they seek ways to accomplish this in the lives of those around them.

And they're not trapped by apathy. They aren't buying into "the opposing ideas of what is falsely called knowledge" (1 Timothy 6:20). They refuse to accept the idea that large portions of Scripture have somehow become defunct or passed out of vogue with God (see 2 Timothy 3:16). They aren't focusing their attention on prophecies which guarantee that the end is so near that there's not much use making Jesus known as Lord of *all* of life. And they reject the "popular Jesus" that so many people have ignorantly fashioned in their own minds, but who's so very different from the real Jesus of the Bible.

You must be spiritually inquisitive if you want to be a champion.

Now, you might be saying to yourself, *most of the time I just don't feel like being spiritually inquisitive.* Well, folks, that's the thing about being spiritually inquisitive—most people don't feel like it, most of the time. Our enemies—the world system, the devil, and our own flesh—are constantly working to make us not feel like it. But you know what? It just doesn't matter if you *feel* like it or not. You can choose, with God's help, to be spiritually inquisitive.

You *must* choose this, if you want God's best.

And how do you go about it?

Almost all of us grew up with an understanding of the kinds of questions that should never be asked. Most of us would be hard pressed to trace the origins of this spirit-crippling disease, but we most certainly have it, and just as certainly are passing it on to the next generation. The way this disease works is that our children can't ask the same questions that we couldn't ask, plus many that we may have added to the list.

There *are* some questions that don't deserve to see the light of day, and it's possible to go too far and allow questions that only seek to satisfy sinful curiosity. Most questions, though, deserve to be answered, *need* to be answered; and yet the very best and most important of them are often the ones that are left unspoken. Your own heart may shelter some questions that you've bottled up in a long-undisturbed area.

Part of the problem, of course, goes beyond how we were trained. It involves our own lack of an inquisitive mind due to laziness, or an unwillingness to expose ignorance (a false pride that guarantees we'll remain in that blissful state), or just the simple fact that we don't really care that much about what God has to say on a number of subjects.

You need to overcome this handicap before you can help your children. If you really think you're too old and set in your ways, you're probably right. So the first thing you're going to have to do is stop thinking that way and prepare yourself for a voyage of discovery.

Take a Voyage of Discovery

You've got to wake up. Montesquieu told us that "slavery is ever preceded by sleep." Your own inertia and inflexibility—what a terrible master to serve!

Next, you must begin to question, to try to look at things — all things — from God's different and fresh perspectives. Your own example will be the best teaching that you can provide to your children. Don't hide your children from a godly question that lurks in your heart, with the idea of maintaining the image of total knowledge and invincibility that you know — and that your children will someday surely find out — is a lie. Quit pretending that you already have all the answers.

How many parents have gone to their graves with questions that they never raised and had answered? How many children, now parents, have the same questions that they will never choose to ask? How many children — born with spirits open to finding God's best — will themselves become stifled and stifling parents, victims of this sad code of silence as it's passed from closed mind to closed mind?

Let your children see the things you're searching through. They'll not only learn that it's all right to get these questions into the open, but they'll also learn how to find the answers as you pour through the Word of God — for only there, of course, are there any answers worth finding. God's operative principle is "Ask and it will be given to you. . . . For everyone who asks receives" (Matthew 7:7–8). He elaborates on this when He tells us, "If any of you lacks wisdom, he should *ask God,* who gives generously to all without finding fault, and it will be given to him" (James 1:5, emphasis added). Ask God in the name of Jesus, and by faith you'll receive the answers you need.

And don't be afraid to ask your own spiritual guides for help in answering your questions. Scripture says, "He who walks with the wise grows wise" (Proverbs 13:20). Your children don't know everything, and — this may come as a shock — neither do you. You want your children to ask *you* for help and to follow your example of inquisitiveness. What better way to do this than for *you* to ask for help in this area and to follow another's example of inquisitiveness? I don't know of a man or woman of God who could turn you down on this kind of request.

If you don't know anyone like this, pray that God will grace you with one — and soon. It may be humbling, but a little more humility never hurt anybody. It may make you less independent and that *alone* makes this prayer worthwhile. God save us from independence in the family of God!

Encourage Questions

Finally, encourage your children to question and look into things for themselves. Make no issue completely out of bounds: not sin or death or fear or anger or sex or why you live the way you do or the effectiveness of prayer, to name just a few. Let them know that you value the desire to learn and grow that prompted their question.

Children *will* get answers to these questions; they *have* to, just to function. The real question is whether you're going to get your input into the process, and the answer is totally up to you. If they never ask the questions, they'll be spiritual dwarves instead of champions; and if they only ask others who have never been trained to ask or learn, they won't be spiritual anythings.

You're probably going to have to work a little to get them to ask their questions, since even if you're asking questions and encouraging them to do the same, they've still got Satan, the world system, peer pressure, and their own flesh working against them. When you come across a question that you know they're thinking, or ought to be thinking, *don't* let the opportunity pass and *don't* ask the question yourself. Instead, reread the passage or restate the issue, and then ask them this: "Does this make you want to ask a question?"

Then have the good sense and patience to wait until they ask it. Don't be bothered if it isn't the one you were thinking about. First learn from their questions, and then let them learn from yours.

In my experience with counseling other people's children, I don't know what's been more frightening: the kinds of questions left unasked by so many young people until a very late age — questions about the nuts and bolts of living for God, questions that were finally brought to me — or the fact that they didn't, or couldn't, ask their own parents.

A Dad Without Honor

The power of an excellent example can encourage your children to honor you and other authorities in their lives. Scripture has a very interesting promise, contingent upon a command: "Honor your father and your mother, as the LORD your God has commanded you, so that you may live long and that it may go well with you" (Deuteronomy 5:16).

Paul finds this so important that he quotes it in the book of Ephesians and adds the comment that this "is the first commandment with a promise" (6:1). God obviously thinks that the authority of the family is of great importance.

"Boy," you say, "I'm glad you're getting into this. I really need to get this idea pounded into my child." This would be all right, if we parents weren't so hypocritical about this command.

How can our relationship to this command be hypocritical? Look again at the verse above. Where does it say that this ends when we get married or for some legitimate reason have to move out of our parents' house?

Where in this verse do you see an age limit on "honoring"? What happens to us as *adults* when we follow this command?

And perhaps more to the point, what happens to us as adults when we *don't* follow it?

In the giving of this command, God uses words that allow and require this to be used throughout our lifetime. He expects us to honor our parents, without qualification, without age limit, without reservation of any kind. Paul, in Ephesians, adds the additional command for children to obey their parents, before he quotes the command to honor them. Even when we as adults are no longer in a position to *obey* our parents, we are always in a position to *honor* them.

Only our own desire for independence and our refusal to follow God's clear command can keep us from acting properly in this important area. The marriage of two people doesn't turn their parents into corpses. God gave people parents as an asset, even if they sometimes seem to be a liability.

So here's the point: If you aren't honoring your parents, how on earth can you expect *your* children to honor *you?* No teaching on respect for parents will be as powerful to them as watching you relate to your own parents—their grandparents. If you honor them, you're a long way into teaching their grandchildren to honor you.

How do you as a married adult honor your parents?

There are many, many ways. You can praise them publicly for their efforts with you and your children. You can ask them for advice and help on important matters. You can write them a note expressing your appreciation for all the times they cared for you and provided for you when they really just wanted to quit and be without responsibility. You can tell them thanks for all the times they could have justifiably thrashed you and didn't. And you can avoid putting them into an institution, when they're still able to be out and in your care.

And if you don't honor your parents, you have no right to expect anything more from your own children.

Many of us may have heard mothers say to their disrespectful children: "You just wait until you have children — you'll get the same from them!" These words are usually said with great emotion — and more often than not, they're true. Disrespect shown to your parents will earn you disrespect from your children.

"But," you might say, "you don't know my parents!"

You can talk at length about your parents' rigidity, cruelty, unavailability, poor teaching, lack of love, and so on. You may believe that you've changed yourself in such a way that you can be honored for your parenting skills by your children, even as you reject your own parents. You can object to this whole idea on a multitude of grounds and reject it as unworkable in your own "special" situation.

But you would be wrong. Totally wrong. This command is for you. You can't reject your parents and expect to be fully honored by your own children. It just won't happen, and you won't have the moral standing to demand it. There you'll be, a hypocrite once more.

Even if your parents are the most degenerate people who ever lived, *this command applies to you!* You must do it regardless of their personalities or any circumstances, because God says so. There's no way around it, no matter how old you are or how far from their home. Nowhere in Scripture can you find God authorizing anyone to stop honoring his parents. Jesus roundly condemned those who took money needed by their parents so they could use it to "serve" God (Mark 7:9–13).

Honor your parents, even when they're obtuse and seem unworthy of honor. It's possible that your children can learn more about this principle when you're honoring such parents than when your parents appear worthy of such honor. To not do as your sinful parents do, and at the same time to show them honor and respect because God says so — now *that's* a powerful example.

So, parents, don't let your dads and moms be without honor. Follow the command, and watch your children follow you. This command is a good one, and it's for you. And, of course, you shouldn't forget the promises that go with the command. They're for you, too.

Men and Women Under Authority

This same crucial idea carries over into your relationships with other authorities in your life. The focus here is on your relationship with church authority, although the principle applies elsewhere—for example, to a man under authority in his vocation. Hebrews 13:17 says it pretty clearly: "Obey your leaders and submit to their authority. They keep watch over you as men who must give an account. Obey them so that their work will be a joy, not a burden, for that would be of no advantage to you."

Pretty straightforward, isn't it?

And yet, the violation of this one verse alone is sufficient to explain much of the decline into irrelevancy by the church. Too many Christians just won't obey their leaders and submit to their authority. People who insist that their children obey them because God says so, won't obey their own authority in the family of God because God says so.

So what happens? In the church, many leaders start compromising and stripping Christianity of its biting truth, so that people won't be offended (convicted) and leave the church (rebel). Spiritual growth is sacrificed for numerical growth. The leaders' work becomes a burden, and their labors cease to be of value or advantage to you. Church becomes entertainment, even as it and the culture dies.

In the family, you get two losses: the advantage that your godly authority could bring to you and the power of your example to teach your children how to be under authority, yours and others.

It's just amazing how people can wander from church to church, picking and choosing, disregarding what is difficult (it's always easy to obey when we are told to do something we already want to do), never obeying or submitting to anyone, and then expecting instant obedience from their own children. Some parents openly criticize and even tear down church leaders in front of their children. Some people have even quit being a part of any church family. I have a question for all of these people.

Who died and left you boss?

If this describes you, did you ever wonder why your children pick and choose and disregard your hard orders? Did you ever think about why they at times chafe under your authority? Can you understand how your own disobedience can lead to a disobedient spirit in your children?

Is it any wonder that so many children want to leave home and go find a place where they're more comfortable?

If you aren't a man or woman under authority, go look in the mirror. You're the reason why your children are having such big problems with your authority. Children might obey for a time by force, but they'll only learn the spirit of obedience by *example.*

Let your children see you do something that you really don't want to do because you've been told by your spiritual authority to do it, and you can save many lectures. Tell your children about it: "You know, I didn't want to help that person, but Bill told me I should, so I did." Let them know that obedience isn't always fun, but that it *is* always mandatory, as long as the command doesn't contradict God's Word.

A lot of people have problems with God's clear teaching on this subject. Since we are free in Christ, surely Scripture cannot seriously mean "obey" like "children obey your parents" (Ephesians 6:1). And besides, what about the Declaration of Independence? Some people say they'll obey the leader if it's "right out of the Bible," but not "other stuff." What if your kids took that approach with you?

Surely we shouldn't do anything immoral or against God's Word, and leaders, like parents, can go too far in dictating the details of life to those under their authority. But these aren't the big problems in most of what today parades as Christianity. The big problems are that too many people don't want to obey things that are from or in line with God's Word, and they don't like any interference at all from outsiders — like shepherds of God's flock.

Far too many men who have a shepherd's role have little or no idea of the true spiritual or other needs of those about whom they must give an account to the Lord. This is a disaster for the church, the shepherds, and the flock. If you're a shepherd, start getting involved and, as the Lord leads, start giving out good guidance and tough orders.

As for the rest of us, for our sake, as well as our children's, we had better start obeying.

Don't You Agree?

One question that parents ask all the time is: Should we argue things out in front of our children, or should we argue them out in private?

The answer is *no.*

I've always been at a loss to know how anyone can think it's wise to argue anything out in front of their children. The only conclusion that seems reasonable is that they're trying to illustrate to their young disciples that adults can be stupid, parents can be obnoxious children, and dads and moms can be fools.

If this is the purpose, then I would have to admit that arguing is a fine technique. It's also pretty good for teaching them how to argue. A few parents actually carry this lesson to its logical conclusion and insist on letting their children "fight it out." Then the children can be "just like dad and mom." Isn't that wonderful?

We parents can be truly amazing. Most of us won't let our children fight or argue with each other or with other children. We tell them that this is absurd, indecent, and otherwise disgusting behavior, and we sound like we mean it. Then we wait for some monumental incident (like the potatoes being cold) so we can launch a modern version of the Hundred Years' War. It's surely wrong to carry this obtuse activity out in front of the innocent.

But is it acceptable to do it in private, away from the absorbing ears and eyes?

Are you kidding? You might be able to fool other adults, but it's highly unlikely that you can fool those who live under your own roof. They'll listen and look and learn from the way you and your spouse talk with each other, look at each other, and touch (or don't touch) each other. You won't like what they'll learn about you or for themselves.

Scripture has an interesting thought on this subject: "He who conceals his hatred has lying lips, and whoever spreads slander is a fool" (Proverbs 10:18). So you seem to have a choice. You can hide your anger or you can spread it around. You can be a liar or a fool.

Thanks, but no thanks.

Don't argue in front of, or behind, your children. Don't conceal your hatred or spread it around. Happily, there's a third choice. You can get rid of it, by asking the Lord to take it. So give your anger to Him, and a legacy of love to your children.

And if you don't have any anger toward your spouse, ask the Lord for the grace and strength to keep it out of your conversations, no matter how strong the provocation might be.

It's also important to be careful with non-angry discussions. Even listening in on the wrong kinds of *discussions* can teach your children much about your attitudes toward each other. If they don't see you, Mr. Husband, loving your wife like Christ loved the church, and if they don't see you, Mrs. Wife, in complete submission to your husband like the church should be to Christ, then you have taught your children some very important, and very sad, lessons. They'll struggle just to be successful spouses, much less champions for Christ.

Paul taught clearly that "the Lord's servant must not quarrel; instead, he must be kind to everyone [even spouses!], able to teach, not resentful. Those who oppose him he must gently instruct" (2 Timothy 2:24–25). Sounds like a *command*, doesn't it?

Discuss if you must and apologize if you forget. But if you can help it (and you can), never, ever, for any reason, argue with your spouse.

Who Will Take Out the Trash?

If you want a champion, you had better be very careful about what your children see you watching and about what they hear you listening to.

Most Christians, and even many non-Christians, are very concerned about the kinds of things that their *children* might see or hear in this filthy culture. This is a totally legitimate concern. Our so-called civilization has become largely degenerate, as its lovely freedom within boundaries has become grotesque sin without limit. We must guard our children's spirits carefully and control the world's input.

There's so much garbage out there that is ready to seep in any crack, any opening. A wise parent will keep his children's spirits tightly shut up against this slimy reality and keep his spiritual caulking—the wisdom and power of God—handy at all times.

To those who say that we shouldn't overprotect our children or leave them unprepared to face the world, we should say, "God *put* me here to protect my children! I want them to face the world prepared with the wisdom of God, not the knowledge of the details of evil." Seeing and hearing this trash won't make your children one iota stronger, but it will probably stunt their spiritual growth—or kill it altogether.

But this isn't the main point; if you don't understand the above, your children are already heading down the chute. Guarding what your children see and hear is a bare minimum required to have a child who's just spiritually surviving. What we are talking about here is what's needed to develop a *champion*.

In this area, as in all others, your best and worst teaching is going to come to your children by your example. While they're young, you can control their intake of information pretty well. But if you teach them something different by your example, all of your control will have been for nothing when they're old enough to make their own choices.

Because they're going to choose to be like you.

We are fond of talking in this country about "adult" and "children's" varieties of books, movies, music, and so on. There isn't any such distinction in the Word of God. He calls all of us to be like little, innocent children in our faith and in our lack of knowledge of the evil that surrounds us. Although there are certain things that your children won't be ready to see, or hear, or learn at certain stages of their childhood, the question should be: What are they prepared for? not: What should we allow them to watch?

Timing of things, yes — *types* of things, no. In other words, you shouldn't watch or listen to anything without your children that you would be embarrassed about if they were present.

"You must be kidding," you say.

"You must be kidding to say that," I say.

If it isn't edifying, and causing you to think on "whatever is true . . . noble . . . right . . . pure . . . lovely . . . admirable . . . excellent . . . or praiseworthy" (Philippians 4:8), then don't watch it or listen to it. It's garbage. Don't exercise your right to watch this corruption because you're an adult. *Act* like a true adult and shut it out.

Do I mean no *National Enquirer* or *People* or evil horror stories or frivolous romance novels (even if they're "Christian") or many articles and sections (including many of the advertisements) of the newspaper or most R and PG-13 rated movies or soap operas or most prime-time shows or a high percentage of commercials or almost all popular music?

Yes, I mean all of these things and many more. A man would admit, if he was honest, that glancing through the female apparel section of the modern Sears catalog would be likely to produce some stray thoughts that a godly man would rather not have. How much trash will your son have to see before it's intertwined with his spirit?

David says, in Psalm 101:

> I will walk *in my house* with blameless heart. I will set before my eyes
> no vile thing. . . . I will have nothing to do with evil. Whoever slan-
> ders his neighbor in secret, him will I put to silence; . . . My eyes will
> be on the faithful in the land; . . . Every morning I will put to silence
> all the wicked in the land. (Emphasis added)

God, as you can see, has a low tolerance for garbage — including
gossip, which is one of the lowest forms that we can choose to hear.
Don't let people tell you things that are gossip, rumor, slander, or slur. If
all else fails, be blunt — lovingly, of course. But *don't,* under any circumstances, listen to this sinful and malicious sewage.

David recognizes that a blameless walk begins in one's own house
and then is carried out into the world. He says that we should not only
avoid watching or listening to junk, but that we should take it as part of
our mission to *squelch* it, to rub it out.

If your children see you pouring this stuff into your spirit, the battle
is over. Guard them all you want — they'll still look with anticipation to
enjoying the forbidden fruits when they're older. Avoid these things like
a new outbreak of the bubonic plague, and teach your children that they
should be avoided by *all* Christians — not just the little ones — because
these things are ungodly and degenerate and destructive of spiritual
health and power.

The advantage of this to your children, and the side benefit of this
course to you, is a delightful one. You'll actually be able to walk with a
pure heart. If you do this, Jesus said in the Sermon on the Mount that
you and your children will see God (see Matthew 5:8).

And He, my friend, *is* worth watching.

Seventy Times Seven

Forgiveness is one of the hallmarks of Christianity and the healing lo-
tion that helps deep wounds to become even deeper love. How many
children have you ever seen actually go up to an adult or child whom
they have offended and on their *own* ask his or her forgiveness? My
guess is that many of us would honestly have to answer none.

Think about it. The whole gospel is based upon the principle of
godly sorrow that brings repentance and a plea to God for forgiveness

(see 2 Corinthians 7:10), and yet we just don't see children practicing this with God *or* their peers. Something is missing in spirits that have no deep appreciation for walking in a forgiven state.

In addition, with regard to other people we are told that: "If you are offering your gift at the altar and there remember that your brother has something *against you*, leave your gift there in front of the altar. First go and be reconciled to your brother; then come and offer your gift" (Matthew 5:23–24, emphasis added).

That's pretty clear, and yet we allow our children on many occasions to run amok, ripping through their peers and other adults with razor-sharp tongues and cruel, thoughtless actions. This forgiveness principle is too serious to overlook their words and attitudes and gloss over their need to seek forgiveness. Otherwise, the passage above indicates that God will not even bother to hear them until they've cleaned out their unforgiven offenses (see Psalms 66:18).

So the bottom line, the foundation of a powerful relationship to God and the beginning of a successful walk with one's brothers and sisters in Christ, is based on actively seeking *forgiveness*. As long as there's an open offense, the whole relationship will be stilted; if the offense is of a certain magnitude, the relationship can be killed. In our own lives, we must learn the importance of this action and keep short accounts with God and His people. With regard to our children, we must understand that this principle is not an option. We must teach them to repent and seek forgiveness when necessary, or they'll *never* be champions for God.

There, however, comes the dilemma. Any parent who has ever tried to force his little charge to ask forgiveness knows that it's a lot easier to get them to scrub their own ears. This asking forgiveness just doesn't come naturally. To do it from the heart is the first step of a supernatural walk on God's higher ground. It requires a supernatural response from a supernaturally trained heart.

It's important, but you can't force them to do it. So how on earth do you teach them to do it? Where is this supernatural training going to come from?

Surprise! You must show them by your example.

Teach by Example

Seeking forgiveness is so sensitive an area of life that it must be demonstrated to the children for them to have any true idea of its importance.

Teach them the Word of God on the subject, of course; this will be their basis for belief and practice of this principle throughout their lives. But if you want them to really know how to do it, and to really actively pursue it, you're just going to have to take your role as a parent seriously and give them an example to follow.

One of the rarest forms of human interaction is for a parent to be seen asking the forgiveness of someone else in the presence of a child (we can start with our spouses). We don't *like* to be humiliated and embarrassed, and that's how we usually perceive this particular action. And so we go on in our pride, refusing to seek forgiveness at all, much less in front of our child. We set an example of pride that belies any of our syrupy teaching about forgiveness.

Even worse, our grudges and bitterness and anger toward the other person can spill out of our spirits and mouths, an outpouring that gives the child something no different from what the world has to offer him. Don't be naive! If this is your direction, your child will learn how to hold grudges and be bitter and angry, even as you mouth the words that Jesus wants him to seek forgiveness.

We must lay aside our satanic-inspired pride and seek forgiveness in the presence of all involved people, including our children. We must ask forgiveness in a genuine, gentle, humble, sensitive, nonrecriminating manner. Then the children can see the beauty of restoration, as the wounds are bound up by God and the relationship with the other person is restored. Your children will have a powerful image implanted into their spirits that seeking forgiveness is an undeniable truth that must and can be done.

Seek Forgiveness from Your Children

And then comes the even rarer form of interrelationship. There's no way that anyone can honestly say that he's never done anything to offend his children. Have you sought your children's forgiveness? Have you been unable to rest until this blot on your relationship is erased? Have you treated your own flesh as well as you might treat some casual acquaintance?

If your answer is yes, praise God. If it's no, you're wrong before your children and God. You need to straighten this out for your own sake, as well as the sake of your children — immortal souls made in the image and likeness of God and of no less importance regarding forgiveness than your friends.

Don't go tell them that you're sorry. Go to them with a broken heart, genuinely sorrowful that you have hurt someone so intimately precious to you. Make no excuses under any circumstances. Let them know that you hate what you did, that you repent of it, and never by God's grace intend to do it again. And then ask them for forgiveness and wait for them to give it to you. If you do this in a godly way, you *will* be closer to your children.

And there's the beauty of it: You'll not only have cleared your account with your children; you'll also have taught them, in the most powerful and commanding way open to a parent, how to ask forgiveness. They may still balk and need encouragement in particular cases, but they'll know that it can be done and that it can end in a beautiful way, because someone they love and respect has walked the path before them and shown them the way.

Make a list right now of the things that must be discussed with your children. If they're asleep or not around, pray that God will give you the right words and the earliest opportunity to ask their forgiveness. If they're in the other room, *go get them now* and teach them what only you can teach them. Humble yourself. Go hat in hand to your children, and be forgiven.

Roberto Assagioli said, "Without forgiveness life is governed by . . . an endless cycle of resentment and retaliation." Please kill this cycle, and ask your child's forgiveness.

When Others Offend Us

And what about the other side, when someone has offended us?

Well, there's much inaccurate teaching floating around Christian circles on this one. It can be summarized as follows: "If you're a Christian, you have to forgive everybody because you're just a sinner who's been forgiven by God. It doesn't matter what the other person has done, or if he is sorry, or even if he has asked for forgiveness; you must forgive him." Have you heard it expressed something like this? If you teach this to your children, you'll be doing them a great disservice.

It's just plain wrong. God never asks us to do more than He does. In fact, He wants us to be like Him, and to do things *just like* He does. And

what does God do in this area? Well, He's *willing* to forgive everybody
and always keeps the way open to forgiveness. He works on the sinner
to prompt Him to seek forgiveness. But actually He only *forgives* those
who repent of their sins, purpose to obey Him, make restitution where
required, and ask for forgiveness through the atoning work of Jesus on
the cross.

God *doesn't* forgive everyone. Hell is going to be full of people
whom God never forgave because they never listened to His rebuke and
sought forgiveness. And we shouldn't forgive everyone, either. And neither should your children.

What? That's right. We shouldn't forgive everyone. When they ask
our forgiveness, we should forgive them or God won't forgive us (see
Matthew 6:14–15; Luke 6:37). But if they never ask, we shouldn't forgive (see John 20:23). We should, like God, always be willing to forgive. And we should be praying for the offender so that he'll seek forgiveness.

Jesus said it clearly: "If your brother sins, *rebuke* him, and if he
repents, forgive him" (Luke 17:3, emphasis added). If someone has
sinned, we should love him enough to go to him with a loving rebuke. If
he repents, we should, because we're God's children and are willing to
forgive, forgive him immediately and gladly. But if he doesn't repent,
we shouldn't forgive. He hasn't satisfied the condition necessary for forgiveness to take place.

How can this be taught to children? Again, start with the Biblical
background. But once again, example is the surest way to victory.

Rebuke your children when they sin. Then take the next step: Tell
your children to—respectfully—rebuke you when you sin. And if they
do, thank them for it, ask their forgiveness, and ask them to pray for you.

Pretty powerful teaching on your part, don't you think?

Help them do this with others, including adults, who have sinned
against them. And if someone has sinned against you both, with God's
help go together and let your children see how to lovingly rebuke a
sinning brother with the intent of restoring him. Let them see you forgive a repentant heart. And let them see you maintain your rebuke, with
love and grief, in the face of an unrepentant heart.

In other words, let them see you be like God.

You'll give them few greater gifts.

Little Samaritans

"But a Samaritan, as he traveled, came where the man was; and when he saw him, he took pity on him" (Luke 10:33).

When we hear this story about the good Samaritan, we usually sit in our seats and smugly judge the priest and the Levite who "passed by on the other side." Either they didn't care about anyone else, or they incorrectly reasoned that the beaten man was not their neighbor. They were wrong, and their callousness rightly offends the hearer of this story.

And all too often, we are just like them.

Most people take pity on their own family and close friends. Many people take pity on their neighbors and others that they would consider friends or acquaintances — whether out of love or because they are embarrassed not to help. But few act like this Samaritan, who without fanfare took pity on a complete stranger. He was a man who gave first and asked no questions at all. He poured out his time and money without thought of repayment. He obviously rested in the fact that "A generous man will prosper; he who refreshes others will himself be refreshed" (Proverbs 11:25).

Even as *we* travel along the road of life, we come upon strangers who need our help. It's not enough that our children observe us controlling our tempers at the obstacles in our paths. It's not enough that they notice how well we deal with inconveniences. They must be able to see us lovingly and cheerfully helping, or they'll never learn the simple lessons that there *are* no strangers in the believer's life and that a person is your neighbor because God has placed him in your path. They will learn that you, then, *become* a neighbor to him by showing him mercy.

We can too easily fail even in the exact parallel to Jesus' illustration. We travel down the highway, and if we see someone in trouble or injured or with a stalled car, we "pass by on the other side."

Is it enough that you don't honk your horn? Is it enough that you don't curse them and vent your anger because they got in the way or slowed you down? Is it enough that you think or say "What a terrible situation for that poor person to be in" or "I hope someone helps him soon"?

No.

We can't think that these responses are enough and expect our own lives to be blessed. And we *certainly* can't expect our children to be generous or blessed as they watch us, as they listen to us, as they follow us. The whole idea of being an ambassador for Christ, of giving selflessly and without expectation of return, of seeing people as Christ sees them rather than as inconveniences, will be lost on your children. By your omission in training you'll be teaching them to be cold, calloused, and aloof.

There's no luck or fortune or chance or happenstance in the lives of God's faithful sons and daughters. All things come from the hand of God. Every person in your path was known by God — even *put* there by God — before you were ever born. But today it's not hard to picture someone driving home from a seminar on evangelism and driving right past the soul that he's supposed to evangelize. We complain of no opportunities when we can hardly get around the ones that God is throwing in front of us.

Of course, we must be prudent. A woman passing three able men on a lonely road at night should still be a good Samaritan. But if her spirit is uncomfortable, she should be a good Samaritan at the next telephone or service station along the road.

By uncomfortable we aren't talking about fearful. If you know God wants you to help but you're just afraid, then put yourself into His hands and believe that His protection absolutely surrounds your every step. Prudence isn't a substitute for mercy; we can be cautious to the point of doing nothing, which God might call faithlessness or sin.

Clearly and boldly teach your children to be little Samaritans. Do this by your own example and by watching their walk and instructing them how to help someone who needs them, for no reason other than it's what Jesus Himself would do.

Jesus told the man who prompted this story of faithfulness: "Go and do likewise."

So go and do likewise.

Poor and Broken

If you've been weaned on the "American Dream" like most middle-class American parents, this may be a tough section for you to read.

I grew up on the philosophy that you were what you made yourself. If someone was down, it was strictly because they were lazy and had too little initiative to pick themselves up "by their own bootstraps" in a country where everyone had the freedom to do it. Anyone can be what they want to be, with a little pluck and luck. I thrilled to the stories of self-made men who found a way to be successful against all odds. I agreed with the man who said that being broke was only temporary, while being poor was a state of mind.

Before I go any further, let me say that I'm not opposed to honest business or financial success, because God isn't opposed to it. Our God is a God of bounty and blessing, and He can pour it out upon us with both hands. Scripture is chock-full of statements and examples of material blessing now, while we are here on earth. God's boundaries are that we accept success as a blessing and don't go after it as though it's our god.

Discerning the Poor

The Bible doesn't promote laziness. Scripture condemns the sluggard and tells him that poverty will come against him like a bandit or an armed man (see Proverbs 6:11; 24:34). We are told that "If a man will not work, he shall not eat" (2 Thessalonians 3:10), and that we are to be ambitious for a quiet life, minding our own business, and working with our hands (see 1 Thessalonians 4:11). Clearly we are to encourage everyone we know to trust the Lord for supply of daily needs, and at the same time to say: "Sow your seed in the morning, and at evening let not your hands be idle, for you do not know which will succeed, whether this or that, or whether both will do equally well" (Ecclesiastes 11:6).

Laziness is a particular problem in a country that has taught people that they're "deprived," "underprivileged," and that they're "entitled" to have a certain share of the pie regardless of what they're willing to do. We have seen the creation, in some cases, of a "gourmet" poor who really *are* lazy, demanding, arrogant, judgmental, and envious. The sight of people taking handouts from the state when they are capable of working must, if Scripture has any meaning, be displeasing to God.

I am not talking about helping *these* people with handouts. The state can't satisfy their cravings, and you can't either. You'll have to learn how to discern true poverty from the "gourmet" variety and then teach this ability to your children. And you can't go by government statistics that declare people poor based upon some arbitrary salary level. You'll have to take the old-fashioned way and simply find out who out there is *really* hurting in spite of their best efforts. The best way to help the sluggards is to instruct them in God's way and encourage them to find work.

But we have to face the plain, scriptural fact that there were a lot of poor people then, are now, and will be right up to the Second Coming. Jesus told us this Himself (see John 12:8). Then there are those of us who need to learn the lesson that we have an obligation beyond our words of encouragement to the truly needy (see James 2:15–16).

In fact, if we really believe Scripture, we know that it's God who bestows wealth as He chooses. We are encouraged over and over again to receive things with contentment, no matter how much or how little, from the hand of God (see Philippians 4:11–13). No one should dare to claim to be a self-made man for the simple reason that these are exactly the kind of men that God unmakes.

We are not to move on to judgment or condemnation either. Mocking the poor is not popular with our God (see Proverbs 17:5).

Helping the Poor

After encouraging and teaching the poor, and clearing out the false ideas of our own and our children's hearts, we have one simple duty, and that is to help. In this regard God has given us a simple truth: "The righteous care about justice for the poor, but the wicked have no such concern (Proverbs 29:7).

You must teach your children to have a deep concern about justice for the poor. There are plenty of poor to help right in your own city. You will *not* be living up to the spirit of the verse to sit around and pray for them — and nothing else. Sending a check to an organization that helps the poor is good, but it's pretty abstract. If you want your children to be champions, you must find ways to help the poor in such a manner that your children can see it, get involved, and grab onto it.

Take the poor food and clothing. Have your plumber fix their pipes or your mechanic fix their cars. Take them to your doctor. Take their kids to tee ball games. If you're really bold, you can invite God's poor into your home and feed them. But remember that the point is to help the people, not just to discharge a duty or salve a conscience, which is the way the unbeliever so often approaches it.

One of the activities that has really helped our family is to spend an afternoon at the grocery store buying food for the poor. Then we deliver the food, letting our children see this aspect of God's world up close. Care must be taken for the feelings and dignity of those that we help, but if you handle it well, your children will learn how to do it and how not to do it.

The children of middle-class parents in this affluent age stand in great danger of being swallowed up by materialism and by the mistaken belief that this is just how things will always be. It isn't true. Most of the world is poor — dirt poor. If your children aren't taught how to relate to this *in a personal way,* they'll be living as though they're on another planet, and they'll be of only limited usefulness to God.

Try to get your church involved with your family in helping the poor. There are many things that can be done more effectively by a large group. And don't limit yourselves to your home town, either. The world has always been overwhelmingly poor. In most countries, there are the very few rich and the very many poor; often, the very few use their position to grind the very many into the dirt. Take your blinders off and show your children the reality that surrounds them, and then *do* something about it with your children. Our church has had great joy preparing shoe boxes full of clothes, toiletries, books, and toys for the poor orphans of Uganda.

Now the Scripture previously quoted says that the wicked don't care about justice for the poor. You might say, "Hey, the government seems pretty wicked at times, and they have a lot of programs for the poor."

These people may want the support, the votes, or the servitude of the poor, or even the creation of more poor to be beholden to them. But if those who hand out cash are wicked, you can take it from God that they really don't care about justice for the poor.

We would all do a lot better if we got the government out of this important business and put God and His people back into it. Too many Christians are sitting around with the attitude that "I'm paying all these taxes; let the government do it."

Well, the civil government is a lousy substitute for real help and misses all of the personal encouragement and spiritual guidance that can go along with it. The government, in many ways, actually teaches people how to be poor. We can teach people how to be truly rich, even while sharing the privilege of helping them with their earthly needs.

Scripture says, "Many seek an audience with a ruler, but it is from the LORD that a man gets justice" (Proverbs 29:26). Take the poor directly to the One who will truly help them. We can do this great work with our children, as we work together to show mercy to the poor. Your children will have much deeper spirits after you've shared such an effort.

This verse also tells us that we are all dependent on God for any justice that we have or want in our lives. The world system is essentially unjust and corrupt. We need to work to bring it in line with God's law, but praise God that we don't have to depend on it for justice! God tells us, "He who is kind to the poor lends to the LORD, and he will reward him for what he has done" (Proverbs 19:17). God actually puts Himself in debt to the kind man!

There is also a warning in Scripture: "If a man shuts his ears to the cry of the poor, he too will cry out and not be answered" (Proverbs 21:13). You don't want to cry out and not be answered. You don't want your *children* to cry out and not be answered. The verse is deep theology in the simplest of words: Help, or you won't get any yourself.

Do you realize the importance of helping the poor? Have you gotten this across to your children? Do you suppose that your prayer for a certain thing has not been answered because the last time a panhandler asked you for money you refused to help him? Is God looking at you or your children as people who stand pleading before Him while you shut up your ears and look down your nose at the poor? If so, you and your children are in big trouble.

For if God won't listen to you, who will?

Conclusion

Your children imitate what you do even more than what you say. Therefore, the greatest teaching tool that you have is the power of an excellent example. You can teach your children to:

- Be spiritually inquisitive by watching you seek after God;

- Honor you by watching you honor your own parents;

- Obey authority by watching you submit to it willingly;

- Avoid quarreling by watching you always respect your spouse;

- Keep pure thoughts by watching you control what you see and hear;
- Seek forgiveness by watching you seek it from them and others;
- Learn to help those in trouble by watching you do it;
- Seek justice and help for the truly poor by watching you give.

Frank McKinney Hubbard said, "The reason parents no longer lead their children in the right direction is because the parents aren't going that way themselves."

I would say he understood parenting pretty well.

PART 2

SIX CRUCIAL
INGREDIENTS

6

FAITH

*This is the victory that has overcome the
world, even our faith.*

(1 John 5:4)

F aith is the absolute essential of the power life.
The Lord God Almighty has chosen to base His dealings with all
people, including children, on the principle of faith alone. No matter
who wants to approach Him — from the nastiest unbeliever to the fully
trusting believer — he *must* approach with faith if he wants to receive
anything. God says to us:

- Without faith it is impossible to please God, because anyone who
  comes to him must believe that he exists and that he rewards those
  who *earnestly* seek him (Hebrews 11:6, emphasis added);

- If you do not stand firm in your faith, you will not stand *at all*
  (Isaiah 7:9, emphasis added);

- To the *faithful* you show yourself faithful (Psalms 18:25, emphasis
  added).

Now you might wish that God worked on a different principle, because faith requires something of you that your pride and your sight will
resist. But "the Lord does whatever pleases him" (Psalms 135:6), and
what He wants is your belief. He doesn't want your sacrifices or your
discharge of duties and obligations instead of real faith.

He just wants you and your children to believe Him.

He wants you to believe Him all of the time. He wants you to believe Him whether or not you understand or agree or feel like it or think that you have any strength or ability to succeed.

When Jesus told Peter to drop the nets for a catch, Peter's mind, loaded with logic and experience, resisted. But his heart believed: "Because you say so, I will let down the nets" (Luke 5:5). This simple act led to the Lord's miraculous response and changed Peter's entire life, as he "left everything and followed him" (v. 11). We should believe God and act on our beliefs like Peter, for the simple reason that God says so.

Many have realized that they can't work their way into heaven. They've accepted God's Word that they can be saved from the awful penalty of their sins through faith in the atoning work of Jesus on the cross plus nothing. Many, perhaps most, of these believers are sure that their faith in this act guarantees their salvation from the hideous presence of sin when they go to be with Jesus. These are fundamental beliefs to which every child must be exposed early and often and encouraged to commit his heart, without restraint.

Walking by Faith

But why do we stop there? Where is our reckless belief in *all* of God's promises? Why do we try to live our new life by a different principle from the one that *gave* us new life? Why don't we teach our children that faith is the key for this *life* as well as for eternal life?

The reason is simple: We are simply not "certain of what we do not see" (Hebrews 11:1). We can be as foolish as the Galatians who saw faith not as a life principle, but rather as a ticket to get into the arena of good works. They got saved by faith but were going to walk the Christian walk by their own strength. Paul, not attacking obedience to God's law but rather the following of it in their own strength, was merciless on them — and us: "Are you so foolish? After beginning with the Spirit, are you now trying to attain your goal by human effort? . . . how is it that you are turning back to those weak and miserable principles?" (Galatians 3:3; 4:9).

Amen!

We tell our kids to "live for the Lord" and to "pay back to the Lord a small measure of what you owe Him." We tell them that they have a duty to "get their act together."

Folks, they can't do it. You can't do it either. Many parents are like the experts in the law, who "load people down with burdens they can hardly carry." (Luke 11:46). No one has *ever* been able to get his act together; Scripture tells us over and over that this isn't even possible.

We must teach ourselves and our children to walk the same way that we came — by faith. We must believe *all* of God's promises, including:

- Salvation by faith from the *power* of sin. We don't have to give in to temptations, or to the world that finds such a willing partner in the flesh, or to re-enslavement from our earlier bondage. We are "more than conquerors" (Romans 8:37) because we have a conquering faith in a conquering Lord. What a joke to believe that we can defend weak flesh by using weak flesh as a weapon!

- Salvation by faith from the *plague* of sin. We don't have to give in to fear, worry, anxiety, confusion, pain, sickness, infirmity, fear of dying "before our time," dissatisfaction with work, or concerns about material needs. God is gracious and compassionate, waiting to fill to overflowing those who seek Him by faith and persevere in this faith: "Whatever you ask for in prayer, believe [present tense] that you have received it [past tense], and it *will* be yours [future tense]" (Mark 11:24, emphasis added). This doesn't mean that you won't have any troubles, or that you're guaranteed health and wealth, or that you can receive God's goodness without fulfilling His conditions or walking a holy walk. But it *does* mean that He's your Papa and cares deeply about your welfare. Don't think He's less concerned about you in these areas than you are about your own children. What audacity to think He's a grudging Father!

- Salvation by faith from the *purpose* of sin. Before you're a believer you *have* to sin; it's your nature. You're part of Satan's master plan. But after salvation, you are "God's workmanship, created in Christ Jesus to do good works, which God prepared in advance for us to do" (Ephesians 2:10). Works do come into play, as a *result* of faith; in fact, "a person is justified by what he does and not by faith alone. . . . faith without deeds is dead" (James 2:24, 26). We just have to get these things in the right order.

Faith is the key to victory right here and now from the penalty, power, plague, and purpose of sin, and someday from the very presence of sin. Pretty simple, isn't it? Does God mean that you just believe Him and He responds? You bet He does. He means that you can take it to the bank before you actually have it in your hand, because He says so.

In Prayer

Some are disturbed that God doesn't deliver everything He has promised to His people, even though they don't believe Him in some areas. They want God to operate on *their* rules. They want deliverance from habitual sin, when they say that they're still "just a sinner" rather than a holy child of God; they want His protection, when they don't think He's guaranteed it; they want His healing, when they aren't sure He'll do it; they want to know His will for their careers and lives, when they aren't sure He'll tell them clearly.

But God has chosen to work only in the arena of belief. He wouldn't even let Jesus do many miracles in Nazareth because of "their lack of faith" (Mark 6:5–6).

Unless you're a universalist, you believe that no sinner is given basic salvation unless he believes. What is it that makes you believe that you have a right to be treated differently just because you're a part-time believer? If God will send some to hell for their lack of faith, how is it that you think He won't deny you, the Christian, His rich blessings for *your* lack of faith? You and I should know better!

God is *completely* fair. All, including your children, must deal with Him on the same basis, and that basis is faith in Him and in His promises and in His commands and conditions.

We must stop praying, "if it be your will" in front of our children. We must either find out what His will is or else throw away our doubts about His willingness to do what He says He will do. We must stop saying, "God didn't choose to do" this or that when He clearly says that He *will* do it. We have to stop blaming things on God, even if we do it piously, when the problem is in our own unbelieving heart.

We must believe God and not men — even good and honest men — and tell them that their failure to receive a promised blessing is a failure of faith. Of *course* this might produce guilt, and so it should, for "everything that does not come from faith is sin" (Romans 14:23). Jesus never pulled any punches when dealing with His followers' lack of faith (see Mark 9:19).

We think that God is always able to help but not always willing. The truth is the opposite: He is always willing but not always able. God *cannot* work with unbelief (see Hebrews 11:6). We try to turn things around, but it won't work.

In Action

Our children must learn God's Word, including His promises and the faith that guarantees their delivery. But these young ones will be poorly taught unless they see evidence of walking by faith in their parents and spiritual family. Only by observing faith in action can their head knowledge of faith ever become heart knowledge. And remember, mental agreement is not faith. Your children need to see Biblical hero-type faith in action in you. "I will show you my faith," James says, "by what I do" (James 2:18).

Many Christians refuse to believe and act until they've got all the details worked out in their heads. Folks, this is *sight*, not faith. Let your children see some good old reckless faith and your confidence that God will give you fuller understanding later. As Augustine said, "Understanding is the reward of faith. Therefore seek not to understand that you may believe, but believe that you may understand."

Step out in faith!

There's a story of a church in a farm community where a drought had been raging for many months. It was agreed that there would be a prayer meeting to ask the Lord for blessing in the form of rain. As the leader stood up, he looked around at the congregation and asked: "Brothers and sisters, if you're here to pray for rain, *where are your umbrellas?*"

Believing always involves attentiveness *and* responsiveness to God. Jesus asked, "Why do you call me, 'Lord, Lord,' and do not do what I say?" (Luke 6:46). Your action should always be based on your faith and must always work with your faith. God doesn't want you to act *instead* of believing; He wants you to act *because* you believe.

A friend was discussing this idea of faith with her little daughter. She told her little girl, "Faith is planting a seed and believing it will be a beautiful flower." Her daughter's reply was right on: "Yes, Mom, you have to believe it'll grow. But you have to water it, too!"

Not in Fear

Faith can conquer fears in your children, including the little ones. Don't try to act as if you don't have any fears; you won't be able to help your kids if they think they've got a problem that you can't understand. Admit to them that you have fears, but tell them how your faith in your Papa-God keeps you from giving in to these fears. Tell them that with Jesus there's *nothing* to fear. Answer a fear of the dark with a ringing description of the angels that are there to serve and protect them (see Hebrews 1:14). The *only* answer to fear is faith.

Faith, at first, is just a little seed. Your refusal to listen to the discourager and your intent to keep throwing yourself on the Lord can seem so shaky and can be so strongly accompanied by nagging questions, tension, and sweaty palms. But if we step out in faith, it will grow deeper and higher and stronger. Soon, you'll be a man or woman of faith in that area.

Faith doesn't mean having a frontal lobotomy. The person of faith faces his fears and doubts, and even the gloomy facts about the situation, and says, "They're all there, but they just don't matter." We can be like our spiritual father, Abraham:

> He is our father in the sight of God, in whom he believed—the God who gives life to the dead and calls things that are not as though they were. Against all hope, Abraham in hope believed. . . . Without weakening in his faith, he faced the fact that his body was as good as dead—since he was about a hundred years old—and that Sarah's womb was also dead. *Yet he did not waiver through unbelief* regarding the promise of God, but was strengthened in his faith and gave glory to God, being fully persuaded that God had power to do what he had promised. (Romans 4:17–21, emphasis added)

Faith can move mountains! It's bigger than everything that you can see, because it taps into a world of invisible majesty that dwarfs the things that surround us. The work of God is to believe in Jesus (see John 6:29), who happens to be the Almighty Creator, the King of kings. No matter what the odds, you and Jesus make up a majority.

You find out about this powerful, invisible world by knowing the clear written Word that God has so graciously given us. Many say it's hard to understand, that it's full of mysteries. But God has a different view: "The secret things belong to the LORD our God, but the things revealed belong to us and to our children forever, that we may follow all the words of this law" (Deuteronomy 29:29).

So learn the Word. Understand it and believe it, because it *belongs* to you. It's part of your inheritance as an adopted son of God (see Deuteronomy 4:6–8). Don't let anyone cheat you out of its fullness. The more you know, the more you can believe in, and the more your life will resemble Christ's.

Teach your young ones to move the newly discovered promises into their hearts, whether or not the words seem logical, or "feel right," or match the experience of most of the world—including the so-called believing world. As they begin this true walk of faith on the true path of power, you should also teach them to remember this: "In fact, everyone who wants to live a godly life in Christ Jesus will be persecuted" (2 Timothy 3:12). They'll need to know this when a faithless world—and maybe a faithless church—opposes them.

And one more thing ought to be kept in mind.

Don't forget your umbrella.

I Know a Person Who . . .

"We live by faith, not by sight" (2 Corinthians 5:7).

As soon as you learn and come to believe this great truth, and teach your children to do the same, you'll make an interesting discovery: This verse doesn't represent the experience of many of the Christians that you know or will meet.

The problem, of course, is that the vast majority has had more experience living by sight than by faith. We teach our children to live by the details of "the faith," but not how to simply *live* by faith. It's easy for a Christian school to fall for this same problem, and many Sunday schools are masters of head knowledge but completely inadequate in their teaching of this simple, powerful truth.

Once you and your children start to grasp the meaning of this "faith" business, you and they will begin to encounter responses that will have a common theme: "But I know a person who . . ."

A person who what?

- A person who asked to be rescued and wasn't and had to learn "why God allowed this to happen to him."

- A person who asked for protection but only got God's consolation in the terrible problems that followed.

- A person who prayed but got no answer.

- A person who asked God to be with him during a period of great trouble and got hard lessons in the "valley of the shadow of death" instead.

- A person who asked to be delivered from some terrible onslaught but received only the grace to deal with the disaster.

- A person who loved the Lord but spent his entire life living in disgrace.

- A person who sought to live a long and powerful life for the Lord and then died "before his time."

No matter what the situation needing faith, or the opportunity needing belief, there's someone who knows someone who didn't receive what they supposedly sought by faith. One man of God published a booklet in which he told us that he knew a person who had sought deliverance from a rapist, got raped anyway, but then found part of an answer in the grace that she received to handle the terrible trauma. We say that God is our Father, but we forget what that means. Would any of you fathers or mothers allow your daughters living under your authority and protection to be raped for any reason? Isn't God a better parent than you?

Note that she wasn't suffering *for* the Name, which is a different matter altogether. This young woman was suffering in *spite* of the Name. There's a big difference in God's Word between mindless suffering — or deserved suffering — and suffering for the Name. God is a loving and protective Father who will guard our lives and keep us from miscellaneous suffering that's unrelated to our life and walk and needs. He's also a God who calls us to follow Him regardless of the cost and a God who may call us to undergo some temporary pain to further His plan, while it brings Him glory, and us maturity, joy, and rewards (see James 1:2–4).

The implication of much that surrounds us in Christianity is clear: We preach faith, but we live by experience. And as a Christian community, we are living with the consequences of this sad state.

In every case of "I know a person who . . . ," you'll be assured that the person used in the example is a Christian. Sometimes, to emphasize the point, you'll be advised that the person was a strong Christian. The evidence seems overwhelming. What can you or your children possibly say?

You can say this: "We live by faith, not by sight." You can, and should, look at Scripture with these people. You'll find much there, and one thing that you'll find is this rebuttal to the "I know a person who . . ." points described earlier in this section:

> "Because he loves me," says the Lord, "I *will* rescue him; I *will* protect him, for he acknowledges my name. He will call upon me, and I *will* answer him; I *will* be with him in trouble, I *will* deliver him and honor him. With long life *will* I satisfy him and show him my salvation." (Psalms 91:14–16, emphasis added)

And when God says, "I will," He means it. You can take it to the bank. But what a sad state we have come to! We are teaching our children and each other about some other god than the One described so clearly in the words above and in so many other passages of Scripture. We are teaching them about a god who isn't really a father, as He says He is; or else who is a perverted father, who doesn't help His children when they need help and when He has the help to give.

It's said all too often that God sometimes chooses not to answer or help. I don't know who this god is that people seem to enjoy discussing so much, but I'm convinced that He's not the awesome and majestic God of Scripture, who *always* chooses to answer and help His faithful children.

The Authority of Scripture

The cardinal truth that you must teach your children is that they should judge all experience (sight) by the Word of God and that they should *never* judge the Word of God by anyone's experience. It's never, ever safe to listen to the "I know a person who . . ." argument. It can never be successfully countered by your own examples of victorious living because it can only be countered by looking at the Word of God and judging the experience (not the person who had the experience) accordingly.

Even the positive experiences of other people can be totally false and misleading if these experiences are not judged first by the flawless and unchangeable Word of God. Godly examples can be extremely helpful, but the Word is the only foolproof guide that we can use to test *anyone's* spirit or experience. We don't know what things — what purity or lack of purity, what wisdom or lack of wisdom, what faith or lack of faith, what obedience or lack of obedience — reside in the spirit of another person. But we do know what truth resides in the Word of God, even if there are *no* examples of this truth anywhere around us.

In all cases teach your children to ask for the Scripture that justifies an "I know a person who . . ." story. When this argument is given, it's usually used to explain or justify an unscriptural position (often due to a lack of faith), so your children will probably find the scriptural "justification" to be pretty thin. Then teach your children to search the Scripture for themselves, and with you, so that together you can find out what the truth is, regardless of what sight has to offer.

Don't be surprised that there are so many unscriptural examples and illustrations out there. Satan has done his homework and has used the world and our flesh to produce practically an entire generation of part-time believers. You and your children should seek to lovingly restore these sad souls to the full expectation that they can *always* count on their God, *even if no one else does.*

Don't ever be discouraged by the scarcity of examples to prove that what you know to be true from Scripture is true. Don't ever be discouraged by the huge quantity of examples that supposedly prove that what you know to be true is false. Sight is always easier and more appealing to the flesh than faith. Just remember that truth is truth even if no one believes it and that the "I know a person who . . ." argument, whether used to prove or disprove, is *always* wrong. Godly examples can be used to *illustrate,* but never to *prove* the truth of the Word of God.

Should you be surprised at the use of this "I know a person" argument? The faithful, those who are sure of what they hope for and certain of what they do not see, can be few and far between. The confused and unfaithful will very often look for a way out.

But there's a simple way for you to prove this argument wrong.

You can exercise your faith.

The Only Thing That Counts

If someone told you that they knew the *only* thing that counts, and if you had any confidence in that person, then you would surely want to know this thing and share it with your children. This would be fabulous *inside* knowledge, juicy information that could make your family a powerful force.

Many of us are looking for such a key to knowledge. We want to know God's first priority, the number one item on His agenda. To say with confidence, "I know the only thing that counts," would give clarity to our hearts and minds and direction to our actions. This is *must* information, if ever such a thing existed.

Does such a thing exist? If it does, on whose authority can we know it?

Scripture says, with incredible directness and simplicity: "The only thing that counts is faith expressing itself through love" (Galatians 5:6). Period. Faith is the primary thing, love is the vehicle, and God is your authority. It's as simple a statement as can be found in Scripture. Believe it. If you clear away the less important, then "the only thing that counts is faith expressing itself through love."

You may have been concerned that *love* was not listed as one of the six crucial ingredients. But love is part and parcel of faith, the first of these six ingredients. Love—for God, His Word, other people—is the mouthpiece of faith.

There is no living faith without love. John reminds us, "We know that we have passed from death to life, *because we love our brothers*" (1 John 3:14, emphasis added). The two are forever intertwined: "And this is his command: to believe in the name of his Son, Jesus Christ, and to *love* one another as he commanded us" (1 John 3:23, emphasis added). Faith without love for God and our brothers and sisters in Christ is dead, cold, un-Biblical, and impossible.

And there is no true love without faith. John says, "If anyone obeys his word, God's love is truly made complete in him. This is how we know we are in him: Whoever claims to live in him must walk as Jesus did" (1 John 2:5–6). Obedience to the Word comes through faith, and it's the only way to let God's love fill us. How did Jesus walk? He walked in love, and only through faith can we claim to live in Him and walk as He did. No eternally intimate and holy relationship between people is possible without faith in God being at the center of it. Love without faith is pointless, powerless, un-Biblical, and impossible.

If you drill this "only thing that counts" truth into your children — by doing it yourself, by walking as Jesus did in faith and love — then you may well be able to write the words of Paul to them someday: "We always thank God, the Father of our Lord Jesus Christ, when we pray for you, because we have heard of your faith in Christ Jesus and of the love you have for all the saints — the faith and love that spring from the hope that is stored up for you in heaven" (Colossians 1:3–5).

We who know Jesus have the hope! For our God's sake, let faith and love spring from that hope. Don't just teach your children to believe, teach them to love. Don't just encourage your children to be kind to others, teach them to believe God, which releases the floodgates that will allow them to love God and the family of God and to lay down their lives for their brothers.

It's so important that I'll say it one more time: "The only thing that counts is faith expressing itself through love."

Sounds like a motto for a homemade plaque, doesn't it?

I suggest on the wall, right by the front door.

Conclusion

You must become a person of great faith if you want to become a champion for Christ. Don't be dragged away from faith by an "I know a person who" or "Nobody else believes this" argument. Instead, let your faith come alive as it expresses itself through love for God and others. If you do these things, you, an ordinary man or woman trying to parent champions, will win a great victory over the world.

7

INTEGRITY

The man of integrity walks securely.
(Proverbs 10:9)

T horeau said it well: "As for conforming outwardly, and living your own life inwardly, I do not think much of that."
Me, either.

We live today in a large compartment complex. We have our work compartment, our church compartment, our school compartment, and our family compartment. And we have our own little compartment in which we hide. Sometimes the differences between these compartments is great, while other times the differences are more subtle.

Compartmentalized living has reduced Christianity and the average Christian to ineffectiveness and irrelevance. If a house divided against itself will surely fall, what about a mouse divided against itself? And that's what too many Christians are — mice divided against themselves.

Integrity is oneness and wholeness, a deep consistency of life and thought. It's a moral soundness that gives its possessor an accurate guide so that he can and will walk with conviction and purpose. God tells us that it's the key to walking securely. Only men and women of integrity can be carefree, not worried about what they said to whom or who will find them out.

Ralph Waldo Emerson described well the man of integrity and character. It's a description that men and women should take to heart:

He conquers, because his arrival alters the face of affairs . . . appointed by Almighty God to stand for a fact, — invincibly persuaded of that fact in himself, — so that the most confident and the most violent persons learn that here is resistance on which both impudence and terror are wasted. . . . men of character are the conscience of the society to which they belong.

A person of integrity clings to his moral consistency as though it's a life preserver — which it is. He guards his reputation with both diligence and vigilance and is relentlessly honest, conducting his affairs with justice (see Psalms 112:5). He's more interested in returning extra change from the vending machine than he is in being reimbursed for a shortage. He knows that "a trustworthy man keeps a secret" (Proverbs 11:13).

And he knows how critical this virtue is to the development of his children as champions. He'll go out of his way to live this out in front of them, and, without pride, to drive this home to them. He'll pile everybody back in the car on a sweltering day and drive miles to return the thirty-five cents that some cashier undercharged him. He'll openly disagree with a compliment about him that he knows to be only partly true. He'll stand his ground in a discussion when he's outnumbered ten to one.

Don't you hate it when you're dealing with the opposite of a man of integrity — a double-minded man? He's a chameleon, changing his colors to fit his surroundings. You never know where he really stands, what he's really thinking, how he really feels about God or you — or maybe anything. And for you, the only thing worse than having to deal with a double-minded man is to *be* a double-minded man or woman. If you are, you can count on God's promise that you won't receive anything from Him (see James 1:6–8).

But *you* can be a man or woman of integrity.

You can be a Daniel, who had 122 men devoting themselves to finding a chink in his integrity, but "They could find no corruption in him, because he was trustworthy and neither corrupt nor negligent" (Daniel 6:4). Finally in exasperation they said, "We will never find any basis for charges against this man Daniel" (v. 5). How many of us could stand up perfectly to this kind of investigation? In fact, how many of us could stand up perfectly to the everyday review of those little people that live in our homes?

But Daniel was a person, just like you. If he could be a person of integrity, so can you. Many of us have sung the song, "Dare to be a

Daniel." It would be better for most of us if we would learn a new tune, "*Try* to be a Daniel"!

You can ask God to give you an undivided heart. You can ask Him to help you to resist the many temptations to compartmentalize your life. You can ask God to make your life a beacon that will shine right through the worldly fog to light the distant shore of a far-off generation.

And along with this shining light, God will assign to you, as a person of integrity, more responsibility, greater trust, and richer blessings. You can be like the man to whom Nehemiah assigned responsibility for Jerusalem, "because he was a man of integrity and feared God more than most men do" (Nehemiah 7:2). If we are Christians, we should love people of integrity. If we are Christians, we should *be* people of integrity.

And it all starts with the understanding that we have a God of integrity who has given us the Bible, which we can use knowing that it has no real contradictions.

Contradictions

Will Rogers once said, "Everybody is ignorant, only on different subjects."

We all know in our heart of hearts that this is true, and yet when we get to the area of so-called Biblical contradictions, we presume that our finite knowledge of the "contradiction" is as far as we can go on the subject. To our unregenerate brains the thing *looks* like a contradiction; why, it might even appear to be a *flagrant* contradiction, one that any honest student of the Bible would trip over. So we either lose some of our confidence in the Word and live with this nagging contradiction, or we blindly tell ourselves that there's no way to understand this before we see Jesus.

And we stop.

I want to tell you something that, if you grasp it, will turn this area from one of constant confusion and frustration to one of tremendous joy. The simple truth is: Every Word of God is utterly flawless (see Proverbs 30:5), and there is not a single contradiction in the Bible.

You might want to know how I know this. The answer is that I *don't* know this; I *believe* it. God says that His Word is firm and reliable. Once you accept in your heart and mind that God's Word contains even the *hint* of a contradiction, you've stripped yourself of any chance to experience the full power of God's might in your life.

And you will have undercut your own integrity.

You must understand some basic things about yourself. You are spirit and body. Your spirit consists of your heart, which is the seat of love and must be purified; your mind, which understands the things taught it by the spirit; and your will, which is the very essence of your spirit and which chooses to believe or not believe the things perceived by heart and mind. Your body consists of your physical makeup, including your brain.

Your brain and your mind are *not* the same thing. We begin to relate to many things through our senses and their interpreter, the brain; an example is our reading of the Bible. But the brain is part of fallen flesh, and your understanding can't stop there if you want a powerful life. You must move these ideas and thoughts as quickly as possible from your brain to your mind.

We are encouraged in Scripture to trust in God and not to lean on our own fleshly understanding (see Proverbs 3:5). Scripture also states that "we have the mind of Christ" (1 Corinthians 2:16). Too many Christians end their reading or study of a passage in their brains, and so the words are just words to them, compel them to no action, and leave them with an empty feeling that there's nothing there for them.

"But we have the mind of Christ" and can go on to believe and obey the Word, which will lead to understanding (see Psalms 111:10).

The Whole Truth and Nothing but the Truth

So you must first teach your children to approach the Bible with an expectation that everything in it matches up perfectly with everything else in it. You want them to be confident that God is only telling them one story, that absolute truth is indivisible and unchangeable and doesn't come in plaids. They must be taught to believe this in their hearts and minds, not in their brains, because the brain is flesh and, left to its own devices, is an enemy of the spirit. The brain works on reason alone and *looks* for contradictions. Reason alone will never understand what only faith can deliver.

Since our initial thoughts about anything, including Scripture, come through our brains, many apparent contradictions will come before you and your children. Since man and creation have fallen from their early sinless perfection, there really *are* many contradictions in the world around us. Doctors kill babies and save babies in the same hospital. Men say that they want peace and slaughter each other by the thousands. We say that we want a less materialistic Christmas and expend our energies in a mad rush of spending and getting. Our lives are full of real, bona fide contradictions — courtesy of Satan, the world, and our own human natures.

You should teach your children to note these manmade contradictions, analyze and understand from Scripture why they exist, and then abhor and renounce them with their whole hearts.

But when their brains hit a stopping point in Scripture, train your children to believe that this is not, *cannot* be, a contradiction. Their fallen, finite brains cannot grasp on their own the fullness and beauty of the Word of God. Their hearts and minds, however, are more than capable of believing these things to be true, if they're taught to *choose* to believe them.

Some of our worldly acquaintances might say that this sounds like brainwashing, and we would have to say that it is: It's washing the brain with the mind-cleansing, heart-purging detergent of faith. But it's different from what they mean by *brainwashing*. They mean that you make your children forget what they know. We simply want them to know what they — and we — have forgotten.

Search for Truth

Next, you should teach them about an interesting phenomenon: Some of the most exciting insights in Scripture are found in the apparent contradictions. God loves to hide His truth so that only His faithful ones can find it. "It is the glory of God to conceal a matter; to search out a matter is the glory of kings" (Proverbs 25:2).

The deepest, hardest things require the greatest amount of faith for understanding. If your children will assume that God's Word is 100 percent correct, believe that no word is contradicted, and ask the Holy Spirit for guidance, they're ready to go to work. They can then begin a study, perhaps with you, that will lead them to magnificent truth. *Only* this determination of heart and mind will produce a full understanding.

If they don't come to the Bible in this way, they're in big trouble. The number of potential contradictions to their brains is tremendous. The one thing that the finite brain is able to produce in infinite quantities is runaway doubt.

We now get excited when we come across an apparent contradiction. We know that there's something very special there for us, and we have not yet been disappointed. Your children need to be excited when they come across these things. They will be, if you are, if they appreciate that it's their *brains* that are fuzzy, not the Bible, and if they are confident that some real treasures await them.

As Kin Hubbard said, "Tain't what a man don't know that hurts him; it's what he knows that just ain't so."

And as far as the Word of God is concerned, there just ain't no contradictions.

Following Through

I don't think most of us have a very clear idea of just how rebellious and disobedient God's own sons and daughters are. There are few boundaries left in much of the church. There's only a freedom run wild, a liberty turned to madness and folly. In our own age, the church is in many ways as hardened and cold as the organized Jewish church was in the time of Christ, which looked good on the outside. But no less than then, the church of our God has become a whitewashed tomb.

In short, the church might look dynamic on the outside, but most Christians wouldn't even *consider* obeying God on something that sounded strange to them or that required some cost or inconvenience or change of lifestyle.

No matter what words or concepts you want to use to describe the situation, the church is in trouble:

- Commitment: Where's the uncompromising and unyielding commitment to the Lord and His Word, no matter the cost?

- Submission: Where are those who submit to God's authority and His true leaders, whether the command is "appealing" (easy to follow) or not (the point where submission actually means something)?

- Obedience: Where is the simple, day-to-day, by-faith following of
  the Word of God in *all* of its particulars, wherever that may lead?

They just aren't there.

I am not talking about the world here. And I am not talking about
the church, repressed and persecuted, in the totalitarian countries. I am
talking about the church in the West, particularly in America, but elsewhere in the West. Commitment, submission, and obedience have almost become a *joke* in this part of the church; only God isn't laughing,
and the joke is on us.

We act as if we have got it all together, and the Rapture would have
to come before it would ever get tough here, because we are *God's
people.* At the same time, the simple and often holy church in other
countries is being hounded into the ground. We are so unfaithful that we
deserve anything and everything that God could throw at us. In one
sense, we deserve to get what our brothers and sisters in those countries
are getting. But in another sense, we are not even worthy to suffer like
them for the name of Christ.

The church in the West, on the whole, has to be an embarrassment
to the Lord. And we are raising a new generation of children to be even
more of an embarrassment. This new crop is being raised in a lawless
culture, in a lawless church, and more often than not in a lawless family.
What do we expect them to be? Champions? When they don't even
know how to obey? It would be funny if it weren't so sad.

We need to teach our children how to follow through on what God
is telling them to do and to hang the cost, and this involves a four-part
process:

- First, they have to be taught to commit themselves totally and without reservation to the Lord.

- Second, they have to be taught to be submissive, including gentle
  and humble and sensitive and everything else that implies.

- Third, they need to be taught to be relentlessly obedient—to the
  point of death if necessary.

- Fourth, they have to see you following through in relentless obedience.

And I am talking about *active* obedience, not lip service to God or His Word. Jesus told a parable that's very instructive here:

> "What do you think? There was a man who had two sons. He went to the first and said, 'Son, go and work today in the vineyard.' 'I will not,' he answered, but later he changed his mind and went. Then the father went to the other son and said the same thing. He answered, 'I will, sir,' but he did not go. Which of the two did what his father wanted?" "The first," they answered. (Matthew 21:28–31)

Immediate obedience to God is, of course, the highest kind and one likeliest to reap rich blessings, even as the devil's foothold is eliminated. But Jesus recognizes that some things might not "sound right" to us at first hearing. There's no severe penalty for taking the time to think about it, even after your initial reaction to say no, as long as your heart is kept open to the Holy Spirit, and the next step is obedience.

But there is a penalty for taking the time to think about it, especially after the immediate response to say yes, if you ignore the Holy Spirit, reconsider your decision, and then disobey. You get no credit for saying the right *words;* to God, it's the actual obedience or disobedience that's the issue. In the parable, the disobedient son even adds the superficial respect of calling his father "sir," which only makes the disrespect of the actual disobedience greater, not less.

If we have taught our children well—primarily by our example, as with everything else—we should see them becoming committed, submissive young people who are more and more instantly obedient to God and to you. This kind of obedience, with time and practice, should become a habit.

But give them a little time, too. If their initial reaction is negative, even if they don't actually say no, don't jump all over them and punish them for disobedience. According to Jesus' parable, they haven't actually disobeyed yet. Give them some time (and perhaps some Scripture) to consider their attitude and decision. This is especially true when the area under question is a new one for your children. If they obey, no matter how great their internal struggle, count it as obedience.

Don't fall easy prey to a quick yes that has no substance behind it. If they tell you they'll do it, and after a reasonable amount of time they don't do it, then it's safe to assume that what you've got there is basic disobedience. They get no points for good intentions. In some ways this is worse than an outright refusal to obey, since it adds lying to rebellion. You need to clean up this act quickly, explain that words without follow-through are meaningless, and expect that the verbal obedience in the future will be followed through in action.

Once you've taught your children to follow through — to be committed, submissive, and obedient in their actions — you've got one big danger. What authority will you allow over them in different situations? If you put them under ungodly authority, such as in school, then their obedience can become a snare for them.

As they grow, they can learn that their obedience must be prioritized, obedience to God always coming before obedience to men. But when they're young, this is hard for them to perceive. A godly and wise parent will emphasize obedience to God first and to men second, and to men not at all if they are standing against God. But beyond that, he'll guard against ungodly authority taking advantage of his child's innocence and trained obedience in the first place.

If you train your children to follow through, they'll stand tall in the Lord's eyes, "For the eyes of the LORD range throughout the earth to strengthen those whose hearts are fully committed to him" (2 Chronicles 16:9). *Fully* committed — like Jesus, who sweat blood and tears as He considered the price He would pay, but who "humbled himself and became obedient to death — even death on a cross!" (Philippians 2:8).

Now *that's* following through.

Following Through for You, Too

Part of the idea of following through involves active commitment, submission, and obedience to God and His Word on the part of you first and then your children. This alignment with the Word is a matching up with God's perfection and is the basis of your being a person of integrity.

And God has His part in the process. When God speaks, He follows through with blessings for obedience and disciplines for disobedience, depending upon our follow-through when we hear Him speak.

And guess what? You should be like God and follow through when you speak, depending upon the follow-through you get from your children.

Follow Through on Promises

Dad, you make a promise to take your kids to the park on Saturday. And it's Saturday, and you're bone tired. All you want to do is settle in a comfortable place and be left alone. And here comes little Alfred, who can't seem to remember an order for twenty-two seconds, but who is a regular computer bank when it comes to your promises. He says, simply, "Dad, I'm ready to go to the park."

Dad, whether you know it or not, you're at a major crossroad. What you do in the next sixty seconds is going to speak volumes about the value of your word. You basically have four choices.

Saying, "No, I don't think I can" and sticking with it is the worst choice; it teaches Alfred that integrity doesn't mean much, that your word doesn't mean much, and that he doesn't have to worry much about integrity either. Saying, "No, I don't think I can" and then changing your mind fairly quickly isn't the best choice, but it shows him you'll follow through, given some time to think about it. Saying, "Yes, I'll take you, because it's important to fulfill your word, even though I don't feel like it" is a good choice, because you're following through and letting him know that you *have* to do this even when you *don't* feel like it. And finally, saying "Yes, I'll take you, because I love you and delight in keeping my word" is the best choice—for obvious reasons.

Follow Through on Discipline

The same principle of following through applies to your commands and threats of discipline as well. "A servant cannot be corrected by mere words; though he understands, he will not respond" (Proverbs 29:19).

Children are action-oriented. Usually even the wordiest children enjoy doing more than talking. Because of this, they pay a lot more attention to what you do than what you say, not only in the example you set, but also in your relationship with them.

Although your spouse might consider your tongue-lashings to be sufficient punishment for any offense, your children may not be so easily intimidated. They need, and perhaps even want, to see some action. Your lectures, no matter how serious, can even become humorous to them if not accompanied by physical reminders. Nothing is as weightless as a threat allowed to float away on a breeze of inaction.

If you're a barking sergeant without any biceps, you'll even find that your children might do things to egg you on so that they can see you (often Mom) blow up. They might be less likely to push Dad over the edge only if they think that he'll be especially nasty when he gets there. Children can play their parents around the rink like professional athletes; but too many parents, even when they get pushed to the brink, respond only with more tongue-lashings.

Tongue-lashings are no lashings at all. They might humiliate or embarrass your children, or make them bitter or angry, or even destroy their feelings about you and themselves. But Scripture says clearly that the best and worst of these are all mere words that alone cannot correct them or make them respond (see Proverbs 29:19). Save the lectures and instead give them something to get their attention, cooperation, and remembrance.

Give them action.

Whether it's a spanking, time in time-out, loss of privileges, or whatever, it's what they need. Tell them once, and only once, why this catastrophe has befallen them. The only other words that will ever get as much attention are "We're going to get an ice cream."

Make sure that the first time you tell them something is the *only* time you tell your children something. Make sure your children know that one time is all they're going to hear it before they see a blur of action. Anything else is mere words. Some of the saddest words parents ever utter are, "I'm going to tell you just one more time . . ."

Which leads to one of the really terrible things about a "mere words" parent: His words are multiplied just like a fool's (see Ecclesiastes 10:14). The words start out as a dribble, run together into a stream, and finally become a raging river that threatens to drown both him and his children. It's no coincidence that some of the worst behaved children belong to some of the most wordy, nagging, verbally obtuse, and inactive parents. The parents have allowed the child to turn into a monster, and the child has trained his parents to be the father and mother of Frankenstein.

This "words without action" approach is as dead as "faith without action." The more wordy the parents become, the more the children learn to disrespect authority, to *ignore* authority, and to be fundamentally disobedient. In other words, this approach will get the parents the *opposite* of what they want their children to be, the *opposite* of what they're demanding with their torrent of "mere words."

If you combine action and words, as in saying a request only one time, you'll not only get obedient children, you'll get peace and delight. In the same chapter of Scripture as the verse that opened this section, it says: "The rod of correction imparts wisdom, but a child left to itself disgraces his mother. . . . Discipline your son, and he will give you peace; he will bring delight to your soul" (Proverbs 29:15, 17).

Loving your children and sharing enjoyable experiences with them can give you fun and pleasure, but the surest way to peace and delight is for you to use the rod of correction and discipline them. It doesn't seem like this ought to bring peace and delight, but that makes zero difference, *because it does.*

Get away from asking your children things "just one more time." Tell them once, expect prompt obedience, and then "hit the beach." If you still feel that you're helpless and that you just *have* to tell your kids to do something ten times, do yourself a favor and reread this section.

Just one more time.

O Promise Me

Most parents like to say that they're men and women of their word; and yet, when the principle involves their children, they can too easily become lax and tolerant. You should know that you're doing your child no favors with this approach.

When your child gives his word to anyone on anything, you should insist that he keep it. He should be encouraged to understand that this isn't optional, and even if it hurts to do it right now, in the end he will be blessed by God for it. This is the meaning of the Scripture: "Lord, who may dwell in your sanctuary? Who may live on your holy hill? He . . . who keeps his oath even when it hurts. . . . He who does these things will never be shaken" (Psalm 15).

A young girl learned this lesson when she told her brother that he could have anything he wanted out of her toy box, from which she thought she had just removed all of the good toys. Well, she had missed something of great value to her, and of course that's what he found and wanted. In addition to not wanting to keep her word, she gave him a very hard time. She was directed by her father to return the item as well as to ask her brother's forgiveness for her remarks.

My concern is that most parents would have negotiated and reasoned with their son on the basis that their daughter had made an "honest" mistake, rather than insisting on her being a girl of her word. They wouldn't have insisted on justice, but only on what they considered was fair and reasonable. They would have made a great mistake. They would have missed teaching her two valuable lessons: to control her tongue and not give her word without thought and to keep her word — period.

The only exception is in a case where by keeping his word, a child would be committing a sin. In this case, the child should be disciplined for both his rashness and his foolishness. The sinful intent of his heart in this situation overrides the fulfillment of his promise. He should be disciplined for the sinful intent, and he should also be allowed to suffer the consequences of not keeping his promise.

Beyond this, you should look for opportunities for your child to make commitments to you and then keep them. This is true training in righteousness. If he wants to do something, say yes if you can; but if there's a logical thing that he should do after that, make him agree to it in advance.

If he wants to make popcorn, let him do it, with the understanding that he must commit to cleaning up the mess. If he wants to go outside in the mud, fine; but make him agree to clean up the mess (or at least help if he's too little to do it all by himself). If he wants to go somewhere, all right; but get a commitment from him on the time by which he'll be back. In short, rather than just giving orders before or after the fact, get him to agree before the fact to be *responsible*.

Then make him live up to his commitment. He might have agreed rashly to it, but it doesn't make any difference. If he doesn't do it, or does it slowly, or does it grumbling, he should suffer two penalties: the loss of the privilege of doing the thing the next time and any other penalties that are appropriately related to his disobedience or attitude.

This approach will teach him responsibility, improve his attitude, improve *your* attitude, make him speak more thoughtfully, and generally clean up your relationship with your child. When a child is old enough to understand what he wants, he's old enough to understand what *you* want. Three years old isn't too soon to start working on this principle.

We live in a society where a man's word isn't worth very much. Even if he puts it on paper, it more often than not just makes the paper worth less. People in every area of life will say that they're going to do something, and then they just don't do it. It wouldn't be quite so bad if they were at least embarrassed, but many people don't even have enough remaining decency to feel guilt or shame.

It's time to squelch this rotten lack of integrity.

One final thought shouldn't really be necessary to express, but observation says that it is. None of this will work long-term unless you're a person of your word: to employers, to family, to friends, to enemies, to your spouse, to your children. When you make promises, you *must* fulfill them, even if it hurts.

Especially if it hurts.

You Scratch My Back . . .

"The devil is compromise."

Although these are Henrik Ibsen's words and not those of the Bible, they couldn't be more true. Compromise is a word that should connote evil to you. It should make you shiver when you hear it. The fact that politicians call politics the "art of compromise" alone ought to be enough to make you drive the word from your vocabulary.

For instance, you and your spouse have worked hard to become the *perfect parents*. You've taught your children God's principles of faith and life, and you're living these principles as an example for your children. You've done everything possible to ensure that a new Florence Nightingale or Hudson Taylor or George Mueller has been prepared inside their spirits.

And then along comes compromise.

Everything in the world around you and your child reeks of compromise. You can't escape contact with it. The majority of books, movies, television, radio, music, and art teach that there are no absolutes, that you have to be pragmatic, that you can't be steadfast in anything and still expect to get ahead—or even get along. The pressure to compromise will come to bear on you, as others try to get you to "be reasonable" in your parenting, compromise on Biblical truth, and understand that "rigidity" on principles just won't work in our modern world.

And then the pressure will move to your children. Peer pressure is a pure pressure to compromise. Satan uses your children's natural desire to be liked against them and encourages them to give up what they know to be right to preserve their "reputation" as flexible, reasonable, friendly, and down-to-earth people — meaning carnal Christians.

Your children can all too easily become like the Jewish leaders who "believed in him. But because of the Pharisees they would not confess their faith for fear they would be put out of the synagogue; for they loved praise from men more than praise from God" (John 12:42–43).

You should constantly remind your children of Jesus' warning in this area, a warning that few Christians take seriously today: "Whoever acknowledges me before men, I will also acknowledge him before my Father in heaven. But whoever disowns me before men, I will disown him before my Father in heaven" (Matthew 10:32–33).

Remind your children that these Jewish leaders believed in Jesus; they were *believers,* which means that your children's salvation doesn't absolve them in this matter of compromise. If they want the maximum from their eternal stay in heaven, then they can't act like they're pagans down here. In fact, if they want the maximum from their passing stay *down here,* they can't act like pagans.

Teach your children the meaning of the word *integrity.* Integrity, as we've already seen, is a oneness and consistency in character. Teach them to build this singleness and stability into their character.

Integrity should mean for them that they're whole people who maintain their principles no matter what crowd they're in. It should mean that they will remain true to their Lord no matter what pressure or trouble comes. And it should mean that they're the same over time, just as their God is. Without this integrity of character, which can and should be seen before they're ten, they'll leave no substantial mark on the people who surround them.

Integrity *must* mean that your children are consistent in their pursuit of God's purpose in their lives. Without this integrity of purpose — and I am not talking only about career choices here, but also about things like being filled with the Holy Spirit and walking a holy walk by the power of God — they'll leave no substantial mark on the church or the culture that surrounds it.

And finally, integrity means knowing with conviction that ultimately there are no gray areas except in our own fuzzy minds and hearts. We have a black-and-white God, with black-and-white principles, who will at the end bless or curse people in a very memorable, black-and-white way. We need to be crystal-clear, black-and-white followers of God and show our children how to be the same.

John Ruskin said: "You may either win your peace or buy it; win it by resistance to evil; buy it by compromise with evil."

This is a day when everything looks as if it's for sale, including peace. It's a lie. Purchased peace is a delusion that keeps a person from seeing that their very lives are being devoured. Don't believe the lie. Win peace for yourself. Encourage your children to win peace for themselves.

No compromise.

Tattletales and Other Stories

Have you ever seen anyone who handled a tattletale in a way that left you satisfied that the right thing had been done?

My guess is probably not.

God wants us who are believers to be a peculiar people. We are peculiar all right, but not in the way that God has in mind.

What's our reaction if we hear about a public official who "blows the whistle" on dishonesty and thievery in government? Or if we hear about a person who walks away from a conspiracy and turns in the criminals? Or if we hear about a person who was told to be dishonest on the job, but who goes to his boss's superiors instead?

Our reaction is not "what a disgusting tattletale!" Instead, we appreciate the courage and integrity that the person is showing to the world. If the person suffers for his honesty, we become outraged and demand justice. When the guilty are brought to justice, we whoop it up. All of this is a good reaction to a stand taken by a person of integrity.

But then our children come to us in exactly the same way, with possible truth about a certain situation, and our reaction becomes fuzzy and unprincipled and, all too often, wrong. We doubt them, assume that they're lying or at least being sneaky or inaccurate, and then holler at them or punish them. It's no wonder that many children and adults end up looking the other way when wrong things are done. Scripture says, "It is not good to punish an innocent man, or to flog officials for their integrity" (Proverbs 17:26).

We chastise children who bring us the truth and warn them sternly not to be so low as to "snitch" on their peers, who may be exercising criminal behavior toward them or someone else. These children will learn the lesson, folks! Far be it from them to ever tell *you* the truth again.

God *delights* in integrity and those who have it. He wants you and your children to be a peculiar people of special integrity. You must not fall for Satan's trap in this matter. He wants parents to discourage both an appreciation for the truth and the telling of that truth. The false code of honor, which says that you should never say that a skunk stinks, is totally bogus and destined to aid evil in running amok.

Obviously, children lie sometimes, and their motives are not always pure. So how does a parent or teacher encourage integrity without encouraging lying, gossip, rumor, slander, and slur?

- You must first teach your children to love decency and truth. If they don't know what's right or wrong, or don't love the right and hate the wrong, you can skip the rest of this section until a later time.

- If they see something wrong, they should follow Biblical principles of correction. They should be taught to go first to the offender alone before getting you or anyone else involved.

- If the other child refuses to listen to the child of integrity, and continues in his bad ways, then it's proper to get you involved.

- You should demand truth, even if it implicates the one telling it and should severely punish any lying. All lying is bad, but lying to get another child into trouble is particularly rotten. The scriptural punishment for perjury was simple: The perjurer got the punishment that the other person would have gotten if the story were true (see Deuteronomy 19:16–21). Perjury will disappear pretty quickly and permanently if you adopt this practice.

- Make sure that the truth-teller is careful in his choice of words. Let him know that you won't listen to gossip or slander and that a self-righteous attitude is unacceptable. You want accuracy, presented in love.

- Motives are important. Watch how the truth-teller reacts to the punishment of the wrongdoer. If he seems to enjoy it, be like God and stop the punishment (see Proverbs 24:17–18). Then have a little chat with the almost child of integrity. Explain mercy to him. Give him an example of mercy by not punishing him for his rejoicing over the problems of another—this time. Teach him that the purpose of this discipline is to restore the offender, not to torture him.

• Make very sure that a "trade war" doesn't get started. Nothing should be done along these lines just to get even. Scripture says: "Do not testify against your neighbor without cause, or use your lips to deceive. Do not say, 'I'll do to him as he has done to me; I'll pay that man back for what he did'" (Proverbs 24:28–29).

• If the truth has been told and the motives are right, then you should praise the truth-teller. Then he'll know that virtue is commendable.

Do you ever wonder why honesty can be so scarce among children? Perhaps it's because adults often aren't honest or don't teach their children about honesty and its value. Or maybe it's just because we don't use the obvious opportunities to teach it.

Conclusion

You have a God of integrity who has given you a Bible of integrity, which you can use knowing that it has no real contradictions. If you align yourself with it, you can become a person of integrity. You can be consistent in word, thought, and deed, and avoid having a compartmentalized life. You can follow through on what you know to be true and teach your children to do the same. You must always keep your word, whether it's a promise to bless obedience or punish disobedience. You can be a person of great humility but no compromise, just like Jesus. And you can, by word and example, teach your children to tell the truth all of the time, no matter what.

8

HOLINESS

Be holy, because I am holy.
(Leviticus 11:44–45; 1 Peter 1:16)

I s it possible, in the midst of an evil age, to live a holy life?
Yes.

Holiness is not only possible — it's *mandatory* if you and your family want to live a life of richness and power and make some real difference in this filthy time. The real question is: Is it possible to truly live
life if it isn't holy?

No.

The body of Christ is in such poor shape that words fail to describe
it. We have little understanding of the holy character of God and what
He means when He says, "Be holy, because I am holy." We have com-
promised on so many areas of doctrine and practice for so long that we
have ended up looking no different from the rest of the world — except
on Sunday mornings.

This isn't only unholiness. This is hypocrisy.

Whom do we think we are kidding? Do we really believe that sin is
no longer important to an absolutely perfect God? Can we possibly be
imagining that God is becoming senile and taking a "boys will be boys"
attitude toward our sinful folly? Are we so far from knowing who God
is that we think He views sin as we do — with a discouraged look and
shrug of the shoulders?

If we look at God this way, we and our children will pay the price for such willfully ignorant foolishness.

Can't we understand that God won't even *listen* to us if we are carrying filth around in our hearts? "If I had cherished sin in my heart, the Lord would not have listened" (Psalms 66:18). *To cherish* means to hold onto, to cling to, to refuse to give up. What are we holding onto that's keeping God from even listening to us? This truth ought to make us tremble in reverent fear.

Set Apart

God wants you — all of you. Every niche, every nook, every cranny. You don't serve fine meals on dirty dishes or refreshments in spotted glasses. God doesn't either. He isn't going to take His joyful and powerful message of hope and love and serve it to the church and the world in a dirty vessel. He never has, and He isn't going to start with you. If you think you're being used by God even though you're cherishing some dirt, you had better think again. You might be used in the sense that God can even use Satan to further the eternal plan, but don't expect to get any peace, joy, blessing, strengthening, or eternal credit for it.

We have been made holy by God: "For he chose us in him before the creation of the world to be holy and blameless in his sight" (Ephesians 1:4). If you or your children know Christ Jesus as personal Savior, *you already are holy.* We have "become the righteousness of God" (2 Corinthians 5:21). We have a "new self, created to be like God in true righteousness and holiness" (Ephesians 4:24). *We are holy. God says so, and that settles it for eternity.*

But unfortunately, we don't have to live up to what we already are. We can choose to miss the special joy of living in intimate fellowship with our holy Father. If we yield to Satan and the world and the old, dead self, we have lost the cutting edge, the peak, the power, the ecstasy of the believer's way. There's no middle ground: "You adulterous people, don't you know that friendship with the world is hatred toward God? Anyone who *chooses* to be a friend of the world becomes an enemy of God" (James 4:4, emphasis added). We still have free will, and we can choose to be, for the flimsiest of pleasures, a friend of the world.

We don't even ask ourselves and our children the right questions. As a minimum, we ought to be asking ourselves all the time: "Is that filthy to me?" We ought to be forcing our children to consider this: "Is this filthy to you?" But ultimately, even these are the wrong questions. The question isn't what's filthy to you. The question is what's filthy to God. How much of your life would have to go out the window if you started asking this question?

God's High Standards

Holiness isn't optional for a believer. It isn't something that we achieve by our own efforts, and it isn't some magical, one-time point past which sin is impossible. But by walking in faith and obedience to God's Word through the power of the Holy Spirit, we can without a doubt walk a holy walk on a minute-by-minute basis. To deny this is to say that we really aren't free from prison, that we really aren't a new creation, and that Satan is stronger than God. Do we really want to say these things?

If we couldn't walk a holy walk, why would God tell us "to be holy in all you do" (1 Peter 1:15)? Why would He tell us to "Be perfect, therefore, as your heavenly Father is perfect" (Matthew 5:48)? He tells us these things because He means them—for you, now. But we can set the standards for our lives and our children too low. We can make too many excuses for our sinfulness.

Why are there so many Christians and so few results? Polls tell us that there may be fifty million born-again Christians in the United States. I only have one question: Where are they? They must all be in the desert in New Mexico, because they sure aren't having much effect anywhere else. Our culture looks more and more pagan because we Christians accept our "fire insurance," and then do pretty much what we please. Do we like the way the culture is going?

God says that "To fear the LORD is to hate evil" (Proverbs 8:13). We are disgusted when we read about sin-crazed people who put things in the temple in Jerusalem to defile it. But now *we* are the temple of God; are we disgusted when we put things or allow things into our very own temple? Fearing the Lord is hating evil—not just not participating in it, not just resisting it, but *hating* it because we serve a holy and awesome God! Fearing the Lord is the beginning of wisdom, so that even wisdom itself depends on purity: "But the wisdom that comes from heaven is *first of all* pure" (James 3:17, emphasis added).

Walking in Holiness

Are there steps to walking in holiness? Jesus has already covered this point: "Sanctify them by the truth; your word is truth. . . . For them I sanctify myself, that they too may be truly sanctified" (John 17:17, 19). God is a very practical God who has given us a written plan for sanctification in the Bible. We walk in holiness as we follow His Word, not by going through spiritual "exercises" or having emotional experiences. Fill yourself and your children with Scripture, particularly Scripture that speaks of the holy walk: Deuteronomy 32:45–47, Psalms 15, 101, and 119, 1 Peter 1:13–2:3, and 2 Peter 1:3–11 would be good places to start.

Controlling your tongue (see James 3:2) leads to holiness, with particular emphasis on doing "everything without complaining or arguing, so that you may become blameless and pure, children of God without fault in a crooked and depraved generation, in which you shine like stars in the universe" (Philippians 2:14–15). And with thoughts and words in check, you can be "clear minded and self-controlled so that you can pray" (1 Peter 4:7).

But isn't this tough? Where do we get the power to walk out of a dirty conversation? Where does the strength come from to turn off the television or radio and open the Word instead? Can we not only avoid sins of commission, but also sins of omission? How do we do it? It's simple. You've already won, if you'll believe it:

His divine power has given us everything we need for life and godliness through our knowledge of him who called us by his own glory and goodness. Through these, he has given us his very great and precious promises, so that through them you may participate in the divine nature and escape the corruption in the world caused by evil desires. (2 Peter 1:3–4)

You do it by an absolute reliance on the power of God—for every breath, every decision, every step, every minute. No turning back or glancing away. If you believe that He's given you this power, it's enough. It's sufficient. In fact, it's all there is that can do the job. Claim it for yourself, and hold your child's hand out to accept it for himself.

Can parents today teach their children how to walk as holy as they already are in God's sight? We can, absolutely. We can hold God's standards high, fill our children with the purifying Word, teach them and show them how to control their tongues, and work with them on self-control by the power of God. We can pick their friends carefully. We can talk to their teachers and others and find out who the godly children are, and get rid of this nonsense about letting little children pick their own friends. We can protect them from much and prepare them for the rest.

But will we, as a Christian community, do these things? I wish I could be more optimistic. Pan is playing his enchanting tune, and the children of God are following him with reckless abandon. We have lost our sense of the loftiness of God, as we have chased after the worthless things of life. We can too easily expect nothing more out of our children than a quick confession and holding rottenness to a minimum. We have lost an understanding of the whole reason God left us here — not to soak up the atmosphere, but to *clean* up the atmosphere.

If you take nothing else in this book seriously, take seriously the holiness of God. Lift your sights, and lift your children so they can look into the sanctuary with you.

If they see it, it will be a vision that will last them a lifetime.

Inside Out

One of the biggest problems that any parent has is how to *internalize* his values into the spirits of his children.

Now this is a very difficult thing to do, and many parents don't even know that it needs to be done. Instead, they go about *imposing* their values onto the spirits of their children, often producing the appearance of obedience and control while the parents graciously accept the applause of their admiring friends.

It looks good right up to the time the lid slides off — or blows off.

An excellent scriptural example of this difference between internalizing and imposing is found in 2 Chronicles 23–24. Here's a young man, Joash, who is made king of Judah at the age of seven, largely as the result of the efforts of the chief priest, Jehoiada. Jehoiada, a godly man, removes the boy's wicked grandmother, who had tried to kill the boy, and places Joash on the throne of David. Jehoiada not only made many important decisions for the new king, but also helped him in his decision-making. "Joash did what was right in the eyes of the LORD *all the years of Jehoiada the priest"* (2 Chronicles 24:2, emphasis added).

Apparently the only thing the priest forgot to do was to internalize God's values into the boy king. This is equivalent to someone saying about your child, "He did what was right in the eyes of the Lord all the years of his parents." Do you really think that's enough? Will that satisfy you as a parent? More importantly, will that satisfy your Lord?

It wasn't enough for Joash. As soon as Jehoiada was dead, Joash went completely out of control. He listened to phony praise and took the advice of false counselors. He abandoned the very temple that he had helped to restore with Jehoiada and went on to worship Asherah poles and idols. Finally, in an ultimate act of gross sinfulness, he had the son of Jehoiada, a prophet, put to death. He "did not remember the kindness Zechariah's father Jehoiada had shown him but killed his son" (2 Chronicles 24:22). Joash paid the price when those who were offended by this incredible ungratefulness killed him in his bed.

Instilling God's Values

You can't allow yourself to make the mistake of imposing values rather than rooting them deeply. You must internalize God's values into your children. Nothing else will do. Imposing these values is a band-aid over a wound that will grow wider every year. As Jehoiada's family found to its dismay, sacrifice for a child isn't enough. Love isn't enough. Kindness isn't enough. Either the values are a part of the child, or they are nothing and will disappear when *you* disappear.

There's no doubt that you can produce a godly veneer if you choose to impose values. If you yourself are a godly and powerful man or woman of God, you may even be able to make this imposition last past high school and college—perhaps even to the end of *your* life.

But it probably won't last to the end of your child's life. Like Pavlovian dogs that respond to the stimulus of the mastermind, your children can be behavior modified and assertively disciplined until their instant and mindless responses impress your friends and family and woo converts to the idea of parental despotism. But again, the question is: When you disappear, will your children's "values" disappear with you?

There's no question that it takes more wisdom and time to internalize, rather than impose, values. This is because internalizing is a process, while imposing is simply an act.

Our daughter hated getting up for school when she was in first grade. I'm certain that I could have simply imposed the requirement to get up on time onto this little child. Instead, we chose to teach her what Scripture says about that ever-present Biblical personage, the sluggard. We looked at Scripture and talked about and observed many applications, both good and bad, of these principles. We didn't do it just one time but went through a process that took months. We got her an alarm clock of her own, so that she would have the necessary tools to do it *herself*.

The result? She's now to the point that she gets up before any of us and is reading before most people shut off their alarms. She doesn't even have to *set* her alarm anymore. It's become a habit to rise early and get a good start on the day God has given her. She doesn't do it because I've commanded her or because she's afraid of what I'll do or say, but simply because she has chosen to rise early. It's an act of her own will. There was a lot of effort in the beginning, but there's no fuss now.

Our oldest son is a first-class storyteller, with all of the hyperbole and embellishments that a spinner of yarns could want. But it was difficult when he was younger for him to pick out the difference between telling stories and telling lies. I could have demanded that he stop saying anything untrue, even when it was just part of a fun conversation. I could have threatened his life and limb if I ever caught him telling a lie. But we chose the process route instead.

We taught him what Scripture says about being a man of integrity. We discussed and observed together the consequences of lying and the benefits of telling the truth. Part of our bedtime routine always involves my asking him the question, "Are you intending to be a man of integrity?" We have shown him why lying about something is usually worse than the thing he's trying to cover up. This process has taken years, but I believe that when we are done he'll be a man willing to tell the truth even at great personal cost, rather than a fool who lies to get something or out of cowardice.

Evaluating Their Progress

One of the best measures of how you're doing in this area is to watch what the children are interested in and what they aren't. Take the issue of friends. If you're like most parents, you want your children to have excellent friends. You can see pretty clearly which of their peers are godly and which ones are godless. If, no matter what you say, your children keep leaning toward and pushing to have godless friends, and you feel like you're in a war of wills, you're imposing—and losing. If, instead, your children with their own judgment consistently pick godly friends and avoid the godless, you're internalizing—and winning.

In a sense, this illustrates the difference between innocence and purity. Innocence is a valuable gift from God to our children, and we should do all we can to guard and protect it in our spiritual greenhouse. But children grow into discerning adults, and there's no way to forever keep them from exposure to things that will chip away at their innocence. Purity, on the other hand, is a choice—on God's part, to want our children to be pure and to give them the wisdom and power to do it; and on our children's part, to accept these things and to walk a holy walk.

If you should hear a bad report about your children, don't say, "Well, so-and-so told me about what you did, and don't ever do it again." Instead, ask them how they did in the particular situation. If they're old enough, ask them to rate themselves on a one-to-ten scale, and then tell you why. Ask them questions that help them get down to the truth. Ask them to tell you what they could have done better. Praise them for their honesty and insight. If you suspect they're holding back, suggest that they and you meet with your source. Either your children will come clean, or you will have a real interesting conversation with old so-and-so.

There are certainly times when commands are called for—when the child has, for example, disobeyed a clear-cut rule. There are times when they're heading for danger, or are merely hyped up and out of control, and the best recourse is to a command. But whenever possible, choose the route of internalization over the easier route of imposition. Teach a child to respond only to a command, and you've taught him godliness for a moment; teach a child to respond also to the truth, and you've taught him godliness for a lifetime.

Internalizing values *can* look sloppy along the way, while imposing values usually looks neat and crisp and effective. But consider the end product and the time when your actual control might be weakened or you are gone. Will your child be a self-chosen man or woman of God? Or will they be Pavlovian dogs, loose in a world without their master, spineless animals listening for someone's direction while they rush pell-mell into the waiting arms of the one who will enslave them?

Be wise. Internalize.

Establishing Holiness in Your Home

Television

We hear a lot about parents who have taken the extreme step of getting rid of their televisions in a protest against what they perceive to be the slime, perversion, ungodliness, and generally disgusting material that pervades television in our day. It has been said that television as a medium is doomed forever to mediocrity, but that would be fine if it just wasn't a sewer, too.

Sometimes trying to find a decent television program is akin to trying to find a ham sandwich in a garbage can, and so I am sympathetic to this point of view. But do we dare to eliminate such a technological wonder, much less one that can double as an inexpensive and unreliable babysitter? Without television how will our children appreciate the diversity, cleverness, and inventiveness of the secular world in which they live. We are awed at the understanding of filth that they can gain from commercials and previews alone.

You can clearly see how important I think it is for you to allow your child not only to have access to a television, but also to watch it as often and as much as possible. In our home; we allow our children to sit in front of their television night after night, for as many hours as seems good to them — *we just don't let them turn it on.*

Appeasement

Winston Churchill described appeasement as a process of feeding an alligator with the hope that he'll eat you last. Many parents are raising little alligators, and the easiest thing in the world is to appease them.

The process of appeasement can begin when any problem or evil creeps into your child's life. When you see something in his life that you know to be unscriptural and which offends your sense of right and wrong in however subtle a way, you have a choice to make.

The right choice is to deal with it in a straightforward and loving way, helping the child through the problem quickly and deliberately, using all of the tools of God and the authority He has delegated to you to bring about a godly life in your child. You can begin to internalize values on this point, hiding the Word in his heart so he won't sin against God (see Psalms 119:11). In the meantime, you can bound his life with clear commands.

This is the way that wins. Don't let any junk get off the ground, and you can fight it before it becomes a part of his life.

The other choice is really destructive. For whatever reason—sentimentality, cowardice, ignorance of the ruinous nature of evil, whatever—you decide to allow the attitude or action to continue, but you decide to "control" it through various restrictions.

The argument goes something like this: I can only do so much to control a child. If I'm too tough on this, it might produce even more rebellion; tough standards will only make the thing more attractive anyway. This world has become too evil to block it all out. He's going to have to learn how to deal with this for himself in any case and surely some restrictions are better than the nothing that other parents are doing.

This, folks, is rationalization, and an acceptance of the worst that worldly wisdom has to offer. It's not as good as internalizing. It's not even as good as imposing.

The results will likely be at least as bad as if you had set *no* restrictions on the attitude or action. First and worst, you'll have left your child on an evil road that leads to all kinds of death and misery. Your child will still struggle with your authority—maybe even to a greater degree, because evil tends to expand in new and horrific ways. He'll probably still view you as a tyrant for putting any restrictions on him, because this kind of "freedom" produces a thirst for more of the same. You'll have taught him that a little evil is okay and that it's all right to live outside of God's boundaries. This can naturally lead him into other areas of violation. His disrespect for your lukewarmness, and finally for you, will grow and perhaps even devour your relationship.

And the joke is on you, because it won't stop what he's doing and it won't pacify him. God never called parents to control evil in their children; He expects us to work with Him to totally weed it out. Scripture says that parents who love their son are *"careful* to discipline him" (Proverbs 13:24, emphasis added). This means that you think about it, and then do it.

This problem of appeasement can be particularly serious when it involves an older child, perhaps one who was adopted, taken in as a foster or spiritual son or daughter, or just not trained when he was younger. You might feel that your whole relationship with him is marginal and that his willingness to submit to your authority is practically nil; you might even fear that he'll reject you totally and, if he is old enough, run away. The result can be a tremendous temptation to appease the child, while rationalizing that you're just trying to be fair and accomplish some good.

Don't do it. Appeasement in parenting is placing boundaries around your child's evil behavior when you know that the behavior itself is wrong. There's no way this path can be blessed. Go back instead to the basics and weed the evil out. Do it as early as possible before it grows into a habit. Do it lovingly, but do it right. The lessons they'll learn and the death they'll experience if you don't do this will be too high. Training in godliness is worth all of the risks, even that of losing the child. And if they aren't trained in godliness, they're not really even yours to lose in the first place.

I'm not saying that you shouldn't try to control your *children.* I am saying that you shouldn't try to control *evil* at a certain level. In other words, you want to put ice into the boiling water, not a lid on the boiling pot.

Don't accept even a little evil, for "a little yeast works through the whole batch of dough" (1 Corinthians 5:6). Jesus was completely clear: We are either with Him or against Him. We should be equally clear. We are to treat evil as a pariah, something so filthy and so bad that the stench drives our spirits from the room — or better, causes us to call on our God so that He'll drive the stench from our presence.

It's the only way to live, and the only way that works. No surrender. No compromise. And no appeasement.

Taking the Fifth Amendment

What goes through your mind when you hear something true but awful about someone whom you've always respected?

Whether it's George Washington or your Aunt Susie, your reaction probably runs toward disappointment—perhaps even bitter disappointment, if your respect was particularly high and the story was particularly low. At some point, especially if the story involves an offense against you or someone else you love, your disappointment can turn to anger or even hatred. That's why Scripture says: "He who covers over an offense promotes love, but whoever repeats the matter separates close friends" (Proverbs 17:9).

Filth dredged from a person's past can really damage his friendship with many people, even close friends. This problem doesn't have to exist in a church that's supposed to be filled with merciful servants, but the problem is that the church *isn't* filled with merciful servants. It's filled with too many snooty, proud Christians who simply love running others' reputations through the muck while they forget what they themselves were once like in God's eyes.

There's too much repeating and too little covering over in God's family. After a person has requested forgiveness from the offended person and the offended God, his time in the spotlight of guilt should end. God is in the forgiving and forgetting business; if we are His children, what business should we be in? Should we be like the prodigal's brother, who wanted to keep his brother's sin on the front burner? Or should we be like the prodigal's father, who wanted to take his son's sin off the stove and start a celebration?

We must stop ruining others, and their friendships and loves, with our passing things along in public displays or private conversations. You wouldn't want others to do it to you; who in heaven gave you the right to do it to someone else?

This matter becomes crucial with regard to your children. You're the pride of your children, one of their highest models on earth and their continual example. If someone—be it pastor or elder or prominent Christian or friend or acquaintance or enemy—starts spreading around some of your past sin, what do you think it will do to your children?

It could ruin their opinion of you. It might even ruin them. Muck sucks people to a lower level. Always.

Be careful of what your children hear. Who knows how much damage has been done by grandparents or other relatives telling children what rotten little beasts their parents were when they were younger? Who knows what children have picked up from the ungodly recollections about their parents given by their parents' old school friends? Who knows what scars are left when a friend or enemy demolishes a parent with reckless words in the presence of his children?

God knows. So do the children. Keep your children away from these kinds of people and discussions. Far, far away.

And don't condemn yourself with your own mouth. It's absolutely terrible to do this in a joking way with someone in the presence of your children. By making light of the "boys will be boys" approach to life and by displaying a twisted view of God and His holiness, you send the message to your children that some sin is okay, especially if it's during your younger years. Don't you think they'll pick up the hypocrisy of sending this message tonight, and then sending a message tomorrow that a similar transgression on their part will be punished?

Parents who avoid the above pitfall can still get into plenty of trouble by sharing in a serious way the details of their past sins with others in the presence of their children or with their children directly. Hearing about what you were like when you were a dead person just isn't going to elevate their view of the possibilities of the Christian life. Your motive — sharing these truths to help others see that you're only human, or to warn or show them what to avoid — might be understandable, but it's wrong.

People, including your children, already *know* that you're only human. Your children are more aware of that than most people you know. They don't need to see how human or natural you are or were; they need to see how spiritual and supernatural you have become by the grace of God. If someone is building a beautiful building and is asked to submit photographs of his lovely new work to a prominent magazine, does he send pictures of the elegant parts that are already finished or some old photos of a slimy hole awaiting the start of the construction?

You don't need details of your past to warn or teach your children or others about the dangers of sin, either. There are already plenty of specifics in Scripture to use for these purposes — and Scripture is inspired by God, while your past life wasn't. If you'll take the principles and specifics of Scripture, and mix them with the general wisdom and experience in God's ways that you've picked up, you'll have a powerful warning/teaching course for your children.

If you're in a conversation with your son and you're talking about purity, to tell him that you committed fornication three times before you married has no possibility of edifying him or achieving your purpose. It'll lower his opinion of God and you and the sacredness of marriage and the supreme value of maintaining his virginity until marriage and the excellence of a holy walk.

But to tell him about what God teaches in His Word about purity and holiness, to illustrate from Scripture the blessings and punishments that accompany following or not following this path, to warn him that this particular sin is a "sin of the fathers" that's been passed down and might be a special problem to watch out for, and to confirm to him that you also know these things to be true from your own experience — *now* you're doing some godly teaching!

In other words, train your children with God's examples of sin, not your own. As far as the specifics of your past sins and life as a dead person, take the fifth amendment. Don't admit to anything.

Some people reading this will disagree with this suggestion. "Nobody should pretend to be perfect," they'll say.

I agree. Nobody should pretend to be perfect. The Bible says, "If we claim to be without sin, we deceive ourselves and the truth is not in us" (1 John 1:8). I'm not saying that you should pretend to be perfect. Admit to any and all that you're not perfect, and that you're praising God that He loved you and saved you when you were a totally befuddled sinner. But *don't* admit to the details of the past. How valuable is it to hear what a corpse in a casket was doing? Weren't you dead in your sins, a spiritual corpse in a spiritual casket? Why not talk about something valuable — like *life?*

Do me a favor. Do those around you a favor. Do yourself a favor. Do your children a favor.

Take the fifth amendment.

To Everything, A Season

One of the most critical areas of holiness is that of moral purity. You *must* teach your children to learn to relate to their bodies in a godly, spiritual, and balanced way.

Parents of an earlier day may have erred on the side of giving too little teaching concerning the importance of the body and a proper view of sexuality. You don't want to be in this category. Talk to your children about these things a little at a time, as they're ready. Dads need to take the lead in this. When children are little, tell them enough to protect them from the twisted people that drive through neighborhoods. When children are older, give them the high Biblical vision of marriage, and not just the biological facts.

Self-Discovery

This may come as a surprise to you, but your children will eventually discover that they have bodies. If they're really astute, they'll also discover that some things bring them pleasure and other things bring them pain. Avoidance of pain comes naturally to children.

Avoidance of pleasure doesn't.

From their earliest moments, children find that certain things are pleasurable and build them into their habits of life. At first, everything is taste-tested. Later, everything not hung from the ceiling will get looked at, listened to, smelled, touched, and very probably dismantled. It's all new to them, and they're just as fascinated by their new location as any parent is on a vacation to an exotic spot.

Inevitably they'll finally discover their bodies. This finding of their bodies might come in the tub or the bed or the backyard, but sooner or later it will happen. What they do with this discovery, and more importantly, what *you* do with their discovery, can have an effect on them so dramatic and life-changing that no parent can afford to avoid the issue.

Many parents in the past, and perhaps many parents even today, simply pretended as though this discovery just wasn't going to happen. "Nice" people didn't discuss such things, and *certainly* not with children. They left their children to discover the truth about their bodies on their own behind the barn or in the backseat of a car or on their wedding night. Millions of mistakes by millions of people is the legacy — one matched only by the terrible tonnage of guilt and shame carried like excess baggage in countless aching spirits.

Some parents of today, however, may have slipped to the other side of the issue. They may be telling their children too much, too soon, too

unrelated to the role their bodies will play in living a successful, powerful, and joyous life.

These parents may admit their awareness of their child's self-discovery and then may allow it to go on without comment. Some, in this day
of no acknowledged sin or folly or restraint, may even encourage it pas-
sively, by allowing unrestricted television or movies or friendships; or
actively, by things too despicable to mention. There might be a feeling
that "it's only natural," and, of course, they're right; but that's been the
problem ever since man cut the natural away from the supernatural. The
natural by itself always leads to death. As parents, we want to have
children about whom we can say, "It's only *supernatural*."

One other possible response is open irritation or even anger if parents find their children in sexual self-discovery. This can be righteous
anger, but it can also be anger that comes from a parent's frustrations
over his or her own sexual life or failures. This response, even when
motivated by a righteous spirit, can produce the very same result as
either ignoring it (so that the sin slowly swallows up the child) or allowing it (so that the sin quickly swallows up the child).

Irritation or anger can send a thousand destructive and confusing
signals to a child but will probably not discourage the child's action.
Your irritation and anger attempt to force a value on the child from the
outside, when it's beyond your ability to enforce it. You must internalize
a godly concept of sexuality. Your response of anger can, in fact, lead to
more sin and guilt and death.

Sexuality Is Created Good

So what do you do with your child's self-discovery program? Do you
ignore it? No. Do you encourage it? No. Do you become angry and for-
bid it? No. Do you tell him it's good? No. Do you tell him it's bad? No.

"Well," you say, "that clinches it. I suspected all along that the only
way to deal with this explosive issue was to lock my children in their
bedrooms until they're eighty." Tied in a chair. No television or radio.
No books or magazines. No visitors.

But you can't ignore this self-discovery. And you shouldn't encourage it. Anger won't stop the confused feelings, even if it stops the actions for a while. And yet, while innocent discovery of self may not be a
sin, unrestrained discovery will almost certainly lead to that conclusion.

The truth is, their sexuality was created to be a good thing, but it can be used in many bad ways.

And this is exactly what your children should be taught: Their sexuality is a good thing and can be used either for proper and noble purposes or the slimiest and emptiest goals. You can show examples from Scripture to your children: from the exquisite poetry of the Song of Solomon and the love of Ruth and Boaz, to the hideous story of the men of Sodom (see Genesis 18–19) and the empty life of the woman of Samaria (see John 4:1–26).

Early in your children's lives, if you see them engaging in self-stimulation or perhaps even innocent activities with others, you should show them that God created their bodies and made them in such a way that they can experience many pleasures. But just because they *can* doesn't mean that they *should*. They need to know that while the physical pleasure may be good for a moment, it's the attitude and circumstances *behind* the pleasure that determine whether they'll have soaring or guilty spirits, powerful or disjointed lives.

Tell them how wonderful sexual pleasure can and will be—at the right time, in the right place, with the right person. Teach them the beauty of being a part of creation, but also teach the truth to the girls that "like a gold ring in a pig's snout is a beautiful woman who shows no discretion" (Proverbs 11:22). Instruct the boys that by improper sexual activity they can give their "best strength to others" (Proverbs 5:7–14). You want champions, not chumps, and failure in this area of life has turned many potential champions into chumps. Don't let it happen to your children.

Our children must know that used rightly, this sexuality is a blessing, but used wrongly, it's a terrible sin that will devour their spirits *and* their bodies. They must be shown from Scripture the results of rightly and wrongly used sexuality. Finally, they must believe that if used in God's way, their bodies and their desires will be able to be satisfied, but if used their own way, there will be no satisfaction and no fulfillment.

And, in the end, not even any pleasure.

Indignation

If your children are going to walk a holy walk in an unholy world, they're going to need to know when and how to be indignant.

It's possibly true that *you* don't know when and how to be indignant. So the first thing to do is define *indignation*. *Indignation* is "anger excited by that which is unworthy, base, or disgraceful; righteous wrath."

Righteous wrath. If I can have that, I have one more thing that makes me an imitator of God, for God displays mighty indignation many times in Scripture. For most of us, wrath comes pretty easily; it's the righteousness part that causes the rub.

You need indignation. Your children need indignation. This is an age which demands that we who believe have indignation. James Russell Lowell said, "The capacity of indignation makes an essential part of the outfit of every honest man." If you want your children to be holy clear to the bone, you must teach them about the necessary ingredient of indignation.

What are the key ingredients of this crowning attribute? These can be seen from the actions of Jesus the two times He cleared the temple of the money changers (see John 2:13–17; Mark 11:15–17):

- Jesus was offended because God the Father was offended. Your children must have the right purpose. They shouldn't become indignant about someone taking their toys. The purpose must be related to a direct and unrelenting assault against *God,* not against your children, by someone who doesn't fear God.

- Jesus didn't participate in the sales show. Your children must not be participating in the offensive act if they want their integrity to shine and their indignation to be righteous.

- Jesus went into action at the right time; He displayed His indignation "on reaching Jerusalem." Your children should allow themselves to become indignant only when other efforts have failed or appear to be fruitless; then they should move without hesitation.

- Jesus prepared for His effort. Contrary to the picture of indignation being wild anger, He took the time to make a whip. Your children should prepare themselves with the whip of Scripture, to have it ready so they can drive out the enemies of God.

- Jesus didn't have a lengthy dialogue with those in the area, asking them politely to leave. He just "began driving out those who were buying and selling there." If your children are sure of their position, they too will know that debates and requests will not work on those who are spitting in God's face. Your children will just quickly and directly go to work.

- Jesus carried out His effort with lots of action and few words, and He wasn't gentle with either. His words were warnings and quotations of Scripture. Your children should know and present the scriptural reason for their action, and without further ado they should act.

- Jesus was so overwhelming that His disciples remembered the prophecy: "Zeal for your house will consume me." How many children — or adults, for that matter — have you known who had *that* kind of zeal? We had better get it into us and our children before the battle is lost. Only the zeal of God's people is capable of turning the tide.

- Jesus offered no apologies. Neither should you. Neither should your children. It's the world that owes *God* the apology. The world might not give it, but that doesn't matter as long as the world has been forced to hide out at the far edge of the cesspool where it belongs.

What should make you indignant? How about millions of slaughtered unborn babies? How about stores selling pornography not too far from your house? How about newspapers printing the horrible details of countless murders while editorializing on more leniency for the murderers? How about your local schools being willing to teach *anything* as long as it's not what *you* believe?

Write some letters. Make some phone calls. Spend some time and money fighting for right. Make a sign and put your faith on the line. And involve your children in all of this. Let them see righteous indignation in action.

If you don't think there's anything "unworthy, base, or disgraceful" going on, then you can forget this section until something comes along.

Or until you wake up.

Conclusion

You can be holy as God is holy. Your children can follow you and be holy as God is holy. If you internalize rather than impose holiness, your children will walk a holy walk even when you're not around or have gone home to heaven. You must deal with evil squarely and not allow even "little" sins to take root in your children's lives. You should be careful not to expose them to the details of evil, including your own past life. You must convince your children of the crucial role that moral purity will play in their lives. Finally, when they're walking God's way and see something that's a stench to Him, they should know how to display righteous indignation.

Do these things, and watch the world change around your family.

9

STABILITY

Once more a remnant . . . will take root
below and bear fruit above.

(Isaiah 37:31)

There have been few nations in which the people were less rooted and less stable than in the United States, a land full of restless nomads.

Nomads? Why, we don't have a nation full of tent-dwellers and camel-riders! But *nomads* are those who are part of a group "that has no fixed location, but wanders from place to place." There can't be a better description of our blighted culture.

We wander from house to house, community to community, city to city, state to state, job to job, school to school, church to church, marriage to marriage, relationship to relationship. We wander as much as another group that spent forty years wandering around a desert. And we create our own desert, a dry and dusty place where nothing living can take root.

There's just not much continuity. In business, for example, many managers and others don't stay one place for very long. The willingness to uproot and move from job to job within a company or from company to company is actually viewed as an asset rather than a liability. And yet, if you give these people a choice as to whom they think would be the most effective—a brilliant manager at a company for only a year or a good manager at a company for twenty-five years—most would probably say the latter.

That's because there's no substitute for stability, consistency, and continuity. Not brilliance or motivation or money or possessions. Not activities or programs or birthday parties. Nothing. If you don't give your family strong and stable roots, then you haven't given them anything that will last for generations. And if you're serious about parenting, you're thinking generations, not just till the end of your children's high school years.

Stable Parents

It has been said that parenting is the only skilled job in the world that requires no prior experience.

A parent is dealing with an entirely new situation, requiring a vast array of skills on a project of many years' duration. Although there are many vital principles that can be learned, each situation will require yet another skillful and varied application. To compound the problem, each new child requires a different application of the principles. Add to this the fact that you're changing at the same time, and being a successful parent can look as achievable as finding an out-of-the-way church when you're late for a wedding.

But your children desperately need you to be there for them. They need you to be stable and consistent in your dealings with your spouse and with them. They need to be able to *count* on things, year after year, regardless of circumstances.

To help your children with these needs, you have to start with yourself. You have to start *within* yourself. Are you an up-and-down Christian, struggling constantly with depression or frustration? You don't have the right to be this kind of Christian, either before God or your children. Are you continually dealing with sorrow about people and things? You have to understand that "godly sorrow brings repentance . . . and leaves no regret, but worldly sorrow brings death" (2 Corinthians 7:10). Are you still wallowing in a worthless, longstanding sin? Run to your God like a rock badger runs into the rocks (see Proverbs 30:26), and let God stabilize your life.

This stability that comes from within must be carried over into your role as a parent. Sadly, you *can* be no more than a physical parent, simply providing food and shelter, and letting "nature" take its course.

Your children will probably still grow up, and they will probably not hate you. You must understand, however, that your substitution of the material for the spiritual will not be appreciated by your child. He'll resent your omission even as he holds his hand out for more.

The state of parenting in the United States has deteriorated in many ways to this maintenance level. People are spending huge sums on education, lessons, and activities for their children, choosing to confuse *spending* with *parenting*. This is simply a higher state of materialism, not a better method of parenting.

A stable home is so important in God's eyes that He makes it a requirement for church and family leadership: "He must manage his own family well and see that his children obey him with proper respect. (If anyone does not know how to manage his own family, how can he take care of God's church?)" (1 Timothy 3:4–5).

Most businessmen don't bother to check out the stability of a man's home life before they hire him; they think this is none of their business. Wise businessmen, however, always check this out as best they can, because they know that this is probably the most important thing to consider in order to hire a wise man, and not simply a fool with credentials.

Training Parents

One of the best possible training courses for young or first-time parents is rarely used. Every church has multiple opportunities to work with other people's children. A wise parent will use these as golden gifts, as he works with children who are older than his own. Young couples who don't have children yet can learn a tremendous amount from working with a nursery or toddler class.

If this approach makes sense to you, don't limit yourself to working with children a little older than your own. If you have a little boy who is four, you would be amazed at how much you can build into his training from working with fifteen-year-olds. It helps to see the end from the beginning, to know what you're working toward and what you're working away from. A side benefit is that you can really help some other parents and kids as you contribute to one of the most undeveloped and undersupported areas of church life.

Some of you might not take this practical approach to gaining experience, but you'll only be hurting yourself. You might be the father or mother of a child about whom people will say, "Look at that little fool—what's the matter with his parents?" Or "Can you believe he (wrecked the car, got caught with drugs, got that girl in trouble, etc.)? His parents must really be out to lunch." Or say about you, "There's no way we want him as an elder or deacon. Just look at his kids!"

Is it starting to become clear why Scripture says that "there is no joy for the father of a fool" (Proverbs 17:21)?

You must do more than just acquire principles. You must use them, over and over. You should be constantly oriented toward *action* in all your dealings with your child: Try it, do it, work with it. You must put what you know into practice consistently and resist the strong push that Satan and the world and your own nature will make to get you to be a nomadic, physical parent only. The time is short, and the time to make your children mighty in spirit is now.

The choice is yours.

Zapped!

If you agree that you must be a stable parent, working consistently in all areas of life to develop stable Christian champions, where does your work begin?

With your marriage.

Even if you follow the rest of the advice in this book, you can still zap your children's ability to be the champions that God wants them to be by missing the lesson of Ephesians 5:22–32.

The bottom line? Your attempts at training your children will be largely ineffective if you who are wives don't submit to and respect your husbands. No *ifs, ands,* or *buts.* You must do these things—all day, every day, even though it's hard, even though your husband might abuse his authority or not always be "worthy" of your respect, even though Satan is tempting you to become a "modern" woman. You're told to submit in everything.

Scripture says that it's "better to live on a corner of the roof than share a house with a quarrelsome wife. . . . Better to live in a desert than with a quarrelsome and ill-tempered wife" (Proverbs 21:9, 19). This is certainly true for her husband, and it's no less true for her children.

In the same way, your attempts at training your children are largely a waste of time if you who are husbands don't love your wives as your own body, giving yourself up for *their* benefit, making them holy, clean, radiant, and blameless. You *must* do this, even if she isn't "beautiful," even if she doesn't submit to you or respect you, even if at times you would rather be on the roof or in the desert.

Why are these things so crucial? First, because in watching your marriage relationship, your children will come to see and understand and appreciate the profound mystery of Christ and the church. God frequently gives us earthly symbols of heavenly truths. If you want your children to see how they should relate to Christ, let them see you moms relating in a submissive, respectful way to their fathers. If you want your children to see how Christ would relate to them, let them see you dads relating in a loving, sacrificial way to their mothers.

Can you see how absolutely indispensable this is? If either parent doesn't do his or her part, then he or she has zapped their children and given them only half of the true and total picture. Either the children won't be ready and willing to submit to Christ, or they won't be ready to accept the love that Christ has for them. They can get over these gaps, but it won't be easy, and they probably won't be champions.

It's been said that the greatest thing a dad can do for his children is to love their mother. It sounds good, but it isn't true. The greatest thing a dad can do for his children is to love God. That's the pinnacle of parenting.

But loving their mother is a mighty good number two.

Two Masters

Just being a stable, consistent parent who is in right relationship with your spouse is very good. But it's not enough. You've got another problem to overcome.

There are two of you.

Now, you might not have thought that this was a problem up till now. You might have even thought it was nice. But in parenting, it can be a real handicap.

Why? Jesus gives us the principle: "No one can serve two masters. Either he will hate the one and love the other, or he will be devoted to the one and despise the other" (Matthew 6:24).

Does the "no one" include your children? You bet it does! Can the "two masters" describe the parents in many homes? Of course it does. And the result? Parents who oppose one another on various parenting issues, children who manipulate their parents against each other, and children who have a higher opinion of one of the two parents.

Don't argue with me if you disagree. Jesus is the one who said it.

You've got to speak with one voice or you're dead as parents. In fact, you've got to speak as one *person,* one *master,* or you're dead as parents. That's what the Scripture tells us. You're two people; you look for all the world like two masters, you can sound like two masters, you can *be* two masters. But you've got to act as though you're one master. How on earth can two people pull this off?

Because of something else that Jesus said: "For this reason a man will leave his father and mother and be united to his wife, and the two will become one flesh. *So they are no longer two, but one*" (Mark 10:7–8, emphasis added).

You can act as though you're one master and miss the two-master problem, because in God's eyes you *are* one master, you *are* one person. You don't have to act like it, but that's what you are. If you'll learn to put this great truth into practice — never giving conflicting instructions, always checking directions with each other, consistently speaking with one voice — you'll keep your children out of a terrible dilemma. And if you don't do these things, you'll be a house divided against itself.

And your home will surely fall (see Luke 11:17).

Staying Home

And now, the $64,000 question: How can you have a stable home, if nobody's there?

Except for not training them to be believers and physical and emotional abuse, there's not much worse than parents letting someone else raise their child. In their unquenchable thirst for pure materialism, Americans have become so irrational that they'll delegate the one job on which they'll be judged by everyone who knows them.

Working mothers have rapidly become the norm. It's easy to foresee a time when the vast majority of mothers with young and needy children will be spending their best times "mothering" a job that could be done by others—if it needs to be done at all. From "having to work" just to pay bills from past or present excesses, to "having to work" to get a bigger piece of the "American Dream," to saying, "I wasn't cut out to stay home and take care of kids. I have to work for my sanity (or self-image)," a large percentage of women have lowered their vision of motherhood.

No matter what kind of care your children get elsewhere, the right kind of care can only come from you. I'll hazard a guess that eventually working moms will be saved from this terrible worry by a smiling and helpful civil government, which will be pleased to set up and administer a nice, clean, atheistic, humanistic, and very empty program, perhaps with mandatory attendance! Thanks, Uncle Sam—we don't know what we would do without you.

In "How to Raise Kids Right—Advice From 5 Experts," an article in the September 24, 1984 issue of *U.S. News and World Report*, we got a sampling of the delights of not staying home. A professor of education told us that:

The main thing a good preschool program has that the average home doesn't is other children. [They took care of that with birth control and abortion.] They can be very powerful stimuli. . . . The young child is a very social creature, but we haven't realized that fully in our society, where we have tended to put too much emphasis on the nuclear family. . . .

Quality preschools also have loving adults [Notice how they never talk about working mothers putting their children into homes with *mothers.*] who are attuned to the responses of children and give them a great deal of attention. In the average home, the child has to share the attention of the mother, who is distracted by housework, shopping, and other tasks. . . .

A basic question to ask is whether the center or home is licensed or registered by the state. . . .

I would say 6 to 10 months is really the very earliest to enter a child into a group. . . . The child develops a primary attachment to the parents within the first 6 months of life, and it's good to keep children in the home setting during that period.

As if this "advice" wasn't bad enough, they had to quiz a professor of psychology, who warmed our hearts with words like:

> Some people look back fondly at the 1950s, when a far higher percentage of women were still full-time mothers and children were closely supervised. I don't share that nostalgia. It seems to me that young children now have a much more enriched experience. . . .

> So mothers should not feel guilty about returning to work while their children are still babies. . . . The reason working women feel guilty is because of all the propaganda in this century over the extreme importance of mothers for their children's mental health. . . .

> Research . . . shows that girls with mothers who were employed had higher self-esteem . . . and were better adjusted than the daughters of mothers who stayed home full time. . . .

> When it comes to choosing a child-care facility, the main task is to find one that will provide sensitive care attuned to the individual needs of your child. [Has this woman ever *been* in one of these places?] If your child is going to spend 2,000 hours a year in a center, it pays to go and spend a little time observing what goes on.

I remember watching a large day-care group on a walk and thinking: "Little girl, I know where you are — even though your mother doesn't." Working moms, your little children would be better off eating bird seed and wearing cardboard boxes than they are without you.

Dads won't get any relief here either. Where have you been while your child was out of your home? Do you think Scripture says that your sole responsibility is your job, and your wife's job is everything else? If you and your wife fail in this effort, whose head do you think goes into the godly guillotine first?

In an essay entitled "Father," my daughter had this to say: "He finds plenty of time to spend with us, too. . . . He usually stays home in the evenings. My dad is wise." I didn't know that staying home was wise, until I read that essay; I do now. If you are wise in other ways but don't stay home, your children might never know it.

Our culture has another terrific idea. There are millions of children who are raising themselves and doing a pretty poor job of it. These are the children who either leave for school after both parents have left for work, or get home before at least one parent has arrived, or both. A recent magazine article gave tips on how to make this time easier and safer. You should lay out their things and have their meals ready; agree on a list of rules to be followed; teach them how to fight fires and disarm burglars; give them money for cab fare; and, of course, you should try to limit the time alone to a "minimum" of no more than three hours per day (U.S. News and World Report, April 2, 1984).

Marvelous.

One or the other of you needs to be home when your children are. Scripture encourages mothers "to be busy at home" (Titus 2:5). This doesn't mean that she can't run a business — even a substantial business — out of her home (look at the Proverbs 31 woman). But her home is her base.

And this is only a minimum. You dads need to start asking yourselves some valuable questions and leave the materialism quest to those who belong to the world and like to be in chains. Many of you need to reduce your time on career and school and outside activities, so that you can increase your time with your wife and children.

Try a few of these questions: Do I really need to work this weekend? Could this report wait until tomorrow? Do you suppose they would let me work just four or four and a half days a week? Do I really need this course? Will my kids be grateful when I make an appointment with them to show them my degree? Is it possible that the church can get along without me just this once? Is there life without fishing trips with the "boys"?

Ralph Waldo Emerson said, "Great men are they who see that spiritual is stronger than material force." This is the only way for you fathers to become great. Your heavenly Father is with you all the time, and because of that you can be great and you should be grateful. How can your child be great — or grateful — if you aren't there?

Dads and moms, there really is no place like home.

Be there.

The Horror of Divorce

"'I hate divorce,' says the LORD God of Israel" (Malachi 2:16). Me, too.

Too many people have written books on this subject. Almost all of these authors are going to give a serious accounting to God for the lies that they've spewed upon the land. A recent secular book, *The Case Against Divorce,* and the May 29, 1989, cover story in *People* magazine, show that the world is beginning to see the horror of divorce, perhaps even more clearly than some Christians who should know better.

This is an age when men, including so-called church leaders, have come to the conclusion that divorce is acceptable, often necessary, and at times even the best option. And of course, if divorce is okay, then remarriage must be okay, too. After all, would God penalize someone with loneliness, just because they've made a little mistake?

God's Views on Divorce and Remarriage

God says no divorce (see Malachi 2:13–16; Mark 10:9; Romans 7:2; 1 Corinthians 7:39). *Remarriage* isn't even a legitimate word, Biblically speaking. Since He never accepts men putting asunder what He has joined together, then two who have become one *are* one in His eyes. Marriage to someone else isn't called *remarriage* in the Bible; it's called *adultery* (see Mark 10:11–12; Luke 16:18; Romans 7:3), even though many think adultery is only when a married person has sexual relations outside of marriage.

Reconciliation with your original marriage partner isn't remarriage; it's just agreeing to continue a marriage that you were bound to by God and your vow all along and should be encouraged unless a second marriage closes the door on it (see Deuteronomy 24:1–4). An outstanding story of reconciliation is that of the prophet Hosea with his faithless wife Gomer (see Hosea 1–3).

And what about the "exceptions"?

The only time we see the so-called unfaithfulness exception is in Matthew chapters 5 and 19, in a book which was written originally to Jews who knew the Law. What does the word mean? Whatever we want it to? Or does *unfaithfulness* mean what God's Word defines it to be: forbidden marriages (see Leviticus 18) or betrothal (engagement) unfaithfulness (see Deuteronomy 22)? It can't mean adultery, because Jesus didn't *use* the word for adultery; He used a different word. He was saying that a legitimate marriage cannot be broken. His answer was so uncompromising that the disciples said, in effect: "It's for *life?* Count me out!"

And what about the unbeliever leaving (see 1 Corinthians 7:15–16)? Paul was writing to people who had become believers after they were already married, but whose spouses were still unbelievers. He tells them to stick with it. If the unbeliever leaves, the believer is "not bound." What does that mean? Whatever we want it to? Or does it mean that the believer is no longer forced to live in a day-to-day unequal yoking, but not that he can divorce and remarry? Divorce and remarriage are never mentioned in the chapter. In fact, Paul closes the chapter by reiterating that married people are bound for life (v. 39). And this chapter isn't for a believer who deliberately marries an unbeliever; that act is a sin in its own right (see 1 Corinthians 7:39; 2 Corinthians 6:14–17).

What about divorces and multiple marriages between unbelievers? Well, where does it say that God's teaching on marriage and divorce and adultery only applies to believers, and somehow people are allowed divorces and multiple marriages if they're unbelievers? Doesn't God's law apply to them? You can count on it (see 1 John 3:4). Hell is going to be full of people who will be held accountable for their breaking of God's law — and refusal to accept the cure.

This has always been a tough issue. The Jewish leaders came to test Jesus with questions about divorce. John the Baptist gave his life for his stand on the issue, when a remarried woman didn't like his preaching and plotted to have him murdered. Preach clearly on this subject today, and a good number of people may want your head, too.

Don't ever consider a divorce. It will certainly devastate your life — how can you expect anything else when you've thrown a God-instituted relationship back into His face and gone your own way? Divorce might look like the way to happiness, but do you think that you can ever really have joy and long-lasting happiness when you've taken a road that seems right in your own eyes but is offensive to God? Even if it's hard to continue in a marriage, do you think that God is insufficient for your need, or that your difficulties will excuse your sin in the eyes of God? Physical separation from abuse, yes; but divorce, never.

Effects on Your Children

But perhaps even worse than the devastation in your own life will be that wreaked upon your children, your grandchildren, and your great-grandchildren. The *People* cover calls the children of divorce "Wounded Hearts." Amen. Your children will be raised in a bizarre, un-Biblical way, as they live only with one parent or become a living beach ball tossed back and forth between the two parents.

Your children will also have a hard time accepting that your love is unconditional and permanent. After all, didn't you make a pledge to their other parent that you would never stop loving or living with him or her? One secular book that accepts divorce, written for parents to use with their children, has the child asking the mother if she'll stop loving her child just as she stopped loving the child's father. The mother emphasizes that this could never happen, but the child is confused by all of this.

Who wouldn't be?

The decision to divorce has another potential effect that will pound through your descendants' lives for decades, even centuries. You will have taught them by your example that God's Word is a lie, that actions don't have consequences, that vows are nothing (see Ecclesiastes 5:4–6), that love is fickle, that relationships exist only for our personal gratification, and that marriage is a triviality. No matter what you *say,* how do you think *they're* going to look at marriage and divorce in their own lives?

Marrying someone else just compounds the sin, the confusion, and the twisted relationships that will surround your child. Who is my daddy? Who is my mommy? To whom do I submit? It's just not God's way. No matter what else you do, can you count on a champion coming out of this goulash?

Forget divorce and marriage to anyone else. Each is a sin and a monstrous satanic lie, which can destroy you and your children. You cannot expect your children to become champions; they might, but it will be in spite of the insanity that you've inflicted upon them.

If you're divorced, ask God's and your partner's and your children's forgiveness. Show your children how wrong it was. Do everything you can to be reconciled to the other half of you. If your spouse has married another or simply won't be reconciled, then you must not remarry. Spend much time in teaching your children the truth about divorce, and why you're still going to be faithful to your covenant by not marrying another. Show your children your sorrow as you show them the consequences of this divorce in your own and other people's lives and as you illustrate the Biblical truths with your personal examples.

One final word. I'm not saying that you should stay together just for the kids, although that's a mighty fine reason. You should also stay together for the sake of your spouse, your friends, and yourself.

And for the Lord. For our God's sake, believe Him on this one.

On the Road Again

Our culture has always had a measure of mobility, but since the end of World War II we have become the rootless society. In a recent year, one-fifth of the U.S. population picked up and moved. This works out to everybody moving about once in every five years. No wonder many counselors consider transience an able competitor for divorce in the race for maximum stress on families and children.

How can there be any sense of community, belonging, or accountability in a nation where nobody stops moving long enough to meet his neighbors?

People, including Christians, will move almost at the drop of a hat. They'll move for a better job, fancier title, more money, a bigger house, a better climate, more convenient access to leisure activities. Most Christians don't even bother to evaluate what the Lord would have them do. Even worse, some do what they want to do, and then blame it on the Lord: "God just won't let me settle down"; "God is moving me around for a reason"; "You won't believe how God opened up the way for that move."

Balderdash.

Our transience is largely the result of "greed, which is *idolatry*" (Colossians 3:5, emphasis added). Paul tells us that "the love of money is a root of all kinds of evil. Some people, eager for money, have wandered from the faith" (1 Timothy 6:10). Because of our greedy natures, we have created our own gods of money and things — nice things, to be sure, but pretty lousy gods. This has led us away from the faith and from the stable roots that we need to support us in our walk with the one true God.

There is such a thing as a move prompted by God. In that case, the only right answer is to go. But if you're honest, you've got to admit that most of the moves you've seen or been part of didn't have much to do with a vision from the Lord. That ripping up of roots will not benefit people who need roots to grow in stable soil.

When you combine this general restlessness and rootlessness with the nomadic nature of the church, you have the perfect atomistic, isolated, lonely, free-from-accountability Christian. Look at how people move from church to church, empty vagabonds needing to belong but avoiding becoming too close. We *go* to church, when we are supposed to *be* the church.

Look at what transience will teach your children:

- It doesn't pay to get close to anybody, because either you or the other person won't be here in a year or two anyway.

- Being close hurts too much when the other person moves away.

- Moving around for more money is a high priority (don't be surprised when they move away from you).

- People can do what they want, because nobody knows them here.

- No one can make a difference with people that aren't going to be around for very long, so why bother to serve people?

- We don't need to fix broken relationships; there's plenty of other acquaintances to spend time with.

- Extended family doesn't have much value. Grandparents are there to send me birthday cards and Christmas presents and to call long distance.

A lot of bad lessons. A terrible heritage. But you can stop it.

You can be the family that puts down roots and says, "This is it." You can become a solid part of your community—maybe, for a while, the only solid part. You can keep your children in the same schools. You can teach and show them how to develop and keep deep relationships for a lifetime. You can commit to your church and involve yourself in life-changing ministry with people you can grow old with.

And then, when you're a grandparent, you can continue to affect the precious people of your life. You might retire from a job, but you can say no to retiring from life. You can use your time to develop the next generation. You can use your money to help those younger ones to plant themselves—like giving a year's income to newlyweds so they can devote themselves to one another (see Deuteronomy 24:5). You'll be a deeper person because you will have roots, and you'll be able to affect those you love because they'll have roots, too.

And, Lord willing, when you're a great-grandparent, you'll be deeply rooted.

And your descendants will be there to see it.

Responsibility

A great number of parents are now giving their children the "joy" and "freedom" of being an adult, without giving them minimum responsibilities. Children are allowed to experience things that are beyond their comprehension, exceed their wisdom, and pervert their emotions and bodies, while nothing is demanded of them in return — or at all.

Does God support letting children reap where they haven't sown? No, you say; and I agree. What, then? Does Scripture support the materialistic creed of giving your child a "better" life than you had? Or the bizarre view of childhood that allows a child to be free from any restraints that would spoil his fun? No, you admit, this isn't right. Then what is it that's allowing us to produce a generation of such cold-blooded, selfish anarchists?

The reason involves parental apathy, ignorance, lack of love, and disregard for the office of parent itself. These things add up to abdication of responsibility on the part of the parent and, as a natural consequence, the abdication of responsibility and responsible behavior on the part of the child as well.

Can you imagine this new generation, irresponsible, street-wise, and stuffed full of humanistic and materialistic garbage at a tender age, as *parents?*

You must exercise responsibility in the things that God has given you. The example you set for your children in this area is more important than the responsibilities that you assign them. If you get up and go to work when you don't feel like it, cook dinner when you have a splitting headache, take in a hurting family member when you don't have room — you'll be teaching about responsibility, loud and clear.

And you don't want to miss giving your children responsibility. It isn't cruel and heartless to give them things to do; it's *vital.* If you can escape from the world's view that children should be allowed to "live it up," you might actually be able to see the truth that mindless entertainment never built anyone's character. It's *responsibility*, in all of its many forms, that builds character upon the foundation of truth that you should be laying in your child.

Booker T. Washington reminded us of this: "Few things help an individual more than to place responsibility upon him, and to let him know that you trust him." Maybe some of us can learn to do this.

I remember a conversation on this point with my son. He said to me, "Dad, I'm the only kid in the neighborhood who has to do chores." I gave him the only appropriate answer that a loving parent can give. "You're welcome."

The Harvest of Discipline

I didn't make discipline a separate chapter, because discipline is the whole process of making a disciple. I chose to include it here, because consistent discipline is such an important part of a stable life.

First, I'd like to say that we don't need another set of child-rearing "quick fixes" to get our children in line and keep them there. Parenting, for the typical Christian father or mother, is an endurance or survival contest, in which a battle is waged for truth and justice for about eighteen tough and often frustrating years, after which we eject what we hope is a decent, relatively nondegenerate quasi-adult into the world. We think that we need all the tricks we can find to help us pull this off, and so we search for some "magic" to help us.

But there isn't any magic. The *attitude* of discipline is the key. One of the main reasons that we have so many mediocre (as opposed to champion) Christians is that they were raised by somebody's gimmicks rather than by some parent's godly approach to discipline. And what is the approach?

As conveyed to your child, it should sound something like this:

I'm your father, and I love you more deeply than you may ever know. I want you to know that there's nothing you can ever say or do to make me stop loving you. I want to spend my time thinking about you in two ways. First, I want to present you with challenges so that you will be a powerful Christian weapon in the hands of God. Second, I want to immerse myself in thinking creatively about how I can shower you with blessings. If you respond to these things, you will become a champion for God on the shorter, softer path.

But since I love you, if you reject these things you'll force me to spend my time thinking about you in two other directions. First, my challenges will turn into punishments designed to shake you off the wrong path. Second, I'll have to think creatively about how I can withdraw my blessings. Actions have consequences, and I love you too much to let you be a fool. I'll still try to help you be a champion, but you'll be doing it on the longer, harder path.

Please give me the freedom to deal with you the first way. Please don't force me to treat you as though you're a fool.

Our children were resisting taking care of a responsibility that we felt was important. They were failing in an area of their lives that was going to cause them problems later on. We had tried all of the "tricks" — do this, ground that, withdraw this, nag there — all to no avail. And then I realized that I was giving them the output of my own shaky thinking, without even knowing clearly what I wanted them to learn or why I wanted them to learn it. I was fighting a battle of details when what I needed to do was let them see the heart that was prompting the details.

The first thing that I had to do was figure out the approach described in the section above. God shows us His attitude in the book of Hebrews, chapter 12, verses 5–11:

And you have forgotten that word of encouragement that addresses you as sons: "My son, do not make light of the Lord's discipline, and do not lose heart when he rebukes you, because the Lord disciplines those he loves, and he punishes everyone he accepts as a son." Endure hardship as discipline; God is treating you as sons. . . . God disciplines us for our good, that we may share in his holiness. No discipline seems pleasant at the time, but painful. Later on, however, it produces a harvest of righteousness and peace for those who have been trained by it.

You can certainly see here God's motive behind the punishment side of the discipline coin. His love for us simply forces Him to spank us, to move us back to where He can really make something powerful out of us.

And I hope that you're able to see God's motive behind the challenge side of the discipline coin: "Endure hardship as discipline; God is treating you as sons." He adds challenges *and* rich blessings to those of His children who are following Him wholeheartedly; He adds punishment *and* withdrawal of blessings to those of His children who are following themselves wholeheartedly.

We should convey our approach to discipline clearly to our children. Make it clear that they're the ones who determine which side of the discipline coin you'll be able to look at. Let them know how it grieves you to be forced onto the punishment side of the coin. When I did this with my children in a clear and loving way, the battle over the problem ended and our relationship moved onto higher ground.

You must let them know as well that you intend to regularly inject some challenge and hardship into their training. Don't be embarrassed to test them so that you and they will know that they can face the bigger tests later. Help them to see the difference between this and the punishment side of the coin. Understand and share with them your understanding that "no discipline seems pleasant at the time, but painful," even when it's meant only for training and not for punishment.

When we conveyed at the same time why we required them to do the thing they had been resisting, and that it was excellent training for their lives, their comprehension of our love and discipline was much more complete.

Finally, help your children to see that both forms of discipline will produce a gigantic and marvelous harvest of righteousness and peace in their lives. Help them to see that they're being built into something strong: "Therefore, strengthen your feeble arms and weak knees. 'Make level paths for your feet,' so that the lame may not be disabled, but rather healed" (Hebrews 12:12–13). It'll be a lot easier for them to head in that direction when they see the goal and not just the details.

Paul says that "we have all had human fathers who disciplined us and we respected them for it" (Hebrews 12:9). If your children don't respect you, odds are that you're probably not disciplining them, at least not in the full sense of that word.

And if you're disciplining them and they're not responding in a deep and powerful way, perhaps you're not giving them the challenge side of the coin; perhaps you're being efficient, but not *effective*, because you've left out half of the entire concept of discipline.

But if you're doing these things, and still don't have the hearts of your children involved in their own development, perhaps you just haven't told your children why you're doing what you're doing.

Tell them. Today.

Conclusion

In the midst of a rootless and nomadic culture and church, you can be the family that puts down roots. You can lay a foundation of stability that can survive for generations. You can give your children a gift that few children receive in our day if you will: develop and maintain a proper husband/wife relationship; avoid the breakup of your family at all costs; find a way to make a home and stay there; and refuse to be a transient chasing after the material gods of our day. You can round out this gift if you will give your children generous amounts of responsibility and godly discipline.

It's a gift they'll still be opening in a hundred years.

10

CONFIDENCE

*He will have no fear of bad news; his
heart is steadfast, trusting in the LORD.*
(Psalms 112:7)

I n a world and nation that are falling apart, there are at least three or four thousand things that could drive you as a parent into an absolute panic. From a little child falling and hitting his head to an older child being kidnapped, the possible disasters that can overtake your children can dominate your attention. And if you're not careful, they will. "If a man harbors any sort of fear," said Lloyd Douglas, "it . . . makes him landlord to a ghost." Too many Christian parents are landlords to a ghost.

Not only can this fear cause you to sin against the Lord and ruin much of your relationship with your children, but it can also be a devastatingly effective method of teaching fear of man, bad news, and sudden disaster to your children. You can talk about your confidence in the Lord until your voice gives out, but if you live fear, you'll teach fear. Fear is disobedience to Jesus (see Matthew 6:25, 31, 34; 10:19). Fear is highly contagious and finds a willing receptacle in the flesh of your children.

The basic question is pretty simple: Who is really and ultimately responsible for the safety of your children? Given the grotesque culture in which we live, if the answer is "I am," your children are in big trouble. The only way that this could possibly work is if you are omnipresent and omnipotent, and I suspect that you aren't.

But has God really said that He's responsible for your child? If He hasn't, then you're going to have a hard time trying *not* to disobey God by worrying about things. If He hasn't, He's put you into a pretty tough position: You have a lot of things to worry about, but you're not allowed to worry about them.

"Fear not" is a hollow command when you're convinced that tragedy may be lurking at your door.

But if God really *does* promise peace and safety for your children, then you can rest from your worry and fear. It will become possible for you to obey His commands not to worry. You'll be able to place your children in God's hands and have the certainty that they won't be dropped. If you really claim and believe His promises, you'll experience a freedom that you've never felt before.

So what does God promise on this important issue?

- "He who fears the LORD has a secure fortress, and for his children it will be a refuge" (Proverbs 14:26). God didn't put your child into a storm sewer; he put him into your family. Your family's safety, spiritual and physical, begins with your elimination of all fear except the fear of the Lord (see Acts 9:31; 10:34–35; 2 Corinthians 5:11; 7:15; Philippians 2:12; 1 Peter 1:17). This proper fear will be safety for you and an absolute place of protection for your children. The downside is the *lack* of protection if you *don't* fear the Lord. Roosevelt said that "the only thing we have to fear is fear itself." This is nonsense. The only thing we have to fear is God.

- "This is the assurance we have in approaching God: that if we ask anything according to his will, he hears us" (1 John 5:14). But sin blocks God's hearing and keeps Him from responding to your cry for help. If you commit a sin, repent and go to the Lord immediately for forgiveness and restoration (see 1 John 1:9). Teach your children to do the same. Their lives may depend on it. If you ignore God's Law, be aware that God says that He *will ignore your children* (see Hosea 4:6). Stay close to God!

- The Lord says in Proverbs that whoever listens to wisdom "will live in safety and be at ease, without fear of harm" (Proverbs 1:33). God says that "her ways are pleasant ways, and all her paths are peace" (Proverbs 3:17). By listening and learning "you will go on your way in safety, and your foot will not stumble; when you lie down, you will not be afraid; when you lie down, your sleep will be sweet. Have *no* fear of sudden disaster or of the ruin that overtakes the wicked, for the LORD will be your confidence and will keep your foot from being snared" (Proverbs 3:23–26, emphasis added). You must learn wisdom for your own safety. You must teach your children wisdom for *their* safety. If you do these things as a family, you'll receive the great promise of the Year of Jubilee, a year Christ proclaimed for believers in Luke 4:19. "Follow my decrees and be careful to obey my laws [which we can do by faith] and you will live safely in the land" (Leviticus 25:18).

- "A prudent man sees danger and takes refuge" (Proverbs 22:3). But where? "The name of the Lord is a strong tower; the righteous run to it and *are safe*" (Proverbs 18:10, emphasis added). We as believers have taken the name of our Father. We are His heirs, to whom He says: "If anyone does attack you, it will not be my doing; whoever attacks you *will surrender to you*" (Isaiah 54:15, emphasis added). Pretty awesome, huh?

- Fearing the Lord only, confessing known sin, feeding on His wisdom, and understanding the power of His Name all must be energized and completed by a faithful walk. "To the *faithful* you show yourself faithful" (Psalms 18:25, emphasis added). "The LORD preserves the *faithful*" (Psalms 31:23, emphasis added). He "will not forsake his *faithful* ones" (Psalms 37:28, emphasis added). "He guards the lives of His *faithful* ones" (Psalms 97:10, emphasis added). He "protects the way of His *faithful* ones" (Proverbs 2:8, emphasis added). "No harm befalls the *righteous*" (Proverbs 12:21, emphasis added). Do you get the picture? You and your children will live by faith, or you'll die without it. Calling yourself a believer is not enough. Being saved alone is not enough. If you want God's protection in this life, you have to live by faith, in obeying His commands and in claiming His promises.

It should be pointed out that godly prudence should be exercised in the supervision of your children. The balance is in trusting your children to God first and then having your children in the right place at the right time. Trusting God isn't an excuse to let your prudence go to lunch early. It's wrong to think that your children are totally in your hands; but it's also wrong to think that they're not in your hands at all.

Perhaps the most important thing that will be accomplished by this joyous way of life is that you won't teach your children to fear what those in the world fear (see 1 Peter 3:14). Think of it: If your children have no fear of anything but God, you'll be able to rest assured that they'll have one of the primary attributes of someone very, very special—*a champion.*

Reasons for Failed Prayer

"God always answers prayer; it's just that sometimes His answer is wait, sometimes it's maybe, sometimes it's no, and sometimes it's try again."

Benjamin Disraeli said that "in politics there is no honor." Will Rogers put it more succinctly when he said, "I tell you, folks, all politics is applesauce." When we hear many politicians, we *expect* to hear applesauce. You could read some politicians' speeches a hundred times and still not know what they stand for or against. *They* probably don't know what they stand for or against.

Why on earth would we treat God as though He's a politician?

Some of us have a close friend or two with whom we can share anything. Show your children how to find and treasure these kinds of friends, who have wisdom and love combined with one very important attribute: a willingness to speak plainly, no holds barred, (see Proverbs 27:9)—for it's only at this level of friendship that anything meaningful ever occurs. And the first friend they should seek at this level is God.

Much teaching on prayer today is applesauce.

I once polled a group of high school and college students in a certain church on the subjects of the will of God and prayer. The highest percentage of time that anyone thought that he or she had known and been in the will of God was 20 percent. When they were asked what percentage of their prayers had been answered, they generally couldn't even put a number on it; they simply said that it was much less than that, and for some it was practically zero.

Why is this? How can this be possible in churches that claim to believe in a personal and loving God? What's the use of talking about prayer and praying if our own children don't even believe that God is faithful enough to answer them clearly?

The first reason for this failed communication with God is our cluttered lives filled with worldly garbage and sin. God wouldn't and *couldn't* hear us, even if we could figure out what to ask Him. If you have sin in your heart, the only prayer He's interested in is a prayer for forgiveness. If your children don't learn this, their prayer lives are doomed to failure.

The next reason is that we pray for things that aren't in Scripture and don't pray for things that are. We don't take the time to find out what God has promised. We forget that "if we know that he hears us — whatever we ask — we know that we have what we asked of him" (1 John 5:15). Sounds pretty certain, doesn't it? And where do we get some clue about His will? Could it be in the Word of God?

The third reason for our prayer failure is that we don't pray specifically enough or carefully enough. Sloppy praying is praying that's not likely to get a clear answer. We shouldn't assume that just because God is all-knowing that He'll answer vague prayer.

The fourth reason for failed prayer is that we pray without the primary motive of giving God the glory — both in our prayer and in the answer that we *know* will come (see James 4:3). Ask God the Father to give you what you request in the name and through the blood and for the glory of Jesus His Son.

The fifth reason is that we ourselves believe the opening statement of this section to be true. We throw a bunch of prayers up in the air and see which ones stick to the ceiling. Most of them return to us "unanswered." The simple truth is that if we want our children to have powerful prayer lives, then we must have one ourselves, and this involves *faith.*

The sixth reason for failure is that we refuse to accept the conditions or obey the commands that go along with the promises. We want the prize without having to do our part — by *faith,* of course. God will not be mocked.

The final reason is that we really don't want just *any* answer. We usually have some idea of what we would like the answer to be, and then we tell God in our hearts that we'll accept any answer as long as it's the one we want. We have to remember that we can't hear if we aren't listening. And we can't hear the gentle voice of God if we are walking by sight.

Eighteen Steps to Effective Prayer

Let's summarize some "prayer pointers" that will help you and your children to have effective prayers rather than failed prayers.

Before the Prayer

1. Prepare to pray and fast when God moves through His Spirit.
2. Repent from sin, confess it, and make any required restitution.
3. Review the Biblical promises that relate to the request.
4. Be ready to accept the form God's yes might take (see 2 Corinthians 1:20).
5. Think through the request and make it as specific as possible.
6. Check motivation and make sure it's to exalt God and others.

The Prayer Itself

7. Pray with intense desire, eagerness, and expectation.
8. Pray to the Father in Jesus' name (see John 15:16).
9. Ask the Holy Spirit to intercede and help.
10. Pray with faith — don't keep repeating, keep believing (see Matthew 6:7).
11. Obey any Scripture attached to the promise or answer.
12. Close with thanksgiving and praise for the answer.

After the Prayer

13. Follow prayer with positive words that show faith.
14. Follow prayer with positive actions that show faith.
15. Refuse, with God's help, to walk by sight.
16. Stay in the Bible and keep reviewing Scriptures on that promise.
17. Ask God to rebuke Satan when he comes in with doubts.

18. Ask others who will follow these steps to pray and agree with them.

Encouragement to Pray

Teach your children to imagine a king. This king has just sent them a message that he'll answer any question they might have. This king wants to relate to them in a personal way, but they have to remember that he's still a king and that they should go into his presence with a healthy amount of fear. Then ask your children this: How will you get ready for your time with the king?

With some encouragement on your part, they'll probably tell you that they would make sure they hadn't done anything to offend the king; work on their question for a long time; ask others how to word the request; leave out dumb questions; make sure their question was clear and called for a clear answer; see if the king had written anything on the subject of their question and read all that was applicable; go over their question again and again to ensure that the question was completely in line with the king's writings; ask the king's messenger to guide them in the development and presentation of their question; and then wait for the right time.

If they're wise, they'll approach the king confidently but respectfully, and let him know that his answer — whatever it is — will be accepted at face value. They'll also be careful not to say in his presence that they've heard that sometimes he doesn't answer, sometimes he answers "maybe," and sometimes he answers "wait." Then they'll sit quietly until the king decides to answer, after they have thanked him for hearing them and, in advance, for answering their question. And finally, when they hear his answer, they'll go and do whatever he says. Show them that this will *always* bring favor from a king. And teach your children one more thing about this king: He is the King of kings.

Apply Faith to Fear

"The ability to worry is a gift from God." This little gem, written by Charles Allen, is one that might find agreement in some quarters. It seems to say that a little honest worry can be a good thing; it can help your children to be realistic and can keep them from some very real dangers.

But this idea fails on the grounds that a skunk by any other name still smells bad.

People who know about God can be really amazing on the subject of worry and fear. We fear men and do the things we shouldn't do before God, when we should fear God and do the things we should do before men. We fear things over which we have no control, like nuclear war, cancer, and muggers, while we don't fear things over which we have control, like the consequences of disobedience to God. We fear what people might say to us if we boldly speak up and stand up for God, while we don't fear the emptiness that our cowardice is sure to bring to the world around us.

Any worry about anything other than whether we are saved or living by faith—in other words, worry about anything other than our relationship with God—is a destructive force that will rip our spirits and bodies apart. Any fear other than the fear of God is misplaced thinking that can bring upon us the very thing that we dread. Job said, "What I feared has come upon me; what I dreaded has happened to me. I have no peace, no quietness; I have no rest, but only turmoil" (Job 3:25–26).

Why is this? Because fear and worry are disobedience to God.

We have to get this point over to our children. When they come to us with their fears, what they need most is for us to tell them, clearly and lovingly, that these fears are ungodly. We need to warn them that if they give these fears a home they're disobeying God. We need to encourage them to run into the arms of God, to cling tightly to Him, and to claim His clear and mighty promises about His care and protection.

The world and its "experts" have a different solution, which can sound pretty good. They tell us to discuss the child's fears with him, to help him rationalize his fears and to teach him to work through them in his own mind. They hold out the potential victory of the child overcoming his fears as we parents try to explain why the thing that they fear can't hurt them—or why they shouldn't worry even if the thing they fear *can* hurt them.

But what else can we expect them to say? They have to try to deal with and understand fear, because there's so much to fear. Parents need help with this themselves and need wisdom in dealing with their children's fears. But the only answer to fear is obedience to and faith in the one true God. Anyone who teaches anything else doesn't know the answer and can only offer trivial and useless "methods" — lies disguised as "rational thinking." The things these people teach have no value because they have no truth and power behind them.

Without faith in God, our usual response to fear on the part of our children is to be sympathetic. We try to put ourselves inside of our children's fears. We might even cater to their fears by letting them sleep with us or by looking through the drawers to assure them that no monsters live there. The worst response is when we ourselves become fearful about what our children fear, giving life to the fears and death to the faith of our children.

Our children don't need our sympathy; they need *God.*

We do need to realize that the temptation to fear is not the issue. Satan, the world, and our own trembling flesh are expert at developing things to make us fear. It's what we and our children do with these temptations that counts. If we absorb these things, we sin against God and push ourselves into the arms of something that will devour us. But if we say with the psalmist, and believe it, "When I am afraid, I will trust in you" (Psalms 56:3), then we are running in the only right direction and into the only right arms.

Fear indicates a lack of faith in God. In fact, fear *is* a lack of faith in God. We can spout fountains of words about how God is all-knowing, all-powerful, and all-loving, but if we fear anyone or anything other than God, we deny all the words and spout fountains of faithlessness instead. The question is, do we really believe that God is sovereign — in total control — and that nothing can touch us except by His permission? Isaiah 8:12-14 says: "Do not call conspiracy everything that these people call conspiracy; do not fear what they fear, and do not dread it. The LORD Almighty is the one you are to regard as holy, he is the one you are to fear, he is the one you are to dread, *and he will be a sanctuary*" (emphasis added). Only when our children have learned this mighty truth will they be able to deal with the countless unholy fears that surround them.

There are dangers that our children must learn to avoid, but we'll have to be very careful to avoid using ungodly fear as a teaching device. If we are only to fear God, then teaching our children to fear anything else is teaching them to sin. We work against ourselves and God when we try to instill fears on the one hand even as we try to drive fears out on the other.

How many of us have been taught to fear water ("Even great swimmers drown sometimes"), heights ("Johnny, you're going to break your neck"), or people ("You just never know what others are saying about you behind your back")?

We think we are using fear to teach, when the main thing that we are teaching is the fear itself. We need to teach our children the fear of the Lord — the trembling at His presence and the awe at His commands — and use this holy fear as a basis for teaching faith with regard to the thousands of very real dangers that exist in this fallen world.

There are dangers this side of heaven, but the only fear that works is the fear of the Lord. This means your child must be taught to fear disobeying God's commands in areas where the danger is under the child's control. And it means your child must be taught to let fears that are outside of his control drive him by faith into the arms of God.

David said: "I do not concern myself with great matters or things too wonderful for me. But I have stilled and quieted my soul." (Psalms 131:1–2). David had learned to fear and obey and have faith in his God. The result was — and still is for us today — a quiet soul.

Teardrops

Many things make us shake and cry and lose our confidence, but we must learn to hold onto our confidence. The first step is to understand that we shed tears for two different reasons.

The first reason is due to our own sinful folly. These are the self-inflicted wounds that come from not getting our own way, from anger and hatred, and from fear that comes from lack of faith.

The second reason comes from outside ourselves. These include the tests and trials that come into everyone's life. We must learn to deal with each of these in a totally different way.

A secular how-to-raise-children pamphlet had this little gem: "During the school years, children begin to develop the capacity for unselfish affection in their friendships. This capacity expands later in adolescence, when companionship is eventually combined with more romantic feelings in attachments to persons of the opposite sex."

Obviously this writer hasn't known a school-age child or ever been a school-age child. This person doesn't understand what unselfish affection is or where it comes from and doesn't understand that companionship + romantic feelings – God = lust + promiscuity + spiritual death.

There's no unselfish affection apart from God; it just doesn't exist. Children without God think about themselves and can often be thoughtless or even brutal toward other children. My wife once told me that a four-year-old's major concern was to remember what's coming to him. I don't think it stops at four.

As for the adolescent capacity for unselfish affection, 64 percent of the boys in a recent study said that they supported the idea of premarital intercourse, while 39 percent of the girls held that view. Anyone who has ever been a boy or known a boy knows that the boys' views weren't prompted by unselfish affection. And more often than not, the girl who engages in these things is looking for something — words, concern, attention — for herself.

Twenty percent of the adolescents said that they had engaged in premarital sexual intercourse by ninth grade.

When your children cry because of any of these self-inflicted wounds, unbounded selfishness, and generally bad attitudes, they *don't* need to be encouraged or receive a helping hand. Rather, they need a helping hand, dropped on an appropriate target with accuracy and forcefulness. Parents have a built-in tendency to run to their children when they're crying or hurt, no matter the reason. Don't do it.

But then there are the true tears. These can come because of the "Lonely Little Petunia in an Onion Patch" syndrome. What does that mean? It means that you and your children, no matter how sweet you are to God, are living in a world of onions that are going to bring you tears. These "onions" can be things in the world or the church or even in your own past life that bring a godly sadness and tears, as they did to men like Nehemiah and Jeremiah and Jesus. They can also result from sadness at a loss of a loved one through death. They can even come from things that cause physical pain. These tears are appropriate and acceptable before God.

But the "onions" can also be tests and trials. One of the hardest things for a Christian to put into practice by faith is the exhortation in James to "consider it joy . . . whenever you face trials of many kinds, *because you know* that the testing of your faith develops perseverance" (James 1:2–3, emphasis added). I know many Cristians who can quote this passage. But how many of these Christians really believe and do this? How many of them live as though they really know that testing develops perseverance? I could count them on one hand and still have fingers left over for snapping.

Our usual reaction to trials of many kinds is to do anything *but* consider it pure joy. We cry and moan and doubt and ask God how He could let such a horrible thing happen to us. Here comes a perfect opportunity to believe and trust God, to watch our faith and perseverance grow, and we mess up the whole deal.

And then we teach our children to do the same.

God doesn't want you to cry when He allows or brings a trial into your life. In fact, He *hates* it when you cry in the face of a trial. How do I know this? Because He commands you to "consider it pure joy." And if you don't but start crying instead, you're disobeying God and He hates disobedience. He wants confidence, not complaints.

He doesn't tell you to "consider it pure joy" if it's not too bad and you think you can stand it. And He's not talking about a phony smile and "joyful" words forced out of your etched and grimacing face. He's talking about obeying Him in faith and considering it pure joy *no matter what.*

If Christians could do this one thing, and teach their children to do the same, we would get all of the promises of God that go with it, experience true peace and joy no matter the circumstances, and present a face and heart attitude to the world that would be awesome and irresistible. Everybody has trials. Christians are supposed to use God's power to deal with them and to show others a glorious response that will surprise them.

Sometimes crying is appropriate; sometimes it isn't. Get your own act straightened out, and then watch your children closely. Drive out the crying that comes from the flesh. Lead out the crying that comes from worldly trials. If you don't, I'll make a prediction.

Your children are going to make you cry.

Singing in Prison

Once, when I was standing up for something I believed in a very public and outspoken way, a man drove by in a car and yelled many gross insults at me. For once, I responded in a godly way and wished him Godspeed and a good day.

I didn't think much about this until later, when I was sharing the importance of blessing your enemies with my then seven-year-old son. As soon as I finished my first statement on the matter, he stopped my whole speech with a single comment, "I know that's what you're supposed to do—I saw you do it with that man."

Nothing's ever brought home to me more clearly the importance of living out the truths of God's Word—no matter how nonsensical they appear to our finely-honed and doubtlessly infallible brain and emotions. God wants His people to do all kinds of things that just seem the opposite of logic and reason.

In this case, Jesus wants us to sing in man's prisons. He says:

> Blessed are you when men hate you, when they exclude you and insult you and reject your name as evil, because of the Son of Man. *Rejoice* in that day and leap for joy, because great is your reward in heaven. . . . Love your enemies, do good to those who *hate* you, bless those who curse you, pray for those who mistreat you. . . . Then your reward will be great, and *you will be sons of the Most High,* because he is kind to the ungrateful and wicked. (Luke 6:22–23, 27–28, 35, emphasis added)

So not only is this God's preferred response, but He emphasizes that this will allow us to experience the fullness of being a son of God and bring us great reward. If these aren't three great reasons to rejoice and leap for joy, then there just aren't any. If you can teach this to your children, in an age of hating and cursing, you'll have opened up to them the exquisite possibility of countless blessings from God.

Be willing to expose your children—with you at first, of course—to attack from the world because of their stand for God as the God of all of life. When you're attacked (see 2 Timothy 3:12), respond as Jesus commanded, and then rejoice and thank God that He has allowed you to suffer because of His name. There is more life-changing power in this course of action than any of us have ever been able to imagine, because supernatural responses get supernatural results.

For those of you who have never once been hated, excluded, insulted, rejected, cursed, or mistreated because of your life being lived for God in *this* world, rotten as this world is, I have only one question: What are you doing?

And someday, your children may have a second question for you: Where were you when God's people were being cursed?

Only one answer will satisfy your spirit as you look them in the eye. "My child, I was singing in prison."

Conclusion

You can depend on the power and protection of God working in your family's life. You and your children can learn the eighteen steps to effective prayer and together see wonderful results. You can, by following God's prescription, recognize worry and fear as sin and overcome them in your life. You and your children can turn your life upside-down and not only "consider it pure joy" when you face tests and problems, but you can even learn how to be calm and sing in the midst of tribulation.

If you learn these things, your family will be untouched by those things that paralyze the world.

11

BALANCE

The man who fears God will avoid all extremes.

(Ecclesiastes 7:18)

Does it seem sometimes as though your whole life is a struggle to find a balance between competing demands for your support, time, effort, and money? That setting and holding the right priorities in the right order is even harder than balancing the family budget? And that the people teaching in fifty different directions through television, radio, tapes, books, and magazines must be talking about fifty different gods?

Man's struggle, both inside and outside of Christianity, is in many ways a struggle with the issue of balance—either to get it or to run away from it. In fact, the reason man struggles is that he usually isn't very balanced. Man swings back and forth on a seldom-resting pendulum between talk of peace and merciless warfare, preaching tolerance and detesting difference, religious apathy and violent crusades, claiming unfailing love and gossiping about a "loved" one.

One area that most Christians constantly need to find balance is in the allocation of time. There's only so much, and it's not recyclable. Unless you're constantly reviewing your priorities with God, you easily become off-balanced. One of the most important things that can for days or weeks at a time slip out of a schedule is a quiet time in the Word of God. You must daily plan this time into your schedule if you want to stay balanced in the other areas of your life.

Have you ever gone to bed and found yourself saying, "Oh, no, I forgot to eat today"? Probably not. But it's likely that you *have* found yourself saying that about your all-important spiritual food, God's Word. How can we be balanced people and parents if we don't say with David, "I will not neglect your word" (Psalms 119:16)?

As a parent, you probably feel the pull, too. From being too hard to being too soft, too interfering to too unavailable, too willing to share adult problems to too unwilling to share "embarrassing" truth, you can go back and forth in a frustrating cycle. One minute you can feel like a rock, and the next like mush. Without a balanced life, you'll be passing a heritage of imbalance and frustration along to your children.

But you can stop the pendulum.

Finding the Balance

"Do not be overrighteous, neither be overwise—why destroy yourself?" (Ecclesiastes 7:16). These are not the words of some Buddhist or Hindu philosopher. These are flawless words from the mind of God and were written by the wisest man who ever lived.

Now there are some who will argue that the book of Ecclesiastes is from the point of view of a worldly man, that somehow you have to take this part of Scripture with a grain of salt. You must realize, however, that there's no basis for this widely held and totally erroneous belief. This book is a vivid description of how the world really is and an excellent exhortation to relate to it in certain ways that are guaranteed to be effective.

The Balance of God

So what does this verse mean?

God is talking here about balance. Scripture says, "Honest scales and balances are from the LORD; all the weights in the bag are of his making" (Proverbs 16:11). Our God is an absolutely balanced being, and this characteristic of balance is evident throughout His creation. Many scientists now believe that the entire universe is poised delicately between complete collapse and runaway expansion.

God asks these questions: "Who has measured the waters in the hollow of his hand, or with the breadth of his hand marked off the heavens? Who has held the dust of the earth in a basket, or weighed the mountains on the scales and the hills in a balance?" (Isaiah 40:12). God didn't just slap creation together; creation is totally precise.

This characteristic of balance is also clearly displayed in His fundamental relationship with man. Our God is balanced gloriously between justice and mercy. If He were an extremist on justice alone, this book wouldn't have been written. You wouldn't be reading it, and both of us would be uncomfortably awaiting judgment at this very moment. If He were an extremist on mercy alone, no wrongs would ever be righted or punished, the unrepentant wicked would not be punished and faith or lack of faith in God would make no difference. We would have a "goody-two-shoes" God who was able to tolerate things that make imperfect beings like you and me sick.

But God is perfectly balanced between justice and mercy. *All* sin is justly punished. God is too just to overlook any sin, but He's too merciful not to provide a way out for those who cry out to Him in truth. So He gave His Son as an innocent lamb to take their place when the blows were struck. Because of justice, each person is faced with damnation; because of mercy, each person is allowed the choice to be forgiven and accept God's grace by faith.

God is a God of balance, and in the verse that opened this section He is telling us something about balance. What monumental, complex truth is He trying to get across to us?

He is simply trying to tell us to be like Him — to be balanced. He says in His Word, "Love and faithfulness meet together; righteousness and peace kiss each other" (Psalms 85:10). He wants us to love people, but never at the expense of faithfulness to His truth. He wants us to mix righteousness with understanding, mercy, and peace; He wants us to mix knowledge with gentleness, humility, and sensitivity. He wants us to stand out, in the same way as His Son stood out while He walked upon the earth.

Can you imagine how tempted Jesus must have been to instantly wipe out the sinful cesspool in which He found Himself? Can you understand how at the same time He could weep over Jerusalem and seek fellowship with those much less perfect than Him? Can you relate to His being able to condemn them for their hardness of heart even as He was preparing to die for them?

He could do it because He had balance.

Even in His two comings we can see His balance. His first coming was not "to condemn the world, but to save the world" (John 3:17). But in His second coming, "With justice he judges and makes war" (Revelation 19:11). He's the Savior of those under judgment and the Judge of those who will not choose to be saved.

Finding Balance Through the Scriptures

So what is this thing called *balance?*

Balance isn't compromise. Compromise is agreeing to combine what you know to be right with what you know to be wrong, while balance is combining two things which you know are right. Balance isn't compartmentalizing your spirit so that you can deal with gross contradictions; this schizophrenic thinking is a refusal to acknowledge that there is absolute truth, while balance is an acknowledgment that absolute truth cannot be refused. And balance is not another word for complacency or apathy or "conservatism." Balance in your spirit is not an excuse to avoid being radical, but rather it calls for being *radical*—"proceeding from the root . . . fundamental; reaching to the center or ultimate source." Jesus was a radical who demanded a return to a balanced view of God's whole truth.

Teach your children to be like God—to be balanced. This means simply that they should try to understand all of God's truth on a particular subject and then believe and apply it with zeal. The balance is so apparent in God's Word that an honest search of the Bible will produce people of balance. It's then and only then that they should become radicals in the application of this truth—even if they're alone in their application and must, like Jesus, die for it.

For example, Scripture tells us to "speak up for those who cannot speak for themselves" (Proverbs 31:8). This would certainly apply to unborn babies facing an abortionist's suction machine, a handicapped baby (like Baby Doe) facing a hospital-wide and court-wide conspiracy to starve him to death, and a helpless elderly person facing the nontreatment, passive euthanasia of our cost-conscious and burden-eliminating medical professionals. God tells us to be watchmen and warn those who are fighting against Him.

But at the same time Scripture tells us to "go and make disciples of all nations . . . teaching them to obey everything I have commanded you" (Matthew 28:19–20). He adds to this that we should be willing to forgive time after time, and that only those of us who are without sin have any right to cast the first stone (Matthew 18:21–22; John 8:1–11).

So what do we do as we look at these Scriptures, and others, on the subject of what we should do with regard to our culture's great moral slide and disrespect for human life? Should we be immobilized by the apparent contradictions? How do we teach our children on this subject?

We should teach them to do *all* of these things, in balance. They should be taught to speak up and work for the helpless, because God tells us to and that's what Jesus did. They should be taught to warn those who are attacking the helpless, and all of the attackers' accomplices, that they're wrong and will be judged. But they also should be taught that they're responsible to hold out the gift of eternal life to any of these people who will listen, to give God the room to work a miracle in seedy and murderous hearts. And they should be taught to be willing to instantly forgive those who seek forgiveness and to leave those who are unrepentant to the balanced and perfect judgment of God.

In short, our children should be taught that they have been commanded and empowered by God to stand up for those who can't stand on their own, and then to leave the results and any required judging in the hands of the Lord.

And what about imbalance? God reduces the results of imbalance to a simple question: "Why destroy yourself?" With that sobering thought in mind, I would like to ask a parallel question: Why destroy your child?

Find the balance.

Separate or Salt?

A question that constantly circulates through serious families and bodies of believers is this: Should we be separate from the world, or should we be salt?

The answer is yes.

We should be separate and we should be salt. To some, this might seem like a contradiction. "How," they will ask, "can we salt the earth if we are separate? And how can we be separate if we are salting the earth?" This contradiction, however, isn't a contradiction at all; it *appears* to be a contradiction because of three failures in our understanding, the first two of which were discussed in detail in the preceding section:

1. We fail to understand God's basic principle of balance. From the delicate balance of the universe to that of the atom, from riches to poverty, from being "overrighteous" to "overwicked," God always wants His creation to be balanced between unscriptural extremes.

2. We fail to understand the difference between *balance* and *compromise*. Balance is spiritual level-heartedness that follows *all* of God's Word, not just part of it. Compromise is thinking God's Word in your head and living the world in your life.

3. We fail to understand that one (to separate) is a prerequisite of the other (to salt). We must separate before we can salt. With children, this means that we must put them in a "greenhouse" and enable them to become salt. We can't afford to expose them to worldly influences too soon. With adults, it means that without the separation—of attitudes, of beliefs and corresponding unworldly actions, and of simple time away with the Lord—their saltshakers will be empty.

So we must do both. We and our children must separate first and salt later. We must sharpen our axes before we try to chop any wood. We must first be people of prayer and meditation and conviction, and then people of action and influence and persuasion. We must train our children for proper responses in their early years, and then gradually expose them to opportunities to respond as they grow older.

Don't push the salting phase, and don't fall for the naive and erroneous push that others will give you to expose your children to the world so they can be "worldly wise." You don't *want* your children to be "worldly wise." The problem with the church today is that too many of God's people are "worldly wise."

The Random House Encyclopedia says, "Salt has been used as a preservative for thousands of years. It extends the storage life of foods by inhibiting the growth of bacteria. Salt and spices are both used to make food more palatable, *especially if it has already begun to deteriorate*" (emphasis added).

There is no question that our culture has already begun to deteriorate. Bacteria-fed decay is proceeding at breakneck speed in our "enlightened" culture. But we can surely preserve and extend lives by being salt. We can certainly make others' lives more palatable by being salt. Without question, we can extend the storage life of Western civilization if we and our children will pour ourselves generously on this gray, smelly, tasteless society in which we live.

But just as salt is only useful when it's been separated from the earth and is fresh and pure, so our effectiveness depends upon our separation from the world. We and our children must have such an intimate relationship with our heavenly Father that we can be used to bring out the flavor of a feast, instead of being good for nothing "except to be thrown out and trampled by men" (Matthew 5:13).

God tells us that we are to "be merciful to those who doubt; snatch others from the fire and save them; to others show mercy, *mixed with fear — hating even the clothing stained by corrupted flesh*" (Jude 22–23, emphasis added). We are to salt the earth, never forgetting for a minute our fear of God and our hatred of evil. Jesus could rub elbows with sinners without getting His arms dirty because He was God in the flesh, because He spent thirty years preparing for His salting ministry, and because of solitary times with His Father after the ministry had begun.

A recent president was called the "Teflon President" because supposedly legitimate charges couldn't be made to stick to him. But as Christians, we can go one better. We can live a separate life so that there *aren't* any legitimate charges to be leveled against us. We can make the dying world around us call out for our involvement. We can do it in our own lives, and with the godly seed which God has given to us.

Pass the salt, please.

Resisters and Adapters

All of us and all of our children have desires to resist some things and to adapt to others. We are all resisters and adapters. Some of us are so resistant to so many things that resistance becomes a way of life, while others are so able to blend into any landscape that even a chameleon would recognize them as a blood brother. We must find God's balance on when to resist and when to adapt.

There are three key questions to ask about your child or yourself:

1. Is this person resisting outside input or is he adapting to it?
2. What kinds of things should he be resisting or adapting to?
3. How do I get him to resist and adapt to the right things?

Those who resist most of the time usually take heart from Thoreau's motto: "Any fool can make a rule, and every fool will mind it." Their first question is usually "Why?" — not the inquisitive why of most small children, but the "you had better have a good reason" form of the question. They hear the different drumbeat loud and clear and hate the parental trumpet blast that, to them, often seems out of rhythm and out of tune. This young person, however, is a potential man of faith in skunk's clothing; if *you* can resist the natural desire to crush this resistance, the body of Christ might have itself another David.

Those who adapt most of the time have a motto of their own: "Every fool can break a rule, but I'm no fool; I'll mind it." Their first question is usually "Why me?" — whether they're being forced by parents to resist when resistance is uncomfortable or forced by peers to adapt to things which are offensive. They hear a flute playing a gentle melody and are usually trying to keep themselves in harmony with those around them. This young person, however, is a potential man of faith in sheep's clothing; if you can resist the natural desire to force him to stand up for himself, the body of Christ might have itself another Abraham.

It's your responsibility to teach each of these bright spirits the importance of resisting or adapting to the right things (see the following table). There really is "a time to plant and a time to uproot" (Ecclesiastes 3:2).

Adapt to	Resist
The mind of Jesus	The mind of humanism
The ways of the wise	The counsel of the wicked
Scriptural principles	Unscriptural traditions
Practices that conform with Scripture	Worldly practices
Walking by faith	Walking by sight
Peace	War
Good peer pressure	Bad peer pressure

Those who are resisting God's way must be taught to adapt to the items listed above—by your words and example, not by sheer willpower and force. If you use the power of example, you'll come to understand the proverb that says: "He who heeds discipline shows the way to life, but whoever ignores correction leads others astray" (Proverbs 10:17). The force method is dangerous as well as ineffective, although it might seem for a time to work. But the rebellion continues to grow, although now under great pressure that will explode when the child is older. He may then dedicate his powerful will to the resistance of all that you supposedly stand for.

This is *not* an argument against discipline of children. It's merely a belief that your discipline of your children had better be totally in line with your discipline of yourself.

It should be no real surprise that those who are adapting to the world's way should be taught resistance in the same way. The method of forcing them to resist will not be effective in producing a person who is mighty in spirit. It will either produce a confirmed adapter who *looks* like a leader but is really leading others in conformity, or a rebellious person who will resist everything *you* say and adapt like putty in the hands of his friends. One is a facade and the other is a monster.

This is not an argument in favor of growing little revolutionaries who will glare in your eye and spit in your face whenever you say, "Do this." But there comes a time when the money changers must be driven from the temple, and only a godly resister can do it. We *must* grow godly resisters to the world and its ways.

Follow Nehemiah's Example

The proper method for us as teachers should be based on Nehemiah's model. As a resister, he hated what he saw, and wept over the evil and what it had done; he went personally into the effort and counted the cost; he explained the situation to those who would be doing the work; he actually began to do the work; he showed what could be done and how to do it; he despised and pushed aside the abuse of the strong men who opposed God; and he encouraged the people until God's wall was rebuilt.

As an adapter, however, he stayed under the authority of God and the king; he kept his knowledge to himself until he himself was ready to act; he trusted all judgment to God; and he didn't lord it over the people.

Nehemiah could dismiss any notion of dominating the people by saying "out of reverence for God I did not act like that. Instead, I devoted myself to the work" (Nehemiah 5:15–16). The result: a successful project built with resistance against resistance, followed by a meeting where "all the people assembled as one man. . . . From the days of Joshua son of Nun until that day, the Israelites had not celebrated it like this. And their joy was very great" (Nehemiah 8:1, 17).

May you and your child have such a project.

And then, such a celebration!

Majoring on the Minor

You only have so many years, so many days, so many hours to spend on the development of your child.

Don't spend them majoring on the minor.

Scripture is very clear that each of us has a significant part to play in his time and place as God's plan unfolds. Satan, of course, is aware of this, too. And one of Satan's most devious schemes, improved upon by millennia of practice, is to throw us a *red herring*.

What is a satanic red herring?

It isn't seafood. A satanic red herring is something that he gives us in the hellish hope that we'll spend an inordinate amount of time pursuing the thing beyond all bounds of reasonableness. Since he's kept his angel-of-light costume, he picks items that seem to be worthwhile to pursue, and then he incites us to "go for the jugular" — often the jugular of our children. We then spend our time hounding them to death to comply with virtually worthless rules.

The effects of this are devastating. We stop spending time on the really important things, which leaves our children in a spiritual vacuum. We get frustrated, as the trivial can never be quite up to our standards. Our children start spending their best efforts to comply with our demands, which teaches *them* to major on the minor. All the while, the majesty of life and the possibilities of affecting it in a powerful way evaporate.

Our children learn to grease the squeaky wheel, when they ought to be putting oil on their engines. They'll finally rebel against this terrific onslaught of triviality, probably after they are old enough to make their rebellion stick.

A list of these red herrings is impossible to make, because even Satan is creative. Even a short list would fill up a library. You'll have to ferret them out by asking yourself questions: Is this really important? If he doesn't do this, will he be a poor witness right now? If he doesn't learn this, will it leave him with a flaw in his character? Does doing this have eternal value? Is not doing it a sin against God? Does God care about this? When something really bugs you, come back to this section and ask yourself these questions — before you launch your attack.

Nagging is usually a sign that the trivial is in action — if it were important, you wouldn't nag; you would *insist*. It's only because it is trivial that you nag instead of taking a stand. If you find yourself nagging, ask yourself this question: Is this worth taking a stand on? If it is, stop nagging and start standing. If it isn't, stop nagging and sit down.

One final note on a clever twist that Satan can put on a red herring: when someone else is doing a little majoring on the minor, say in a Christian school or in your church, Satan can get you to respond in kind. I know some parents who rightly rejected a Christian school's overemphasis on things like hair length, and then responded by dramatically withdrawing themselves from even *considering* such a school for their child.

What starts out looking like a stand against the trivial can become a trivial stand against the trivial. We can pride ourselves on being free of this disease, when we are in fact living it out in front of our children. And they'll learn the terrible lesson that it's valuable to enter their spirits in a battle against the valueless.

This is not to say that we are to let minor offenses slip by when they're offenses of *principle*. On these we should take a stand, for two reasons. First, because these minor offenses will grow into major ones pretty quickly; and second, because violations of principle are despicable to God even if they are small.

So many minor things can swallow up our precious years. It's so easy to focus on the things that irritate us and the little details that surround us and never seem to be exactly right. Even as Christians, we can spend our time on this planet in an entirely insignificant way. Too many

children today—and since they will be the parents of the next generation, it will probably be true tomorrow—are being immersed in the insignificant by their dim-spirited and short-sighted parents.

This is perhaps the greatest damage that majoring on the minor can
produce. It leaves no time to do anything but minor on the major. It
causes us to make the same mistake as the Jewish leaders of Jesus' day,
who watched the Lord of glory, the object of their hope, with envy and
hatred to see if He would break some minor and overemphasized rule.
They majored on the minor—and as a result, minored on the major
question of their lives.

I wonder how many parents, when they're standing before the Lord,
will tremble when they hear Jesus' questions about why they didn't
teach their children principles and help them to live by them. Will their
only answer be a pathetic, "But, Lord, I was too busy trying to get them
to eat their turnips?"

Listen, if he won't clean his plate or button his coat or go right to
sleep or stay out of the mud or wear the exact ensemble that you like or
sing out during the Christmas program, then know this very major thing:
It's no big deal.

Conclusion

You and your family can avoid extremes and be balanced like God. You
can avoid thrusting your children into the world too quickly or holding
them too long. Your family can learn to be separate so it can then salt
the culture. You can learn to resist worldly influences even as you adapt
to God's principles. And you can major on the major instead of the
minor. Be balanced. You'll never be more free.

PART 3

CARRYING OUT
THE PLAN

12

NINE THINGS THAT WILL ADVANCE YOUR VISION

With your help I can advance against a troop.

(Psalms 18:29)

I n this chapter, we're going to look at nine ideas that elaborate on what we have already discussed. Don't just read it through; stop after each item and ask yourself how this can be built into your life and your parenting.

1. Learn to Be Pilgrims

A *pilgrim* is defined by Webster's as "one who travels to some holy place as a devotee."

Parent, are you a pilgrim?

You're not traveling to *some* holy place; you're traveling to *the* holy place. Or at least that's what you're supposed to be doing. Are you a devotee—one whose entire life and walk is dedicated to the goal of arriving at the holy place spiritually intact? Or are you clinging to your "fire insurance" while you sink your roots into this barren, dying world?

There are those who, in every place and age, have wallowed in affluence. They've built palaces, named lands after themselves, given themselves every available luxury, and spent their days dreaming up new desires in which they could then indulge. Some have had more things than most men can even imagine. Those rich in material things can become beggars in spirit, however, when their hearts become set on these gifts from the God who allows and enables them to receive. "The wealth of the rich is their fortified city; they imagine it an unscalable wall" (Proverbs 18:11)—but "when a wicked man dies, his hope perishes; all he expected from his power comes to nothing" (Proverbs 11:7).

We live in an age perhaps unparalleled for its vast affluence. More to the point, we live in an age where the affluence is widespread and generally available. Most Americans and others in the West would be called "the rich" by the overwhelming majority of all the people who have ever lived or are living today. And just like the rich few in other lands and times, we can have a general tendency to fall for "the deceitfulness of wealth" (Mark 4:19).

A thing is deceitful because it looks like one thing, but it is really something else. Wealth is deceitful because it looks like it's valuable, when in fact it isn't. Now, material things aren't wrong in themselves, and they can be used in many valuable ways; but the simple truth is that they can't buy anything of real value: salvation, faith, filling of the Holy Spirit, hope, love, peace, joy, and satisfaction.

I am not talking about a false guilt because we have so many material things; God has been very good to us, and we can thank Him for His breathtaking generosity. But at the same time, we have to realize that wealth has a powerful ability to distract or pervert, and that no one has ever spent his way to fulfillment. We must enjoy and use these things, without letting them distract us from the holy place.

In an age of incredible materialism, you must teach your children that "wealth is worthless in the day of wrath" (Proverbs 11:4). You must teach them that wealth is deceitful and can distract them from God's mighty purpose for them. You must teach them that they're just pilgrims, traveling to a holy place, and that they should look "not on what is seen, but on what is unseen." Why? "For what is seen is temporary, but what is unseen is eternal" (2 Corinthians 4:18).

Do you even believe this? Others have.

All these people were still living by faith when they died. They did not receive the things promised; they only saw them and welcomed them from a distance. *And they admitted that they were aliens and strangers on earth.* People who say such things show that they are looking for a country of their own. (Hebrews 11:13–14, emphasis added)

Following this is a warning to be continually aware of our immigrant status: "If they had been thinking of the country they had left, they would have had opportunity to return" (v. 15).

And why on earth would we want to return to the world's ways?

Wealth, affluence, the physical world around you, and the earthly things that you treasure can all cause you to stop traveling and to start building your dwelling here, on the flimsier side of reality. You must set the example for your children in the rejection of this foolishness. Enjoy your possessions, care for your possessions, and share your possessions, but don't send signals to your children that these possessions have any eternal value. If they see you wrapped up in a house or car or clothes or junk of any kind, they'll take the cue and start building up their treasure here as well.

It may not keep them from heaven, but it'll surely keep them from enjoying the trip.

Kids in the 1950s and 1960s made an attempt to stand against the "American Dream"—not the real dream of God-given life and liberty for each and every man, but the counterfeit dream of a house with a big debt, twenty charge cards, three cars in every garage, and two videocassette recorders. These kids failed as their humanistic idealism was replaced at first by music and drugs and sex, and now by an even grosser materialism than that of their parents. Their efforts failed, but that doesn't mean that the stand itself was wrong. They knew there was no fulfillment in materialism; sadly, the majority seem to have never found true fulfillment.

Scripture gives another warning and another promise: "The *house* of the wicked will be destroyed, but the *tent* of the upright will flourish" (Proverbs 14:11, emphasis added). Let the wicked and the fools build their houses in this sinking sand. As for you and your tent, be ready to flourish. People live in tents because there's nothing of any lasting interest where they're traveling. We should do all we can to reconstruct this place we are traveling through, while at the same time remembering that the only thing of lasting interest here is the other pilgrims in the tents next to yours—and those who might consider trading their earthly mansion for a heavenly tent.

And the result of learning to be a pilgrim family? "Therefore God is not ashamed to be called their God, for he has prepared a city for them" (Hebrews 11:16). Wow! God is telling you and your children that *He* is building the real palace. And He would be *ashamed* to see you turn from His architectural delights to build your own grubby little dump down here. So He says:

> Blessed are those whose strength is in you, who have set their hearts on pilgrimage. As they pass through the Valley of Baca, they make it a place of springs; . . . They go from strength to strength till each appears before God in Zion. . . . Better is one day in your courts than a thousand elsewhere. (Psalms 84:5–7, 10)

You must constantly remind your children that they're just passing through; there are too many blessings that will come their way if they'll remember and live this. It's truly an age of incredible affluence, but in the midst of it, God needs and wants you and your children to be pilgrims.

2. Learn Who Your Best Neighbor Is

The literal translation of John 1:14 is delightful: "The Word became flesh and pitched his tent among us." You're a pilgrim, and your children are pilgrims, if you and they know Jesus. Jesus Himself came and lived here with us as a pilgrim; His tent is right next to yours.

Never let young people forget one crucial fact: Our faith is ultimately in a person, and not just in things that speak of the person.

In all things, the Word of God stands. But it doesn't just stand to be read; it stands to be believed and followed. The church in America basically disrespects the Word of God. That doesn't mean that we don't read it and even study it; on the contrary, few countries have more Bibles in print, more churches, or more Bible studies than this one. But we disrespect it by not taking it seriously, by throwing parts of it out, by laughing at things that seem outdated, and mainly by not believing and acting upon what we know. We somehow think that just reading the Bible is enough.

But there is no magic in the words themselves. As beautiful and deep as they are, they've left many who have read them unsaved and powerless. The one who reads these words must encounter the one who wrote the Book. The same Scripture that says that His every Word is flawless goes on to say: "He is a shield to those who take refuge in *him*" (Proverbs 30:5, emphasis added). Our sanctuary is a person, not the Book that leads us to Him.

The words must be believed—not just agreed with, but *committed to*—if they're to provide any power to the one who hears or reads them. And they can *only* be believed because of the absolutely faithful nature of the one who speaks the words.

In fact, it's an insult to God to claim to be a believer and yet not take Him totally at His Word. It's immeasurably more valuable to know only one promise or command of God and to believe and act upon it, than to know a thousand of His promises and commands in your head and not really believe any of them.

We must teach our kids to meet with Jesus, their personal God. We must show them that the Bible is important because its author is alive, watching, judging, saving, and coming again. We must root them in God's Word, but we should not elevate the Bible to the status of an idol. Churches that have done this have lost their power as surely as churches not rooted in the Bible have lost their way.

Remember that the scribes revered the written Word of God even as they supported the slaughter of the living Word of God. Jesus warned unbelieving Jews: "You diligently study the Scriptures because you think that by them you possess eternal life. These are the Scriptures that testify about me, yet you refuse to come to me to have life" (John 5:39–40).

In short, the Bible has value because it's the Word of a *living* God that describes the perfect character of the God of creation and eternity. It's the seedbed for our faith, the anchor for our new lives, and the touchstone next to which all ideas and knowledge must be placed. With the Holy Spirit's help, a human spirit under conviction can use God's Word as the map into the sanctuary. But the goal of our new lives is to know the person who leads us in, Jesus, and the one who awaits us there, God the Father. The directions are a means to our destination, not the destination itself.

Certainly, beware of teaching that emphasizes experience apart from or contrary to the Word of God. But also beware of teaching that emphasizes knowledge of the Word apart from living the words by faith. Beware of kids that can parrot verses and Christian cliches which they don't really believe or who can discuss Scripture using words and terms which they don't really understand. Reading and memorization by our children are fine, as long as they—and we—"live up to what we have already attained" (Philippians 3:16).

Give your child a belief checkup. When he is looking at a claim or promise or command of God, ask him if he's ever believed it and what the effect was in his life. If he hasn't, share with him your experience in the matter and the experience of Biblical characters and other men and women of faith. If neither of you has ever believed this particular truth with boldness, then do it now.

To sum up: Far better that a child live out one verse by the strength of Jesus, than memorize ten thousand verses that dangle from his mouth "like a lame man's legs that hang limp" (Proverbs 26:7).

3. Learn to Sacrifice

What is worship? "Therefore, I urge you, brothers, in view of God's mercy, to offer your bodies as living sacrifices, holy and pleasing to God—which *is your spiritual worship*" (Romans 12:1, emphasis added).

What? You thought that worship was praising God in word and song? Enjoying a powerful choir explode with power on a beautiful hymn? Lifting your hands and dancing before the Lord? Being in a meeting where spiritual gifts are exercised? Finding a creative way to pay homage to God?

Nope. These things can be an overflow from a worshipful life, but they themselves aren't worship.

According to the Lord, the "offering of your bodies as living sacrifices" is the *only* way to worship. Most churches have *worship meetings*, but if we were being accurate we would talk about having meetings for "worship people"—or better, for showing Christians how to better worship God by their "holy and pleasing" lives.

And what about worship meetings full of people who haven't fully offered their bodies as living sacrifices? Is it really proper to call them worship meetings at all? How does God really feel about worship meetings that have no true worship, or sacrifice, at all? Here's what the Lord says: "I will spread on your faces the offal [waste] from your festival sacrifices" (Malachi 2:3). Think about it—God being so displeased with the lack of sacrificial worship that His response is to smear your superficial worship all over your face.

Sacrifice. It's a word you don't hear much in our culture. And yet, it defines worship; it *is* worship. Lives lived out in a sacrificial way always catch our attention: the man who gives up his own life to save a drowning child, the woman who gives up her own interests to care for needy parents, the child who gives his favorite toy to his friend who really likes it. We like hearing about sacrifice a lot.

We just don't like *doing* it.

It's a simple proposition: Learn to sacrifice, and your life becomes a pleasing aroma to God. Teach your children to sacrifice, and their lives will please both God and you. Let your children see you give your time when you're tired, your money when you'd like to buy something for yourself, your convenience when somebody you really don't like asks you for help.

Then suggest ways for them to sacrifice. Urge them to use their money to buy food for the poor. Exhort them to help the elderly neighbor do some yard work that the older person just can't do. Encourage them to spend their Saturday afternoon showing a younger child in your church family how to make a cake or a go-cart. As their lives actually become a living sacrifice, you'll come to know with certainty that you're parenting champions. Go give them a big hug, and let them know how pleased you are with them, and praise God in their presence for their sacrificial lives.

Now *that's* a worship meeting.

4. Learn That You're Not the Only One

You believe that you're the sole guardians of your children's spirits and welfare. You believe that you must protect them from any and all outside influence. You believe that no one else has the right to instruct or discipline your children. You believe that you're truly the only one— outside of God—destined to be and acceptable as a source of wisdom and as a model for these developing spirits.

You are wrong.

This pride is presumptive and wrong.

What can even begin as a good idea, in guarding against rotten outside influences, can become a rotten influence in its own right as it expands to include family, pastors and leaders, Christian teachers, and fellow believers. How *dare* anyone be so bold and out of line as to take a special interest in *my* child!

Those who take this approach often don't see the counterproductive double-mindedness of deliberately eliminating godly adult influences even as they allow their children to be intimately and extensively influenced by godless scalawags who happen to be their children's peers.

What is it that produces this unscriptural and unhealthy attitude? Certainly, if we are insecure in our own beliefs, we won't have the confidence to allow our children to be exposed to other Christian adults. We can be stifled if we aren't close enough to these other adults to know what they believe. With the garbage flowing through the culture, we can simply be frightened by the dangers lurking behind every smile.

But the basic reason is, I believe, just plain old pride. We just can't shake the idea that somehow we are *it,* and anyone else is just second best or worse. We cover over this pride with a lot of quasi-religious and pseudo-Biblical comments or arguments about the all-important role of the parents alone as a guide for their children.

But this is unscriptural hogwash. After God, you might be expected to have the *primary* influence. But the *only* influence? Come on! Whatever happened to the body of Christ, the ministry of all believers toward one another, the exercise of spiritual gifts for the edification of every believer, and going and making disciples of everyone, and confessing our faults one to another, and provoking one another to good works, and Paul's relationship to Timothy? Where in Scripture are children ever exempted from any of this? Are children just second-class citizens in God's kingdom, or are they the most important part of God's kingdom (see Matthew 18:1–5)? Aren't all people told to "submit to one another out of reverence for Christ" (Ephesians 5:21)?

If you set yourself up as your child's only authority, you'll reap bad news. First of all, they'll rebel against and reject other authority. This will produce a negative attitude against authority in general, which will inevitably come up against *you.* In fact, they may use these others as an outlet for their rebellion only until they can get around to rebelling against you.

If you encourage or support your children in their rebellion by your words ("that teacher is a fool," "that woman is really out to lunch," "your uncle really doesn't know what he's talking about,") or by your actions (like boycotting people or schools or Sunday school classes), then the rebellion will be just that much worse.

The worst of it, though, will be that your children will miss incredibly rich blessings from interrelating with these other adults and incredibly important help with those problems that need insights from people with a different background and spiritual gift from yours.

Most people won't do this for your children automatically. We find ourselves constantly on the alert for some excellent Christian whom we can provoke to take an interest in one or more of our children. Where do you look? Try your church family. If you don't have anyone there that you'd trust, then you don't *have* a church family. You're just going to "church." Your need is to find a church family first.

Many believers will respond to your request for help and love. However, it's sad but true that most adults are so unsure of their position with you and their responsibility to your children that the slightest resistance on your part will stop them absolutely cold. Even if they're *convicted* about helping, many won't do it because of their fear of alienating or offending you.

"Too bad, so sad," as my son Peter used to say. Your mission is to recognize those who would be important to your child's development and who would "show the way to life" (Proverbs 10:17), and to encourage these people, while at the same time keeping the rotten influences away. Not *all* influences, mind you; just the rotten ones.

In the final analysis, God is the primary influence; all the rest of us are just His helpers, to build up the body of Christ so that God might be glorified. No matter how high an opinion you have of your role, you aren't the only one. I don't want you to misunderstand me; you *are* a helper, and even a critically important helper, for your children.

But, after all is said and done, you are only one.

5. Learn to Grovel

Although most parents don't realize it, groveling is one of their most critical activities.

Most people, sadly, don't have very many people who care about them, at least to the point of spending any truly valuable time with them. This is true for adults as well as children, and it's a tragedy of the modern Christian noncommunity. After the parents and perhaps a few relatives, there aren't many godly disciplers around your child.

Many parents, if they think about this at all, assume they've got the solution to this in several important directions. They put their child in Christian school (good); they involve their child in a church with a strong Sunday school (good); they allow their children to attend all of the church youth group's activities (maybe good and maybe not); they enter their child into a whole list of other clubs and associations and organizations that will be glad to tell you about their importance to your child's growth (probably not good); and they generally figure that they'll just so immerse their child in Christian activity, that some sound growth has to occur. Right?

Wrong. So many of these things never reach into the deep part of the child's spirit. Sound doctrine alone won't do it. What your child needs is an intimate relationship with a few outstanding men and women who will dedicate their *lives,* and not just their time, to your child. Most of the people running these activities have good hearts and good intentions. But face it, some of them haven't even planned their time with the group until about forty-five minutes before the activity starts. They don't have, or won't make, the time to individually disciple your child. It's one-on-one time that will make the difference. This is where the rubber meets the road. This is where contact is made with a fledgling immortal spirit.

"Ah," some parents will say, "we have tried to help with this one-on-one business by making sure that our child only associates with decent, respectful peers."

Now if your children associate with their peers, the "decent, respectful" variety is the best kind. But think about peers for a few minutes. If your child is thirteen, and he has four close peers who are also thirteen, ask yourself a simple question: How much did you know when you were thirteen?

If your answer is honest and you were anywhere near typical, your answer would be "not much" (or maybe "nothing"). Your child's peers usually can't help your child, at least in a significant way, *because they don't know any more than he does.* It's the blind leading the blind. Any parent who emphasizes peer involvement is a person who has forgotten the confusion and turmoil of his own youth.

Your kids may need some organizational activity and peer involvement, but they *desperately* need one or two or three godly men or women to disciple them. These people won't be easy to find, and the best choices will already be so busy that they won't be easy to involve with your child. So what are you going to do if this approach to parent assistance makes some sense to you?

Grovel.

That's right, grovel. *To grovel* is defined as "to humble oneself; to lie or crawl with the face downward, as in abject humility." This is a good Christian activity before God at any time; in the matter of finding people to help you parent champions, it's absolutely essential.

Ask the Lord to lead you in your thoughts and observations, and then look around to see if there are any likely, albeit unsuspecting, candidates. Watch them in action. And then, if they look like what the Doctor ordered, start groveling. Why? Because your child is *important.* Provoke these potential spirit builders, encourage them, tell them you'll do their chores for them while they spend time with your child, pay their way out to dinner together — do *anything* within the bounds of Scripture that will help your child to find, in addition to you, his very own Paul or Paula (your child will need a big sister no less than a big brother in the Lord).

If you don't think this is important, may God help you and your child.

And if you do think this is important, start groveling.

6. Learn to Whisper

"Then a great and powerful wind tore the mountains apart and shattered the rocks before the LORD, but the LORD was not in the wind. After the wind there was an earthquake, but the LORD was not in the earthquake. After the earthquake came a fire, but the LORD was not in the fire."

"And after the fire came a gentle whisper" (1 Kings 19:11–12).

You may not believe it, but after showing your child how to have a close personal relationship with God, whispering may be one of the most important things that you can do to parent a champion.

Many parents appear to their children to be more like wind, earthquake, and fire than they do anything else. In the parents' dialogue with their children, they can blow their children back and forth like a fierce gale that won't let anything settle to the ground. The parents can boom out their commands, shaking the spirits of their offspring. And the parents' voices can rage like a scorching fire, burning up part of the children's love in the process. Many of us act as though parenting, to be effective, has to be *loud.*

God isn't like that. Why are we?

How would you like it if God yelled out at you in your next church meeting, "Hey you, John Doe. Would you mind getting your act together?" Or how about, "Jane Smith! Would you please pipe down for once?" And, "Would you look at yourself, Robert? What's the matter with you?" How would you react — even if these things were *true?* You would be totally humiliated and embarrassed and more likely to resent God than to follow Him.

Jesus said: "In everything, do to others what you would have them do to you, *for this sums up the Law and the Prophets*" (Matthew 7:12, emphasis added). The only thing that we would like less than God doing this to us is for another person to do this to us. No one reading this wants to be treated with open disrespect, and yet that's exactly what vocal correction of our children in front of others is.

When you're in a group with your child, and he starts doing his Goliath impersonation, your natural reaction is going to be to let him and everyone else know that you're not laughing. You're going to want to nail this behavior before it turns into a road show. The *temptation* to bellow and blow at your child will be as natural as breathing but a lot less edifying.

Instead, go to him, or ask him quietly to come to you, and whisper into his ear what you want him to know. There's no correction, counsel, or command that won't go over a hundred times better this way than with the old earthquake approach. The same comments that can sound like scolding or rebuke when spoken out loud can become encouragement when whispered into a lovely listening ear. Your child can even feel special to you in a way that no one else in the room is.

In short, you will have turned a potential lemon into a big, cold glass of lemonade.

So don't disrespect your child. Treat him with the dignity that his Creator intended him to experience. Remember that he is an immortal, valuable, irreplaceable spirit, brought to you Special Delivery by the hand of a God who—praise His holy name!—won't broadcast *your* follies in public.

Don't roar into your child's consciousness like a wind or an earthquake or a fire. If you want him to really hear you, do what God does with you: just whisper.

Gently, please.

7. Learn to Test with Praise

What's the best way to tell if your children are developing any character to go along with their skills and abilities?

God gives a very clear way to do this:

"The crucible for silver and the furnace for gold, but man is tested by the praise he receives" (Proverbs 27:21).

It seems pretty unlikely that any parent would come up with this as a test, but there it is in scripture; it must mean *something*. After some very careful analysis, I have come to the conclusion that it must mean that man is tested by the praise he receives. God obviously does this with *us* (which is a fairly disconcerting thought). How can we come up with anything better for *our* children?

Watch your children when they receive praise from others. Some tell-tale signs of problems are:

- They begin doing things with the primary purpose of receiving praise.

- They begin actively seeking and soliciting praise (". . . nor is it honorable to seek one's own honor" Proverbs 25:37).

- They begin praising themselves ("If you have played the fool and exalted yourself . . . clap your hand over your mouth!" Proverbs 30:32).

- They forget to be "completely humble and gentle" (Ephesians 4:2) and answer with little gems like, "I know" or "What do you expect?"

- They answer praise with questions like, "Do you really think so?", which sound humble but are really efforts to secure more praise.

How should praise be answered? The answer comes in three parts: thoughtfully, outwardly, and upwardly.

They should first think about the praise; if it's flippant, or deceitful, or dishonest, or about something that they didn't do, or about something over which they have no control (like physical appearance), or just idle flattery. They should be taught to act accordingly. They should know that they should reject the praise and politely correct the one who is a flatterer or who made the mistake. Work with them on sample statements, like "Do you really mean what you just said?"; "Thank you for thinking of me, but I really didn't do that"; and "If you really like something about the way God made me, you need to tell Him, not me."

Your children will be tempted to listen to this bogus praise. There's no value in it, but most of us get so little of any kind of praise that we can be willing to accept the fake variety. How sad!

The "outwardly and upwardly" work together. Once the value of the praise has been determined, your children should know what scripture says about dealing with this honor that they have been given. It says: "Like tying a stone in a sling is the giving of honor to a fool" (Proverbs 26:8).

Think about it. What happens when you tie a stone in a sling? You defeat the purpose of the stone and the sling, for one very simple reason: The stone goes in but it never comes out. A fool is recognized by the praise he receives, because he still has it all with him! He has it stuffed in his pockets, and is quite sure that it's all deserved and well short of what he should have. A fool is marked by his confidence that he is *owed* praise. If he cannot get it from others, then he will do the job himself.

Don't let your child get marked as a fool. Teach him to be gracious to the one giving him praise. Teach him to be humble and gentle, but not falsely humble by denying the truth of valid praise. Teach him to love the person who's praising him, and to look for ways to encourage and praise his friend—but not to praise his friend falsely just to "trade" praise. Have him thank God in his heart for this honor that he's allowed, and give aloud to God the praise that belongs to Him.

One thing more: You must praise your child. No praise, in fact, is more important to him than yours, since "parents are the pride of their children" (Proverbs 17:6). This advice isn't new; many have told parents to praise their children, and praise has value to your child in its own right. But you must know that praise without testing and teaching is incomplete at best, and can increase your child's foolishness at worst. Show them by example how to receive praise. Praise them, and encourage others to praise them.

And then give them a test.

8. Learn to Have Family Nights

If you aren't dedicating one night a week to the spiritual development of your family *as a family,* you shouldn't be surprised to find out someday that you really aren't as close a family as you could be.

Many families today don't even take one meal together on a daily basis. The idea that a family is a very special refuge is being eroded by the attitude that living in the same place makes a group of people a family. Things to distract you from your family — jobs, activities, television, and the often rude and thoughtless telephone — abound. Our belief that these things are an inescapable part of our modern, fast-paced society shows us just how ignorant we have become.

Meals should be eaten together whenever possible. These are everyday regrouping times that get you face to face when often you could stay busy doing something else. At least one meal a week should be the start of an extended evening of joy around the Lord. We call ours "Family Night," and have been enjoying it on Friday nights. We think Fridays are the best because they're the end of the busy week, and because they refocus our attention on resting in the Lord. But the main thing is that it be done generally on the same night so that all eyes are focused on it, and so that everyone, including the little ones, can look forward to it.

After a while you won't feel like doing it anymore, but we have found that if you lie down for a few minutes, the feeling will go away. This is too important to quit.

We have a nice meal, that all of us like, followed by a nice dessert that we wouldn't normally have. Then we have alternated among several activities:

- Reading Scripture, and then drawing individual pictures to describe what impressed each person. (We read through the Bible, unless someone has a passage of particularly good interest to the group.)

Each person then holds up and describes his picture, which includes a pertinent verse from another part of Scripture. We have a large notebook full of these pictures, which we then use for review. It's amazing how well kids (and adults) respond to the Bible as recalled by their own art work.

- Working on a longer-term project, like an oil painting of some special Scripture story or a plaque or a sculpture.

- Playing one of several available Bible games, or making up a game, like Bible charades.

- Singing, with each person picking out a song on a rotating basis. If the talent and skills are there, write a song together, using a favorite Scripture passage or words of your own creation.

- Listening to tapes of Bible stories or music.

- Doing a project for someone else — making a meal for a shut-in would be one good example.

- Taking the Scripture we have read and asking ourselves how we can put it into practice as soon as possible — like that night or the next day. If we have read about selling our possessions and giving to the poor, then we could find something to sell, go as a family to sell the things, and then buy some things for the poor.

- This night can involve eating out, if the funds are there. Sometimes we go home for our activity, but sometimes we do it right in the restaurant. It can provide an excellent opportunity to witness and share with those around you.

You might say, "This sounds pretty good — why only one night a week?" If you can do it more often, by all means do it — although you need to be consistent and work to keep it fresh. But fight like crazy to keep it in your schedule at least once a week. There'll be many things that will try to squeeze it out. Treat these things like a contagious disease.

Can you raise a champion if you don't have family nights? Possibly, but you've hampered your efforts, as well as missed a lot of fun and growth together. You don't have to have family nights. If you don't start the practice, you'll surely never miss it. And if you stop it later on, you'll probably never miss it. You'll be too busy.

Doing something.

9. Learn to Create Memory Pockets

Think back to your own childhood. There are probably some very special and gentle and mellow pictures that will come back to your mind and heart.

Perhaps you see a little child — you — sharing a quiet moment with his dad in a park, or a special look of joy on a mom's face as she let her joy in her child shine through. Maybe you see a drive to the country to visit a grandpa and grandma, or a little one sharing hot dogs and snow-cones with that awesome but loving creature known as a parent. Perhaps you see the strong arms of a father as he carries his sleeping child from the car to the bed, or the gentle face of a mother as she tucks her baby in. Or maybe you see those special holidays or vacations, which have a special hue to them, no matter how simple they were. I used to feel guilty about taking vacations, but now I know that the return on the investment is very, very high.

Take a few minutes to quietly remember those days. List the first five that come to your mind.

Where have these paintings been kept all these years?

In memory pockets.

Any parent who has the vaguest recollection of what it was to be a child should know how important these times are. These were the things that were anticipated and lived with such special intensity, and are now tucked away safely in a pocket of your heart. Your pockets are unique. No one else has ever carried around your particular and exquisite collection, and no one else ever will.

You are who you are and what you are in part because of these pockets of joy. If you have a diary from your childhood, it can add color to the memories; but in truth you *are* a diary, written in by your parents in indelible ink, and you'll carry these memories with you to the end of your life on earth. This should be a sobering thought for you as a parent. Your own parenting will live in memories far beyond your own time here.

It takes three things to make a memory pocket: time, love, and softness. Time, because nothing of value is ever built without it; love, because nothing can be fully enjoyed without it; and softness, because there will be no smiles without it. You must give your child your time and your love and your softness — and if you do, you'll reach across the gap between your hearts and impress a rich treasure on your living gifts to the years beyond your life.

Now there's a problem with this idea of memory pockets, for no one carries around empty ones. Far too many adults have had their memory pockets crammed full of nightmares: cruelty, hate, brutal and reckless tongue-lashings, broken promises, and sweet moments turned sour by a parent remembered only in the blackness of the night, and only with a bitterness that lodges where love wanted to dwell.

Both good and bad can be imprinted on a heart. It's true both ways: "Each heart knows its own bitterness, and no one else can share its joy" (Proverbs 14:10). Nightmares can take up all of the space where joy alone should be, and no one can fully convey the depth of pervasive sadness. All children start out, to be sure, with folly in their hearts; but it's just as certain that they start out with bitterless joy. Children *learn* to believe in parent-created nightmares.

Scripture says that "even in laughter the heart may ache, and joy may end in grief" (Proverbs 14:13). We live in a culture that specializes in turning laughter to aching and joy to grief. This is a dirty business. Stay away from it, by the power of God.

One of my oldest son's favorite stories was about a boy named Peter, who always stuffed everything he could into his pockets. Your child will do this too. Are you giving him nothing but "whatever is true, whatever is noble, whatever is right, whatever is pure, whatever is lovely, whatever is admirable" (Philippians 4:8) to think on and remember? And if you're giving him other things, how will he remember you?

So, you had better start thinking. And stuffing. Every day contains some untapped treasure, and every experience can be turned by a creative parent into an unfading smile. Make this a priority.

And watch the good memories go into those tiny pockets.

Conclusion

Go back over each heading, and make a mark by the one you want to start on this week. Then do it.

13

NINE THINGS
THAT WILL HINDER
YOUR VISION

Let us throw off everything that hinders.
(Hebrews 12:1)

I n this chapter, we'll look at nine things that you can do to really make your mission of parenting a champion much more difficult.

1. Make Your Child a Clone of You

It's appropriate that you encourage your child to become like you — but not *exactly* like you.

As you look at the many wonderful faces of children in a Christmas program, you start to become aware of the fabulous variety of God's creation. Each child is a physical and spiritual package that's absolutely unique; he should be treated like the treasure that he is and respected for his magnificent design. Jesus died for him, lives for him, and loves him; Jesus has placed this "diamond in the rough" into your hands and will allow you to help Him produce a masterpiece.

But don't go too far. The principles you live by should be impressed upon him by word and deed. You can thank God that your child is designed to absorb these principles. But let these principles take their special form in this new being that is most emphatically *not* you or your spouse.

Don't try to make your child choose the same career, ministry, music, or food that you've chosen. The principles of life that you're going to give him will stand by him no matter which of these things he chooses.

Instead, try to do what God so obviously enjoys doing: Relish your child, delight in his diversity, and be filled with joy at this one-of-a-kind creation. God is enjoying your child. You should do no less.

A classic statement on this principle of unity and diversity is this: "There is one body and one Spirit — just as you were called to one hope when you were called — one Lord, one faith, one baptism; one God and Father of all, who is over all and through all and in all" (Ephesians 4:4–6). *This* is unity, and this is where our spirits and our children's spirits should be alike. The next verse, however, has a startling contrast: "But to each one of us grace has been given as Christ apportioned it."

We are the same, but different. If you look at yourself properly, you should be *glad* that God threw away the mold after He formed you. You should rejoice that your child was a special order. You each will affect people that would be untouched by just one of you and a clone.

The power of the Spirit that you and your child share will be magnified through God's all-original cast. He has unique people, planned for specific times and places, to make a dramatic difference for Him. This thought should not only direct your parenting; it should please you that He has chosen you to prepare His warrior for the battles he or she will face in his or her piece of history, perhaps long after you've gone.

I discussed earlier training a child in the way he should go with God's principles. The idea has been presented by some that this could mean that we should train him in the way his particular gifts and abilities would take him. I think it means both: Train him in the way he should go with God's timeless Word, and train him in the way he should go with his own unique life. The two can and should fit together perfectly.

So don't make your child a clone. You don't need a clone. God doesn't need a clone. Help your child to be what God wants him to be, and not just a carbon copy of you.

Besides, hasn't one of *you* already tried God's patience enough?

2. Be the Bland Leading the Bland

Have you ever noticed how easy it is to fill up your days with activities? Golf, tennis, skiing, camping, racquetball, gardening, stamp collecting, watching movies, shopping, while all fine if kept in perspective, can take the place of thought, research, questioning, creating, imagining, seeking, and challenging. We act as though we were put here only to enjoy the cover on the book of our lives, rather than to enjoy the good things in the book itself. Our children will pick up this empty way of life, if only because they *are* our children.

We settle for so little when there is so much to have. It's possible — perhaps even likely — that the greatest potential achievers in every field are those who never enter it. A potentially great writer may spend his entire career working in a factory; a potentially great statesman may spend his entire career as a writer; and so it goes, multiplied by many millions of potentially great someones who persist in a given direction even when it bores them to death and they're not the best at what they're doing. Why would we even get close to allowing our children to be consigned to the wrong place?

So many people are potentially everything, but practically nothing. We can teach our children to punch in and out on a giant time card, "enter life here, exit life there," without a single thought or effort directed to the question: "Why did God put my children here, in this time, in this place, with these abilities and gifts, with these people?" We can teach them this by the example of our own spiritually apathetic lives, lived without expectation from God or enthusiasm for God. We teach them to be worldly wise and worldly successful, and to lead lives without godly exuberance. For this, we most certainly deserve to be sent to our room.

How many children grow into their maximum potential spiritually? How many men and women are truly fulfilling God's purpose for them? How on earth can we waste the wisdom and power that are available to achieve the dramatic goals that God has set for us? How many of us can say with David: "You give me your shield of victory, and your right hand sustains me; you stoop down to make me great" (Psalms 18:35)?

Great — that's what God is talking about. *Getting by* — that's what we talk about. I don't mean greatness in the world's eyes, although that, too, can come. I am talking about greatness in God's eyes, because we have allowed Him to use us for the reasons and purposes behind our being here in the first place. The world might think you're strange, but when has the world ever been right about much?

In other words, *every* believer has an important appointment with God's purpose. God has a unique and special place for each person in your family. Can you as a parent grasp this? Find out what your purpose is, and go for it; then help your children find what their purpose is, and urge them to go for it. Don't let Satan, the world's distractions, or your own inane fleshly desires make you forget your appointment with true destiny. Too many have already forgotten.

The way that you avoid becoming bland or staying that way is to force yourself to be interested in things, in God's plan for you. It doesn't happen naturally because it's a little scary and a little too easy to put new things down or avoid them. Satan is a master at keeping you dull. He likes you that way.

Satan will, of course, try to get you to lead a spectacularly sinful life, or even just a despicable life. But if he can't get you to go along, if you insist on being on the straight and narrow path, then his best available course is to frustrate you and make you boring to your children and others who might be interested in Christ. Then, at least, no one will want to follow you in this Christianity business.

To Satan, boring is better.

You have to watch for new things from God, dig into them when you find them, and develop new patterns of spiritual thought from this mosaic of wisdom and knowledge and experience. I am not talking about just knowing a lot of things about a lot of things; this isn't enough. I am talking about bringing your and your child's God-given individuality to bear on every subject, on every area of life. Each of you is by edict of God different from every other human being that has ever graced or disgraced this planet. Because of this, each of you should ask: Why me? why now? why here? God will give you the answers, if only you and your child will ask Him, seek Him, and knock on His door.

Don't be bland. Don't let your children be bland. There's no good reason why one of you couldn't show up in a history book. Remember, if the bland lead the bland, they'll both slide into the pit. They won't fall. They'll just slide. Know why?

Falling is too exciting.

3. Abuse Your Child's Spirit

Just as there are many ways to be dead, there are many ways to be abused. Some hurt worse than others and leave deeper scars. Schools are prohibited by law from effectively using physical discipline, while they rip kids' hearts to shreds and numb their minds. Businesses pay lip service to employees' "higher" needs and capabilities, while management rigidly enforces the mindless trade of money for hours. Employees measure success not by satisfaction level, but rather by salary level. Church organizations build more magnificent buildings, in which sermons can be preached against the pitfalls of materialism. Parents claim that they gave their children everything, when what they mean is everything money can buy.

We live as though what we see is what we get.

Even psychiatrists, who claimed that they were treating minds as well as bodies, are now becoming technicians. They dispense chemicals that work on physical symptoms, while the person's heart is left in the slimy pit that's been dug by its owner. People are made to appear physically calm, while their hearts are still raging infernos.

We need to break out of this "physical only" way of thinking.

Physical child abuse, whether violent or sexual or whatever, is certainly repulsive and should be punished, but it isn't the most frequent type. Spiritual abuse is foremost. We abuse kids by the lack of consistent teaching and discipline and by our outbursts of crushing hate and anger. Wounded spirits heal even slower than wounded bodies — if they heal at all.

Jesus said, "If anyone causes one of these little ones *who believe in me* to sin, it would be better for him to be thrown into the sea with a large millstone tied around his neck" (Mark 9:42, emphasis added). Jesus wasn't mincing any words on this subject. These children belong to Him, and He doesn't appreciate those who push the little ones around. God certainly detests "hands that shed innocent blood" (Proverbs 6:17), but an offense against an innocent spirit is also a stench that will surely bring down His great wrath upon the unrepentant perpetrator.

In what ways can we spiritually abuse our children? First and foremost is by neglect of spiritual things in the home. Whatever your home is full of is what your children will be full of. If it's full of endless television and grotesque radio stations and gossip and coldness, the reading on your children's spiritual gauge will say "empty."

You should certainly keep your hearts off of your children if you only have anger and gruffness to share. But it's far more common to find baby Christians who have simply been abandoned even while they're physically living at home. The long, brutal abuse of starving a child to death is a hideous display of the worst of human nature. In the same way, spiritual starvation may win the award for the worst in parenting—especially Christian parenting, by people who should know better.

What do I mean? I mean simply that your home ought to overflow with the Lord. All thoughts and words and actions should trace their way back to Him. His name and Word should reign supreme all day, every day. You probably don't skip many meals in your home and would certainly hate to see your children go hungry; don't skip any spiritual meals either and hate even more to see your children spiritually malnourished. Spiritual starvation all too often leads to spiritual death. Don't let it happen in your home.

But if your home is full of prayer and Scripture and faith and confidence in God, your children will surprise you with the quality that they'll exhibit—-now and later. Like a little baby who with care can grow to be a seven-foot man, so a little spirit with care can grow to be a Christ-like champion, even if he or she is only fifty inches tall. As the professional baseball player responded when asked what it was like to be the shortest player in the major leagues: "It's a whole lot better than being the tallest player in the minor leagues."

In other words, if you love the Lord, please feed His sheep so *they* can be at least the shortest players in God's major league.

Perhaps equally destructive of little spirits is the deadening or hypocritizing or trivializing influence of "church" in America. Too many parents are content to shuffle their children off to Sunday school classes with absolutely no idea what goes on there. As long as the kids aren't crying when they get out, have some take-home papers, and can parrot a few well-worn verses, the parents assume that all systems are go. Well, they may be go, but *go where?* is the question.

Sitting through spiritually draining meetings with you is another sure-fire way to abuse their spirits. I'll bet you can't stand those kinds of meetings, either. Do yourselves a favor and don't go to those kinds of meetings anymore. Find a church family where they're teaching something *real.* There's suffering for the name, and then there's just suffering. Abusing yourself and your children in a dead or dishonest church is just suffering. Say good-bye.

School can be a great source for spiritual child abuse. Sadly, even "Christian" schools can miss the boat by two weeks. Spend a lot of time checking out every possible Christian school—no matter how much driving you have to do to get them there—until you find one that doesn't abuse your children's spirits. A bad school can destroy the very best efforts of the home and the church; in fact, what a bad school pushes can be just as bad, and probably more destructive, as the stuff palmed off by your local drug pusher.

To sum up: Don't abuse your children's spirits.

And don't let anyone else do it, either.

4. Pick a Formula and Pigeon-Hole Your Child

I have a confession to make: *I'm a wintry, right-brained, first-born, strong-willed, irregular choleric.*

Does this surprise you?

Well, it's probably no surprise to you that we live in an age of generalizations and categorizations.

There's nothing wrong with this if the generalizations are true and the categorizations have some truth-related value. These can be a help in understanding life and the world around us. They can provide a way to deal with new situations and problems and can provide a framework in which this information can be placed.

But what if the generalizations only *sound* true? What if they only give you enough information to agree with the generalization, but not enough to know where its holes are? And what can happen to the success in our lives and the lives of others when we take widely different people and slap them into the same category?

One of the lures of astrology is that it allows people to explain things that happen to them on the basis of some implanted, uncontrollable, predetermined characteristic. People are neatly divided into twelve categories based on their date of birth, and this one event sets the tone for the rest of their lives. Unsuspecting individuals can read a "horrorscope" and be amazed at how accurately it describes them. They don't understand that this is due partly to their desire to *be* amazed and partly due to the manner in which the "forecast" or description is written.

So it is with most attempts to generalize on God's exquisite and intensely varied creation; and this is particularly true with His masterpiece, man. Each person is so completely unlike anyone else that to categorize people into a few broad groups based on the finite capabilities of human research is to say, I know how God did it; I have the key to knowledge when it comes to understanding man.

As the man said, no matter how thin you slice it, it's still baloney.

These generalizations about God's people — "third-born children are thus-and-so, unless they're the second boy and over five-feet tall"; "melancholies tend to be that way, unless they spend two hours with a choleric in a stuck elevator" — have several attributes in common:

- They speak to us about things other than our spirits — and our spirits are the very things that make us unique. They're dealing with things that can be outwardly observed. Paul said: "As for those who seemed to be important — whatever they were makes no difference to me; God does not judge by external appearance." (Galatians 2:6). Scripture makes it very plain that man constantly errs in judging by what he sees, while God concerns Himself with what can't be seen.

- They can lead to prejudice in our dealings with others. Once you think you have someone placed in one or more of these categories, it's hard not to treat him differently, to treat him as though he *is* that kind of person. This artificial division has caused great tragedies in the history of races, and won't do you and those around you much good, either. It misses what Paul was saying when he told us that "from now on we regard no one from a worldly point of view" (2 Corinthians 5:16).

- They can confuse your parenting ideas until you don't know what kind of concoction you're trying to raise. You can end up with a mish-mash philosophy and a flock of self-fulfilling prophecies. This is out of line with Scripture when it tells you to train a child in the way he, not his "groupings," should go.

- They can lead you to explain away legitimate needs, problems, or sins because your child fits one of these categories that "explains it all." You think he's right-brained when really he's wrong-spirited; you think he's suffering from first-born "dependence on self" when really he is suffering from a lack of love or attention; you think he's strong-willed when really he's a slave to his flesh and *weak*-willed; you think he's irregular when really he's just obnoxious; you think he's choleric when really he's impatient and insensitive. We have developed a lot of cute descriptions for plain old sin and self.

- They can actually *prevent* you from getting to know the immortal spirit that's dwelling inside that fleshy cover. This knowledge will only come through a large investment of time and love. You have to get into the details of your child's life, instead of stopping just below the surface. You must *disciple,* not designate.

- They can cause you to be unlike your God who, from the beginning of the Bible to the end, is depicted as a God who is not a respecter of persons (see Galatians 3:28).

Many people have gone to a lot of work to convince you of their particular formula. Perhaps it's okay as long as these things are limited to humorous conversations over tea and cookies, but I doubt it. We humans tend too easily to latch onto the "rule of thumb," the short-cut, the quick way of explaining things, the clever analysis that represents our feeble way of converting the gray areas of life into blacks and whites. We listen to these theories and end up agreeing, laughing, and then, horror of horrors, putting them into practice.

There is one who has already divided men as much as they need to be divided. He has divided us into two groups. On the one hand, there are the spiritually alive, eternally joyful, holy and blameless, adopted sons of God; on the other hand, there are the spiritually dead, eternally ruined, despicable and guilty, adopted sons of the devil. There are the sheep and there are the goats. There are the faithful and there are the unfaithful. And none of this is inflicted on you or your children from above; you choose with which group you'll spend the rest of forever.

The truth is that all of us started out in God's eyes as wintry, no-brained, once-born/twice dead, strong-willed, irregular, and temperamental people. All we had was pride to offer our pride-hating God. But thank God, He allowed each of us the delicious choice of getting out of these categories by getting into grace. He was gracious enough to let us leave behind all that we *really* were (whether we appeared that way or not) to become something brand new.

Don't categorize your children. Give your children the same opportunity with God that you have, to be in the only category that counts: the
Redeemed.

5. Hide Out in the Christian Ghetto

One of the forces operating on the Christian community is the idea that
Christians, if we are to be tolerated at all, should be roped off and isolated from having any effect on anyone or anything else. We are different, even strange, and should be treated as though we have some horrible communicable disease that would pollute the environment which
secular man has worked so hard to build. In short, they want us out of
the way.

Believers have been rounded up and stuffed into the Christian ghetto.
We can have our little churches, our underequipped private schools (for
now), our radio stations, and our bookstores, as long as we don't bother
anyone else. Just like Polish and Hungarian Jews who were allowed to
live in the smothering ghettos of Europe under Hitler, we can go about
our business only with the approval of those who would be god.

The only problem is, they won't let us go about our *Father's* business, which is to invade and pervade every area of life and reclaim it all
for Him. Their approvals will be fewer and fewer, until we are clinging
to life by the ends of our fingers, and they can stomp on them until we
fall off.

Look at how we have fallen for this evil attempt to push Christians
out of the way. One by one, ten by ten, things which were once dominated by Christian ethics are being stripped from us by relentless humanists: literature, radio, television, movies, education, politics, law,
economics, welfare. Are the Christians in the streets doing battle with
these greedy thugs for the soul of America? Are Christians even making
mild protests? Are they even *thinking* about it? No way. They just move
a little closer together, as God's enemies squeeze a few more Christians
into the ghetto.

Instead, we listen to the poppycock of the humanists as they mouth
absurd platitudes about the separation of church and state. Worse, *we*
mouth the same sinful junk. What are the statist humanists protecting us
from with this cancerous by-product of the Enlightenment? Why, they're

so thoughtful, keeping us from allowing God to influence people, and keeping Biblical values out of the public forum, and keeping mankind chained to the brilliant things that they can cook up out of their own heads!

These people don't want separation of church and state; they want the elimination of the church by the state. Under this principle, Christ would be prevented from taking the throne in His own kingdom; in fact, under this principle, Christ would be *crucified.* And He was. "'What are we accomplishing?' they asked. 'Here is this man performing many miraculous signs. If we let him go on like this, everyone will believe in him, and then the Romans will come and take away both our place and our nation'" (John 11:47–48). They didn't allow this to happen. They separated church and state — with a cross.

Your children need to be bold in breaking out of the Christian ghetto. No legitimate area of life or creation is off limits to a child of God. Eliminate this pietistic and pompous talk about "full-time Christian work," as though there's any other kind. Your life, and your children's lives, are either committed totally to God or they aren't. If they aren't, you might as well start teaching your children to enjoy the ghetto.

Christians aren't rabble, put here to be dominated by godless fools. We were put here to be the body of Christ and to exercise authority over a creation that Jesus has already redeemed. True, we are not U.S. citizens first, for "our citizenship is in heaven" (Philippians 3:20). But the King of our country — heaven — also happens to be the King of this world.

This world is, in fact, just a *colony,* under the authority of the King of kings. We don't belong in a ghetto, and we and our children shouldn't allow the world to put us there. If anything, it should be the other way around. Christians should be cramming all that stands against God into the ghetto of endless ruin.

If we don't break out, can we really believe that our enemies will let us keep our little niche? Did Hitler stop there? Do you think they'll let us talk about God on the public airwaves or the public streets? They'll want it all. They'll want to push us off the face of the earth, to devour us, to erase our memories. We can't afford to be helpless sheep, herded into the slaughterhouse and gassed by secular humanism. We must break out and take control of this colony for God. We must do it, or our children will die — in the ghetto.

6. Nurture Your Own Blind Spots

It's amazing to me how many parents think that their children are perfect, right up to the moment that they can't understand them at all.

We as parents have a God-implanted love and concern for our children. God wants us to treat our children with mercy and understanding, not just a cold and sterile justice. He wants us to help Him mold an essentially imperfect being into His kind of person, and for that effort we need patience and acceptance.

Satan, however, can turn these attributes of parents into gross and destructive qualities. He'll use deceit and treachery to develop major blind spots that prevent parents from seeing the folly and stupidity of their little wonders. He'll help parents make excuses for their children when they do things that would make Ghengis Khan look like an angel of mercy. He'll help parents put up walls to keep out other Christians who might be able to point out the blind spots.

You've probably heard a few of the great lines:

- "He's just a little boy."

- "What can you expect from a child?"

- "He'll settle down as he gets older."

- "He might have a few rough edges, but he's basically a good boy."

- "No one else has the right to correct her."

- "They just don't know her like I do."

- "With all due respect, I don't think that she's any of your business."

- "He's no different from anyone else."

Satan then gets you to cover over these blind spots with a syrupy coating of sentimentality, and you and your child are doomed. You may never get a good look at this blooming monster. And it'll be your fault—not that you made him to be a monster, but that you allowed his fallen nature to take over his being.

Parents who fall for this are then totally shocked when their little Shirley Temple turns into Jacqueline the Ripper. They'll tell you that they're totally amazed, can't understand it in a million years, don't know what sudden occurrence could have caused such a change. If you try to point out gently that you saw this coming, say, fourteen years ago, they'll look at you in disbelief. They might even hit you with: "If that's true, then why didn't you *say* something?" They might even accuse you, possibly behind your back, of being judgmental.

In no way can they even allow the possibility that they might have caused their own cardiac arrest. Many of them will end up combining two thoughts. First, that they did the best they could; and second, that they should feel guilty in some vague and general way. The truth is that they didn't do the best they could. And if they tell you that they feel guilty, you shouldn't try to convince them otherwise or make these feelings go away. If they feel "somehow responsible," it's because they are.

The only way to avoid this malady is to look hard (but still with love) at this little being placed into your hands by a loving but very realistic Father. *Don't* excuse rotten behavior at all. Call a skunk a skunk. Seek not only the counsel of your Christian friends, but also ask the wise ones to disciple your children as well. Be assured that your child has at least one shelf full of garbage somewhere in the basement of his spirit. You make him clean up his room. Make him clean up his spirit, too.

God is clear: When children reach the age of making choices, *they are not basically good,* "for all have sinned and fall short of the glory of God" (Romans 3:23).

And that, my friend, includes your little marvel.

7. Allow Complaining in Your Home

The Moslems have a very interesting practice. They're very careful to never complain about the weather, for fear that they will in some way offend the Almighty One who designed the product.

Many Christians are not so careful.

This Moslem idea would be a good practice everywhere, particularly in the churches that claim to fear and revere the Lord and to know Him as a personal and saving God through His Son, Jesus the Anointed One. For God *does* design the product: "He sends his command to the earth; his word runs swiftly. He spreads the snow like wool and scatters the frost like ashes. He hurls down his hail like pebbles. Who can withstand his icy blast?" (Psalms 147:15–17). After having a week of sub-zero temperatures, most of us would agree that the answer is "no one." And yet every winter, believer after believer complains about this decree from God. We think nothing about joining in with unbelievers in complaining *about God* and His handiwork.

Can you see how destructive this is? You must teach your children to never complain about *anything* received from the hand of God. Teach them by your own example, and teach them by making complaining an unacceptable family activity in all situations. Teach them that complaints about the wickedness and evil of the world should be taken to the Lord who can do something about them. Teach them that complaining to men is discouraging and totally useless, in addition to being offensive to God.

The key is "in everything, by prayer and petition, with thanksgiving, present your requests to God" (Philippians 4:6). This thought should be drummed into a complainer, whether it's you or your child. "And the peace of God, which transcends all understanding, will guard your hearts and your minds in Christ Jesus" (Philippians 4:7). This is the way to peace in your child's inmost being; no one, old or young, will ever have peace if he's a complainer to men — particularly if he's a complainer about God.

The believer who walks in full trust of the Lord knows in his heart that all things come to him from the hand of God, whether or not they come from other people, whether or not they appear on the surface to be good or evil, whether or not the natural reaction is to complain. *Nothing* can get past God unless He allows it; there are no accidents or bad breaks, and there's no luck (good or bad) or chance in the life of a child of God.

All that's required of you is to acknowledge that God knows what He's doing, to thank Him for it, and to wait and watch with excitement to see how all things will be used for your good (see Romans 8:28).

You can't truly worship God while you're complaining about what He's brought you. Complaints are encouraged by the father of lies, and they can only destroy your family's confidence in God and negate the power that your family has available to it.

We don't complain in our house anymore, for three simple reasons:

1. God tells us not to (see Philippians 2:14), which is sufficient.

2. We don't want to miss anything from the Lord.

3. We are wisely fearful. We don't want to offend anyone that powerful.

And even though I am talking about *all* complaining, just think about the time you and your children will have for interesting and valuable conversations when you stop complaining about the weather alone! Henry Ward Beecher said, "The test of Christian character should be that a man is a joy-bearing agent to the world." Are you a "joy-bearing agent" to the world? Are you training your child to be one? How will you explain yourself to God if your family falls short?

For many of us, *complaining* is a "joy," but it's the wrong kind and will never edify. It can't edify. It can only depress everyone: you, your child, your spouse, your family, the church, and the world.

The choice is simple, complaints or peace.

Be different. Choose peace.

8. Never Forget a Grudge

Jonathan Swift seems to have hit the nail on the head when he wrote,

> Hated by fools, and fools to hate
> Be that my motto and my fate.

Anyone who has tried to live for God has experienced being hated by fools. It seems only natural to hate them right back, too easy and too natural. Scripture does make room for us to hate *God's* enemies (see Psalms 139:21–22). Although we might tell our friends that our hatred is because of the fools' stands against God, the real truth is that it's usually because of the abuse that they've piled up on us.

But God has no room for petty grudges, and He wants His people — both big and little — to have no room for them either. Jesus' attitude was: "If your brother sins, rebuke him, and if he repents, forgive him. If he sins against you seven times in a day, and seven times comes back to you and says, 'I repent,' forgive him (Luke 17:3–4). That's why "the apostles said to the Lord, 'Increase our faith!'" (v. 5).

On the part of the offender, this passage shows that we should ask forgiveness even if we are only a little wrong, and that we should keep our account with others clear. But on the part of the offended, this passage shows that our basic posture should be to be ready to forgive, until we actually get the opportunity to forgive.

I know people who are still holding grudges twenty or thirty years after the offense took place. Usually it's more of an alleged offense than a provable one. Sometimes the people can't even remember the specifics of why they're holding a grudge, but that doesn't stop them. Even if they can't remember the *basic* reason behind their grudge, they're enjoying holding it too much to put it down.

We must teach our children to never hold a grudge no matter what. We must teach them to develop a speed-of-light forgiving spirit. And then we must teach them to love these people, to do good things for them, bless them, pray for them, and give them things. We must teach them to do this because God tells us to; but He holds out a higher reason than that.

The reason is because we want to be like God. And how is God? God is, remarkably, kind to the ungrateful and wicked (see Luke 6:35). You are living proof. There are probably times in your life when you deserved to be creamed and God kept showing you kindness. Can we and our children do any less for others? If we are like God in this, He says we'll be sons of the Most High (v. 35). We'll be showing the family likeness to those who need to see it the most.

Practically, what does this all mean? If your child has someone who has wronged him, hurt him, insulted or embarrassed him, you have a golden opportunity. Don't miss it. Teach your child to follow the Scripture. Talk with your child only in loving terms about his nemesis. Ask together for God's blessing on him. Pray together for him as often as you can. And then make a project out of the good things that you can think of to do for this other child.

Encourage your child to make or buy something for the other child. Exhort him to do it more than once. Invite the other child along on some exciting family outing. Have your child send him nice notes and cards. If your child does enough of these kinds of things, it'll probably blow the other kid's socks off. It's so weird because it's so godly, and it has a good chance of reducing him to emotional putty.

But don't teach your child to do it for that reason, or you both stand to be disappointed. Teach him to do it for God, because we are His sons and daughters, and not for the potential results. If the other child turns around, praise God together. If he doesn't, together leave him in God's hands.

Many of the people to whom God shows great kindness never thank Him or turn around, but He keeps doing it anyway. If your child is looking at results instead of God, his discouragement can cause him to quit doing something that may be one of the most godly things he'll ever do.

As with everything else, your own example is the best teacher. If you are hurt by someone else, and your child learns about it through other means (you can't tell him just to use it as an example, or you'll be slandering), then involve him in your love and blessings and prayers and projects. I guarantee that it'll make an impression on him so deep that he'll never forget it, even if he sometimes forgets to apply it.

To be fair to Jonathan Swift, look at another of his thoughts: "We have just enough religion to make uᵣ hate, but not enough to make us love one another."

May we and our children have enough religion—enough faith in God and desire to be like Him and follow Him—to make us love one another.

9. Don't Take Full Responsibility for Your Failures

It was appropriate that, in our modern age of rapidly increasing failure accompanied by rapidly decreasing responsibility, we would see the introduction of "don't-blame-me" parenthood.

It goes something like this. You give parenting your best shot. You think you've hit a home run, and then your child turns out to be more like Attila the Hun than your lovely Aunt Rose. You analyze it carefully and determine that you couldn't have done any better, that it's really nobody's fault, and now you can go on to hoping that she will solve her problem, wherever it came from.

This theory was justified a few years ago by Dr. Bertram J. Cohler, a sociologist, who told us that "kids create their own craziness" because they're preset genetically to become what their genetic coding says they will be, and "parents can do little about that" (*Kansas City Times*, November 18, 1977). He went on to say that there's no statistical evidence that parenting affects a child's later well-being.

In fact, this is such a fabulous theory that only one minor problem with it has ever surfaced.

It is totally wrong.

Children don't come out of a box of Wheaties. Actions have consequences. Inaction has consequences. *Everything* has consequences. His behavior didn't come from *nowhere*. Poor results are somebody's *fault*.

Odds are it's yours.

Most of us don't want to accept this idea. I once had a father of four tell me to do as much as I could when kids were little, since that was the only time you could really influence them. He thought that children were out of your hands by the time they were teenagers. Needless to say, his children *were* out of his hands.

The sociologist said that children have an innate ability to survive and cope with problems that they face. What nonsense! If this were so (and anyone who ever had a five-year-old knows that it isn't), why would God go to such great pains to establish the family to direct the growth of children? Why wouldn't He have made children more physically capable at a younger age, so they could go their own way (as is the case with so many animals)? Could it be that you're exactly what God had in mind to direct the spiritual growth of His children?

Your children aren't robots or self-sufficient; they need you to do your job. "Train a child in the way he should go, and when he is old he will not turn from it" (Proverbs 22:6). This doesn't say that he might drift away and then come back to the path again; it says that he won't depart from it in the first place. In other words, if you're right on the money in your teaching, the child will be right on the money in his learning.

Dig in and spend the time and effort on each child that so great an assignment cries for, or as a mother once told me, "I want each of my four children to be a first child."

And remember that parenting is *your* job. Don't pass it along to your mother or anyone else. If God wanted your mother to raise another child, you would have had another brother or sister. Your mother is equipped to be your child's *grandmother,* not his mother. Other choices, like day-care centers, are even worse. Even if your surrogates love your child, they're still not you and can't do for you and your child what God wants you to do.

God doesn't want other people to raise your child, even though they can help you in your role. God has assigned you to the job and has equipped you to be the best person for it. You *can* be effective in guiding your child to be just what God intended. I'm convinced there will be many rewards on earth and in heaven for parents who do the job with Scripture and with gusto. And lots of blame for those who say, "Don't blame me."

And if you do fail along the way, recognize it, repent of it, ask God and your child for forgiveness, and purpose to do better with the wisdom and power of God. Don't sit around and beat yourself for the failure. Press on! (See Philippians 3:12–14.)

You should help your child solve his problem; but please, please spend the time to find out where things went wrong, where you missed giving him the best, and where and how you could have done better. Scripture says, "A simple man believes anything, but a prudent man gives thought to his steps" (Proverbs 14:15). Part of your steps, if you're a parent, involves the training of your children. Don't naively believe that everything will somehow work out.

So review and correct your failures. Absolutely, for his sake. Certainly, if you have another child at home. Especially, if *he* has another child at home — for by rectifying a wrong even at this late point, you can keep your error from being inflicted upon yet another generation.

In other words, if you don't accept responsibility and clear up the problem, this final failure may be worse than the original mistake, for this bad parenting on your part will be passed down and allowed to repeat itself.

And bad parenting tends to repeat itself to the fourth generation.

Conclusion

Go back through the headings and put a check by any item which you feel is a problem. Pick the biggest one, and start to work on it today.

14

EDUCATION AND SCHOOLING

*These commandments that I give you
today are to be upon your hearts. Impress them on your children.*

(Deuteronomy 6:6–7)

W hen we come to the subject of education and schooling, we have
hit an area that can cause great consternation for Christian parents. Which option is best? Public school, private school, Christian
school, church school, home school? Are several of these good choices,
at different stages of my children's development? Should my children be
witnesses in the public school? What if there aren't any good Christian
schools? What if I don't have the money for anything but public school?

In the first place, the Bible doesn't talk about *education* and *schooling,* but rather about *instruction* and *discipling.* It tells parents that we
should train ourselves "to be godly" (1 Timothy 4:7), for our own success as well as our children's. Even young parents can set an example
"in speech, in life, in love, in faith and in purity" (1 Timothy 4:12).

But instead we fall for the idea that schooling — formal education —
is the way to success. It *can* be the way to a job and material success,
and it can even be a tool to help our children achieve success in the
really important things; but it's not the critical thing for success with
God, the one who will give our children their final exam.

Perhaps Mark Twain had it right when he said, "I never let schooling interfere with my education."

We have got to get hold of the idea that schooling and formal education are only tools that we can use to shape the character of our children. *We* have to keep control of the tools, because God's going to hold us accountable. If a school ruins our children, those in the school responsible for the problem will have their own account to give to God, but *we are* going to have to give account for why we let them ruin our children in the first place.

We must use this tool to shape the character of our children. Samuel Johnson defined this as the very purpose of true education: "The supreme end of education is expert discernment in all things—the power to tell the good from the bad, the genuine from the counterfeit, and to prefer the good and the genuine to the bad and the counterfeit." (See also Hebrews 5:14.)

And so we have to ask the question, are you as a parent ecstatic about the school where your child is spending a fourth of his life?

Non-Christian Private School

You can spend a lot of money on private schools.

But the problem with non-Christian private schools is *not* their cost. The problem is that most of them, including many "religious" schools that have nothing to do with recognizing Jesus as the Savior and Lord of each person's life, are of no more value than and are no different from the public schools.

They leave God out and push humanistic—man is the center of all things, even though man descended from apes and is *nothing special*—doctrine down so many innocent throats.

To the regular horrors of public school, private schools can often add an elitism—the sense that I and we are not only the center of our own universe, but we are also the center of *everyone's* universe. No thanks.

The bottom line: You can spend a lot of money to give your child a good education and a credential that the world will admire, but your child might not look very much like Christ.

Home School

Home schooling has a lot of potential value, with emphasis on the word *potential.* It puts the parents in direct control of their children's training. It forces the parents to be involved in what their children are learning in all areas. It *can* serve to bring the parents and children closer together. It lets the parents be more regular models for their children. If done well, it causes the parents to grow spiritually and show the way to their children and can be a delightful experience.

But it can also have problems.

I'm not going to bring up the usual argument about the child missing "socialization" with peers. Many of the peers running around these days would have embarrassed Al Capone. If your main reason for not considering at least some home schooling is that your child will miss this tingling experience with other children, forget it. This isn't a reason to avoid home schooling and may be one of the blessings.

But there are several Biblical problems with the way some parents approach home schooling. In the first place, about 50 percent of parents in many home school situations aren't really involved. The fact is, a home school that doesn't heavily involve the father in both leadership and instruction just won't succeed. Scripture says, "Fathers, do not exasperate your children; *instead,* bring them up in the training and instruction of the Lord" (Ephesians 6:4, emphasis added).

Many people quote the first part of this verse when trying to teach or rebuke a father that he shouldn't exasperate or frustrate his children. But the rest of the verse talks about how this exasperation takes place. It happens when the father *doesn't* bring up his child "in the training and instruction of the Lord."

A child may get exasperated when his father disciplines him or when the child doesn't get his way, but that isn't Biblical exasperation — that's fleshly frustration and rebellion. Biblical exasperation is when the father isn't doing the main thing Christian fathers are supposed to do: training and instructing their children. Paul gives a beautiful summary of a father's role in 1 Thessalonians 2:11–12.

Solution: Involve dad in the home school or reconsider home schooling.

The second problem is that mothers alone — even mothers and fathers alone — aren't totally equipped to minister to all of their children's training, instructional, and developmental needs. If they were, we wouldn't need churches; all ministry on all points could be handled by parents. Even adults could rely only on their parents for their spiritual and educational development.

If this were the case, the only people who would need a church would be those whose parents had already died. We need to understand and accept the fact that our children are also part of the body of Christ and need intimate input from their brothers and sisters in the Lord. Even excellent parents are going to have a difficult time training their children alone.

Solution: Rotate training with other home schools, find special activities—do *something* to involve others in the training of your children.

The third problem is that parents don't know everything. I know this comes as quite a shock to some of you, but it's true nevertheless. There comes a point when the parents can't teach what needs to be taught. You need to go to school before you can train your child, but this means that the child may be ninety-seven before he gets everything he needs. Other people have spiritual gifts, talents, abilities, knowledge, and experience that can benefit your child. You would be foolish not to tap these resources. But the way some home schooling works out, this other input doesn't get in.

Solution: Organize a discipling center (more on that later).

The fourth problem is that home schooling might not work as planned because many parents haven't even learned *self-discipline* yet— much less daily, hour-by-hour discipline of another creatively procrastinating and unfocused person. The child can end up as a *free spirit,* meaning he's learned to do whatever he bloody well pleases.

Solution: Get organized—or get out of home schooling.

Christian and Church Schools

My experience tells me that there are a lot of kids in Christian and church schools because they seem to be the only choice left, rather than because the schools are excellent.

Many Christian schools are patterned after the public schools from which so many people are trying to escape. Certainly there is more freedom to talk about the Lord and His Word, but other than that, there are usually the same classes (except for the mandatory "Bible" class), same methods, same activities, same everything. Maybe a little better discipline, although that's complicated by the fact that some of the kids are there because they were disciplinary problems somewhere else, — like in the public schools.

Often, even the academic training isn't superior to the private and public schools. All too often, there are fewer electives, much less in the way of facilities (things like science and language labs, for example), and little in the way of meaningful extracurricular activities.

If it's a church-affiliated school, you can add two more problems: first, whatever denominational distinctives the church is excited about at the moment; and second, the limitations that many of them will put on hiring "outsiders," even if the outsiders are excellent disciplers and the insiders are unholy and incompetent.

The worst problem with many Christian schools, though, is that they don't emphasize grounding the children in the Word of God across the whole range of the Bible's teaching. This includes not only the hearing and learning of the Word, but also the *doing*. More Bible quizzes and memorization programs and contests aren't the answer. More *wisdom* is the answer.

Whatever happened to training children to do what they hear? Where are the classes and the outside experiences that will teach Christian values, morals, and ethics? Where are the Christian teachers and parents who look at training children as a dedicated ministry — with all that this implies — instead of as a job?

The light is on in many Christian schools, but nobody's home.

Discipling Centers

What do we need? Consider this section as a call to a new concept of Christian training.

First, what do we not need? Well, we don't need public schools and we don't need private schools, and we don't need very many of the ideas that they use. The only thing we could use from them is some of their money to support facilities, laboratories, electives, and extracurricular activities — money which they're not likely to give up.

What do we need? We need a new combination of the best of parental training, home schooling, Christian schooling, and some old-fashioned moral instruction. Detailing this is beyond the scope of this book,
but some major ideas to be incorporated include these:

- Real support (both moral and practical) from the Discipling Centers so
  that parents, including both mothers and fathers, can provide decent
  home schooling until the child is ready for more (around ages 7–9).

- A transition period between home schooling and formal schooling,
  and a flexibility that allows even later moving back and forth between the two.

- Parental involvement in the real work of formal schooling — not just
  riding along on field trips and serving Kool-Aid at the Christmas
  party. We must use the gifts of all parents who can and will help; in
  fact, consider not letting families in if the parents *won't* share in the
  ministry.

- Selection of teachers on the basis of their holy lives, spiritual gifts
  and other abilities, experience in the thing being taught, and love for
  the Lord and His children, and not on the basis of credentials or on
  having the "right" denominational pedigree — or being "available" or
  not demanding much money.

- Lengthy training in the breadth and length and height of the Bible
  and lengthy training in character — the building of solid morals and
  values into the heart, and not just the head, of the child. About a
  fourth of the day ought to go into each of these areas.

- Solid, intensive training in academics and practical skills the other
  half of the day. Reading, writing, mathematics, history, geography,
  and other academic subjects need to be taught with an intensity that
  is usually missing in all types of schools. Practical skills — trade-
  school, home economics, and other things ranging from public
  speaking to computer programming — are usually missing from
  Christian schools, and these skills are often taught only to the unmo-
  tivated in public schools. Yet these are the things that make up a
  large part of most of our lives.

This concept could work with a school that's set up to support parents of younger children so the training could be primarily at home. The

work could involve training of parents, accountability, testing, recommendations, direct school support on things the child is struggling with, extracurricular activities, and field trips. I am not talking about something to keep the state off the backs of home-schoolers. I am talking about making home schooling truly excellent.

Later, the school could take on a role that supports the parents' needs even while involving the parents in the work. The school day could be set up with "Basics" blocks; for example, one two-hour block for language and humanities and another two-hour block for math and science. Parents could teach these things at home (on the teacher's schedule, for accountability, and also so the home-taught student could come in to take the tests with his class). Or they could enroll in one or both blocks, making their choices on a year-by-year or semester-by-semester basis, like college. Spiritually and otherwise qualified parents could be involved in the teaching.

The other part of the day could be a special activity time, in which some children could get further training in areas like crafts, carpentry, and computer work, or could be taken home for further instruction by the parents. Classes in these areas could be organized and taught by the school or by the parents, with the school's facilities being used either way.

These Discipling Centers could, of course, be used by parents who wanted their children to get in on all of the available training and be at the Center all day. But these parents should still be required to be more involved than just sending their kids and checks in to the school. The bottom line? If you're involved with a school, you would be foolish to let parents delegate something to you that they're not involved in or doing themselves.

I don't know of many who are trying to pull all of these things together. If you are, or know someone who is, please carry it through. If you're not, but you're interested, now is the time.

For how will we raise champions, if our tools—our schools—aren't excellent?

Sunday School

Here it is, thirty to sixty minutes for your child to get direct training in the Word of God in the place where you're professing to be under authority. Is your child getting it?

There's only one way to know. Get to know the teacher intimately. Have him (yes, there *can* be male Sunday school teachers) over for dinner and real discussion about real things. Find out what he believes. Take the time to look over any materials, including teacher's manuals, very carefully.

Don't waste this precious time. And don't let it waste your children.

Public School

In the United States the materialistic, humanistic world view is being taught exclusively in most state schools. . . . There is an obvious parallel between this and the situation in Russia. And we really must not be blind to the fact that indeed in the public schools in the United States all religious influence is as forcibly forbidden as in the Soviet Union. (Francis Schaeffer, *A Christian Manifesto,* Ch. 8)

We are more and more convinced that despite the differences in our political structures, the educators in both countries are the same. (Soviet First Deputy Minister for Public Education Vladimir D. Shadrikov, speaking in San Diego to the National Education Association; as quoted in *World,* May 20, 1989)

Get and keep your children out of public school.

Some say: "But then the humanists will take control of the public schools."

Friend, they already *have* control of these schools. Believe it. They have control of the government, the school boards, the teacher's schools, the teacher's union, and the curricula. Not everywhere, of course; not yet. But more and more every day. We each have too little time to spend it fighting a battle that's been over for decades.

A while back there was the report about a Christian group that threatened to pull their children out of public school because the parents were opposed to classes in *computers*—and in general to "modern" equipment. These parents are saying, in effect, "You can teach my children things that are totally opposed to Christianity, but don't teach them about inventions." They are fighting the wrong battle.

Some say: "But if Jesus is Lord of life, shouldn't we fight for control of the public schools?"

Jesus *is* the Lord of life. He wants control of everything, but He doesn't want us to spend our lives trying to fix something that's structurally wrong in itself, and He doesn't want the sacrifices offered by such a system. He wants the truth, and He wants everything else out of the room. Remember, our fight isn't for the public schools; it's for *the spiritual lives of our children.*

Good education can drive out bad education. So build a system of education that does things God's way, and watch while the dead carcass of government-controlled, secular instruction rots away.

Some say: "But don't I have the responsibility of supporting the local community's public school?"

God gave the responsibility of training children to parents and the family of God. God gave the responsibility of bearing the sword to the civil government. How can we be so dull as to have allowed the sword-bearers into this unrelated area? Where are the Christians who should be demanding the separation of *school* and state?

You should support God, your spouse, your godly relatives, your fellow believers, and a private, non-government school that teaches all of God's truth. All you're doing by supporting your local community's public school, however, is supporting those who know how to manipulate the power of civil government to train your child's spirit *their* way. How can we so gullibly allow ourselves to be yoked with unbelievers? The government only has one tool—the sword. How do you think they'll use it in your child's training?

Besides, most public schools aren't local community schools anymore. They're run by state boards of education, and increasingly dictated to and controlled by the federal government to produce little model humanists.

Some say: "Public schools were pretty good when I went there."

They may have been. If so, you were fortunate. Things have changed.

Some say: "But we want our children to be salt and influence their friends."

Scripture says: "Do not be misled: 'Bad company corrupts good character'" (1 Corinthians 15:33). If you send your child to a humanist school populated more and more by humanist administrators, humanist teachers, and blossoming little humanists, do you know what you're likely to get? A *humanist.* Does it make sense to let God's enemies train your children? Wasn't even Jesus thirty before He began His public ministry?

Some say: "But we want our children to be witnesses in the public schools."

Witnesses to what? Illegal drugs? Immorality? Disrespect for authority? Teachers who can't or won't talk about God? Evolutionary bunk paraded as science? History books that leave God out? Sex education courses? Values clarification indoctrination? Maybe being witnesses would be a valuable idea if the government schools were on trial.

Some say: "But we'll keep our children out until high school."

Great. You're on the home stretch, and you hand your kids over to the *high-level* humanists.

Some say: "But our local public school still offers a good academic education, and the children do still get to sing Christmas carols."

Your children can get the academics elsewhere. Given the partially disguised decline in government school standards and the explosion of illiterate children, they can possibly learn better out in left field. But even if they can't, they would be better off not getting the basics at all than to get the garbage, subtle and otherwise, that goes with them.

God's plan of instruction is primarily concerned with learning truth about Him and His creation, learning about good and evil, and learning to prefer the good to the evil. Brain improvement at the expense of spiritual growth is a ticket to carnal Christianity.

Worse, the government schools would like to pretend that they're "value-neutral," which is a poor way to teach even if they could pull it off, which they can't. They will teach your child values. You won't like the values they do teach, and it'll be tough to cancel out their effects in a few after-school discussions. In other words, how can you have a "good education" when you leave out the most important things — God and His Word?

The best situation would be a school with excellent Biblical values *and* excellent academics; short of that, go for the one with the excellent Biblical values. Even illiteracy isn't as bad as spiritual death.

And as for the leftover religious "trinkets" in the government schools, let me say simply: hogwash. They don't mean much, and they won't be there long.

Some say: "But my children can't get the extracurriculars they want except in the public schools."

Basketball and volleyball can be fun, but how important do you think they are in terms of eternal values? Do you think God's going to say, "Well, you let the enemy ruin your child's spirit, but he did letter in four sports"? *Priorities,* folks. Extracurriculars can't be priorities.

Some say: "But I can't afford to put my children in a Christian school."

This can be a real problem, but put it another way: You can't afford *not* to put your children in a Christian school. You're going to have to answer for their training. Cut all expenses to the bone. Sell things. Take in sewing or laundry. See if your children can work around the school for part of their tuition. Ask or beg your church for help. Move into a tent. But do something.

Home school, of course, is a valid option. Even if you don't think you're qualified, it would be better to have them read books and use video and audio tapes at home than to have them become even partial humanists. Watch another mother's little children while she teaches your older ones. Ask your parents to help teach. But again, do something.

Some say: "But what will happen if we pull our children out?"

You'll save your children from great harm and very possibly from disaster. What do you expect? Many children of believers aren't even *believers* yet. How can they be salt?

If you're so all fired up to have salt in the government schools, then go get or use your teaching degree, and *you* go into the government schools. Stand up there for your principles. The Lord is always looking for missionaries and sometimes calls for martyrdom. But *don't* sacrifice your children. Under any circumstances.

Please.

Reading

The minds of children are starving for the simple reason that we haven't taught them to read.

Now, I am talking here about the *mechanics* of reading, although we haven't exactly distinguished ourselves in this regard in our homes and especially in our schools. What I am talking about is the *love* of reading, the preference for reading over the continual nonnutrition of watching television or movies or playing video games, and the reading of only those things that are worth reading.

Many parents, though, worry about giving their children the mechanics of reading, but they spend little or no time teaching them how to use those reading skills selectively. It's like training someone to be a carpenter, but not teaching him to see that it's better to build a refuge for the unwanted than a clinic for the abortionist.

In other words, even when we teach kids how to read, they don't know what to read.

You *must* start reading as a family: you to yourself, so your children can see it isn't torture; you to them, so they can sense both your appreciation of good writing as well as how to give the proper sound and sense to the words; they to you, so you can share their interest and determine if they know what they're reading; and they to themselves for wisdom and knowledge.

Some parents think they've done enough when they've gotten their children to read. But they may have done *damage. Insist* that they read excellent books and only excellent books. Sixty-six of them are in their Bibles. There are enough other good ones available that they should never have to — or be allowed to — put sewage into their spirits. Your children will learn from whatever they read, and whatever you allow them to read will, even by default, have your stamp of approval on it.

Until your children reach a deep spiritual maturity that mirrors your own, you should read or at least skim through everything before you allow them to read it. *Everything.* If you haven't read something in a while, you should reread it with the new spiritual eyes that the Lord has given you as you've grown in Him. You'll be amazed at the things that used to sound good that now will sound unholy and unspiritual and of no value. You can have a godly spiritual authority or friend do some of the reading for you and recommending to you.

But the bottom line is that someone has to read everything before you give it to your children, and he has to read it currently. If you're slow, let your children read the same good books over and over again until you can plow through another one. But be a censor of all that goes into your children's hands and spirits.

What? Don't I know how much time that would take? Don't I know that you have a lot of other things to do?

Yes, I know these things. And my response is: start reading.

Mark Twain said: "The man who does not read good books has no advantage over the man who can't read them."

Illiteracy is a creeping destroyer of civilized life. As a person loses words and phrases, he loses the ability to express his ideas, and ultimately the ability to have an original thought. Even if he has the desire to think, he won't have the means to do it. Our children are failing in droves in this very important area.

But they're being failed in an even worse way if they're allowed to read blasphemy, lies, errors, half-truths, filth, and mockery. In the case of bad books, ignorance is indeed a joy and probably also bliss.

As a parent, you have the responsibility to teach your children to read. You must teach them to read well.

Looking Things Up:
Are You Sure We Have the Same Bible?

Did you ever wonder how much of your Biblical "knowledge" doesn't come from the Bible?

We absolutely *know* things are in the Bible when the truth is that they're not. We are confident that other things are not in the Bible when the plain fact is that they are. And my suspicion is that much of the rest of our "understanding" is so mangled and unbelievable that we wouldn't recognize it if it were tattooed on our hands. We are lazy, and we teach our children to be the same.

You've got to get your children to read the Bible (not books about the Bible, or Bible summaries for children, or quarterlies from Sunday school) as early as they can read anything. Give them their own Bible early to encourage interest, and make it a Bible translated into the modern language that they speak with their friends. Up until the time that they can read, you must read it to them over and over. Skip "Humpty Dumpty," talking train stories, and baby badger adventures if your time is limited (although those can be fun).

Never let your children "not have time" for God's Word. This is where faith will be built up; this is where wisdom will be stored for future use. Many people say you can give children too much Scripture at too young an age and somehow make it boring or worn-out for them. What a lofty vision of God's Word!

If you only teach them bits and pieces, or teach that it says the opposite of what it says, or teach without practicing it, then they might not have an enthusiastic interest in it and might react negatively to the Word of God later. If their convictions are based only upon slogans and proof texts and non-Biblical traditions, then the world, science, and logic will devour them and their "convictions." This is because their convictions aren't based upon the Word of God, and anything not based on the Word of God is dead meat, waiting to be hacked to pieces by the warriors of hell.

Use any practical device you can find to encourage this personal interest in the Bible itself.

- Set up a poster, a Wisdom Chart, in your kitchen. Let your child put a sticker on for each day that he's read a particular portion. Make a month's worth of stickers worth an ice cream or dinner out.

- Read some Scripture after one or more of your meals. You can have a different person read anything from three verses up to an entire chapter each night. As an alternate, bring an interesting verse or story from the Bible to the table and start a discussion about it.

- Ask your child a question of interest to him, and when he asks for the answer (he will if it's of interest to him), tell him where to find the answer in the Bible. If he's little, give him the verse; if he's older, give him the chapter or book; if he's twelve or older, give him the concordance.

- Have your child look things up and get back to you with an answer from Scripture.

- Teach your children that bad dreams are most easily disposed of by reading Scripture. Don't tell them to go back to sleep; tell them to read Psalms. This is infinitely more valuable and effective than tricks like leaving a light on or looking under the bed with them.

- Instruct and encourage these innocent spirits to be young Bereans who look everything up for themselves (see Acts 17:11), no matter who tells them that it's in the Bible.

- Here's the toughie: Tell your children that you're really trying to live your life according to your belief in the Bible. Ask them for their help in correcting you if they see an inconsistency between your life and the Bible. You'll be amazed at how much Scripture some of them will start reading! They should, of course, be loving and respectful when they present their findings. You should also let them know that they'll have to put this new discovery into practice too. They'll almost always change if you do. And what a benefit to you!

We deplore the ages when the common man didn't have and couldn't get a Bible for himself. Many people had to rely on secondhand information, tradition, and the authority of the mother church, instead of the actual words of the actual King. But in many ways our age is even more deplorable.

We have access to dozens of Bibles, and we hardly use them. Not for life. Not for decisions. Not for obedience. Not for claiming promises. God says repeatedly, in awesome and powerful words, that this wandering from His word will bring confusion, heartache, and spiritual death.

And if you don't believe me, you can look it up.

Conclusion

Get your children in the right Christ-controlled school. Teach them to read only excellent books. Teach them to be men and women of the Word.

And then get out of the way of these godly juggernauts.

15

TRAINING THE YOUNGER CHAMPIONS

Even a child is known by his actions, by
whether his conduct is pure and right.

(Proverbs 20:11)

E ven little children can and will be known by the purity and right-
ness of their conduct. Don't make excuses for the poor behavior of
little children. If they're old enough to tell you no, they're old enough to
tell you yes!

In this chapter, we'll look at some ideas that apply directly to your
younger children.

Center of the Universe

One of the first barriers you'll need to get over with your young children is the idea that they're the center of the universe — that all roads
used to lead to Rome, but now they lead to your children.

This is often complicated by the fact that we start out treating them
like they *are* the center of the universe. This is an easy fault to fall into
because nobody can resist pampering a baby or toddler. Why, they're
cuter than the center of the universe!

Parents can compound this by focusing undue attention on their children. We are to seek first the kingdom of God; no matter how cute they

are, your children aren't the whole kingdom of God. They're an important part, but still just a part. Moms especially can compound this when they say things like "My kids are my whole life." What about your husband? Your church family? Yours and your husband's families? Unbelievers? The poor and needy? If you see a family where the mom puts *everything* related to her children ahead of almost *everything* else, you know for sure that you're near the center of the universe.

When you mix special treatment with the fact that human nature always tends to think it *is* the center of the universe, you can very easily end up with a demanding, egotistical little . . . well, you know.

This can be even more of a problem for "only" children, even if the only child is one who doesn't have any brothers or sisters *yet*. If the child is a first grandchild, the grandparents can add to the onslaught. Perhaps one of the reasons God gives children siblings is to eliminate the idea that a first child is the center of the universe.

Don't cause a problem or add to a problem in this area. Don't jump every time your children call. Don't give them everything they want. Don't let them whine and complain and generally act like little tyrants. Life's too short.

Nonviolence, Little Person Style

It's absolutely amazing that so many adults allow so much wanton and mindless violence on the part of the young folks, on the unscriptural and nonsensical premise that they're "just kids." Parents tolerate despicable behavior that would cause them to prosecute an adult to the full extent of the law.

Think about it. If most people saw an adult go up to another adult on the street and hit him on the head with a Tonka truck, they would probably call for the nearest policeman and demand the attacker's arrest. But when little Billy or Susie commits mayhem on their defenseless peers, what do they say?

They say "boys will be boys," and "you have to let them have some freedom," and "you can't expect too much from children." They justify it and rationalize it and choose at times to look the other way. They might whisper something real tough, like "that wasn't very nice," into the little hoodlum's ear. They're sure their little angel couldn't really be so rotten to the core.

But what does Scripture say about this?

It tells you that "even a child is known by his actions, by whether his conduct is pure and right" (Proverbs 20:11). When your beloved hits or kicks or pinches or pulls on another child, or throws a book at an adult, or threatens someone with imminent bodily harm, take it for what it is: senseless brutality that shouldn't be tolerated — not even once, not even for a moment. Violence has no symbolic value, nor is it a healthy release of tension and frustration. It's exactly what it appears to be: ugly. Clear to the bone.

You should set a peaceful example. If you holler and rage, you shouldn't be surprised at your imitative children. I can recall the little boy in the kiddie "bump" cars at the amusement park. He would scream and curse and shake his fist when anyone got in his way. He was already a miserable excuse for a driver, and he was only four or five years old. You've probably had his father behind you in traffic.

You should certainly restrict a child's intake of violence to as near zero as you can. Kids are just like big people: They do what they see. They just do it a little harder and louder than most adults. Turn off the television violence, and keep GI Joe and the guns out of your house. Don't let your children spend time with violent peers; remember that the biggest danger isn't that your children will get injured, but that they'll learn to be brutal. Physical wounds usually heal faster than spiritual ones.

Most certainly of all, stop the violence in the hearts of your children. Don't tolerate it in even the smallest measure, and let them know how much you abhor it. Moan and grieve in their presence when you see it or hear about it. Discipline it carefully, so that they'll know that it is a serious crime.

Scripture says that we should let our "gentleness be evident to all" (Philippians 4:5) and that we should be "completely humble and gentle" (Ephesians 4:2). Scripture makes no exceptions. *You* shouldn't, either.

When my son was five, he said about his older sister, "The days that we fight — those are the days that aren't fun."

Amen.

A Mouthful of Tongue

Almost everyone has a loose tongue to one extent or another, but nowhere can it be more prevalent, outspoken, and obnoxious than in children. We adults can think some gross things about other people, and this is sin enough—but at least we don't have the courage to say everything we think.

But children can be very brave. In the absence of control, if they think it they'll say it. They need help in controlling the little organ between their brain and their lips, and in learning to reject the 90 percent of their thoughts that ought never see the light of day.

It's in your own interest as well. It'll be painfully obvious to others if your child and his spirit aren't under God's and your control. All they'll have to do is listen to him. If he sounds like a verbal Godzilla run amok, they won't want him around, and you'll have zero credibility as an effective parent.

Lying is the most serious form of tongue abuse. Lying is totally devastating to the liar as well as its victims. "A lie," said Mark Twain, "can travel half way around the world while the truth is putting on its shoes." God says He hates, He *detests,* a lying tongue (see Proverbs 6:17), and no one can be a champion who is not a person of integrity, accuracy, and thoroughness. Lies should be dealt with severely, since they deny the presence of God and the authority under which He has put the child.

If a child lies to cover up a wrong, he should generally be punished more for the lie than for the wrong—because the lie offends God, because the lie hurts you and others, and because the child is saying that he would rather commit another wrong than repent.

Children can even outdo adults in using their tongues to exalt themselves. God is clear on this: "If you have played the fool and exalted yourself . . . clap your hand over your mouth!" (Proverbs 30:32). You should be just as clear. Children are more than capable of understanding pride and its despicable odor in the nostrils of our God. Whenever you see pride sprouting—in exaltation of self or tearing down of authority or smarting off to adults or peers—dig it up immediately and burn it.

Keep an eye on a tongue that constantly falls into a pattern of silliness. We want to be careful on this one. A sense of humor and the ability to laugh at difficult circumstances can be very valuable in a world that has much to laugh about and much to laugh at. God enjoys the little things, and so should we and our children. And certainly we can feel relief in laughing at the absurdity of self-important people as they come to their ridiculous conclusions about God and life—witness Elijah encouraging the false prophets to shout louder because their god might be "deep in thought, or busy, or traveling. Maybe he is sleeping and must be awakened" (1 Kings 18:27).

Godly sarcasm can be both appropriate and devastating. But plain old foolishness or ungodly sarcasm or cynicism or just a silly, flapping tongue can ruin both the flapper and those who listen to him. "When words are many, sin is not absent" (Proverbs 10:19).

Obscenity, especially that which involves the name or person of God, is so out of place in Scripture and in the life of His people that not much needs to be said. Your children are going to hear more of this than children of earlier generations, and what they hear is going to be more offensive: in movies, on television, in books and magazines. Everywhere children turn, obscenity is lurking at the door. You must teach them to turn their ears away from it and treat it like the unspeakable slime that it is. We and our children need to resensitize ourselves to the slightest obscenity and take upon ourselves the attitude of David: "Every morning I will put to silence all the wicked in the land" (Psalms 101:8). Don't put up with this vulgar muck from anyone, and especially not from your children.

Perhaps hurtful comments are the most common examples of children's tongues not under control. I remember when one of our children, at the age of four, said about an overweight relative in his presence: "I'd like to be like him when I grow up, except I wouldn't like to be fat." I could almost see the big, ugly scar being struck across the man's spirit. God says that "reckless words pierce like a sword" (Proverbs 12:18), and adults can be pierced mortally by the tiniest of reckless people.

Children can be ruthless in their comments about adults, other children, the handicapped—about anyone who has the slightest difference from their perceived "normal." Don't ignore these comments or humor them or tolerate them or brush them away by saying "he's only a child." Treat these reckless words as poison and crush them swiftly and completely.

We have all heard about "wisdom from the mouths of babes." Much more common is lying and complaining and pride and silliness and obscenity and insult and nastiness from the mouths of babes. God will hold all of us, including our children, accountable for every word we have spoken (see Ecclesiastes 5:2–4; Matthew 12:36–37), and we should do no less with these little ones. Show them how to follow Scripture and weigh their answers.

And then teach them how — and when — to speak.

Who's That Knocking at My Door?

Kids by nature aren't courteous beings.

They can't conceive of anything more important than what's on their minds at any given moment, and they can't imagine why everyone else wouldn't want to hear it — immediately. They feel it to be their solemn duty to explode into your private times and areas to lift you out of the darkness and misery that they suspect is the normal state of adulthood. Their motto is "he who has an ear to hear, let him hear — loud and clear."

To many kids and adults silence isn't golden unless it belongs to someone else. This is a serious character flaw that must be eliminated. Teach your children to be "quick to listen, slow to speak." (James 1:19).

This teaching should be started as soon as your children start talking and continued until they stop talking or get married, whichever comes first. Your motto should be: "If they're old enough to talk, they're old enough to keep quiet."

Remind them of a few key proverbs: "He who guards his lips guards his soul, but he who speaks rashly will come to ruin." "A fool's mouth is his undoing, and his lips are a snare to his soul." "He who guards his mouth and his tongue keeps himself from calamity" (Proverbs 13:3; 18:7; 21:23).

Courtesy in word and interaction should be extended to other people's privacy. Explain to your children that the reason you have doors is to send them a message: Open doors mean it's all right to come in; closed doors mean knock before entering. Even very little children should be taught to knock on doors. The operative verse here is "knock and the door will be opened to you" (Matthew 7:7).

And they should be trained to wait for an answer.

No child who is big enough to open a door is too small to knock instead. He might think that it just seems right to run in on Dad or Mom or brothers or sisters. Our key verse here is: "There is a way that seems right to a man but in the end it leads to death" (Proverbs 16:25).

If they do come crashing in, you should invite them right back out and not listen to whatever they have to say. The reason for this is that rudeness seldom has anything to say, nor deserves the right to say it.

By the way, you have to return the courtesy. The strongest teaching will come from your listening (instead of interrupting), leaving (instead of barging in), and knocking (instead of opening).

Ask the Lord to help you to respect your children and to command their respect. And if you fail, ask the Lord to help you seek their forgiveness of your discourtesy. And then?

Go seek your children's forgiveness. But knock first.

Please Treat Us Alike

The parents in any family that has more than one child are sooner or later going to hear the call from that bizarre socialistic root that must grow in all of our natural selves: "Please treat us alike."

Children can persuade themselves that all they're asking for is justice, when they really want more privileges (if the child is younger) or less responsibility (if the child is older).

Jesus has a better idea: "From everyone who has been given much, much will be demanded; and from the one who has been entrusted with much, much more will be asked" (Luke 12:48). The younger child must understand that many responsibilities go along with age and privileges, just as the older child must understand that much that has been given to him must be taken away if he isn't willing to meet the demands of responsibility.

The way to conquer this problem is to reverse the "hidden" request of the child. If he's the younger one, you offer to give him more responsibility and put all of your emphasis on that (he already thinks he understands the value of the privileges of being older, so you don't need to waste any time on that). Less childishness, less room allowed before discipline, more chores, more time spent in study—on and on, let him know the other side of the coin that he so eagerly wants to take into his hand.

If he's the older one, you offer to give him less privileges, and spend all of your discussion time on that (believe me, he *totally* understands the advantages of having less responsibility). Less time out in the evenings, fewer adult conversations joined in, more early bedtimes, more restrictions on activities with friends—as before, let him know that the coin he seeks has two sides, *before* he decides to take it.

It's perfectly legitimate to tell them that they'll get the other side of the coin after you see how they do with the "rough" side first. Don't give in to phony guilt over not being fair; your objective is to rid them of the foolishness that's bound up in their hearts, and that includes the elimination of this phony demand for fairness. Kids are masters at laying false guilt on their parents. Don't let them do it to you.

It's amazing what this approach can do. We have never had to carry on this kind of conversation for as much as five minutes before the complaining party sees the folly of his statement. Even if your child is a tough case, just implement the plan for a few days and see how he likes it. (This process does wonders for the other children who are watching as well.) Don't let him back into his normal role until he cries "uncle."

And he'll think twice—or more—before he says anything the next time.

Losing the Right Things

One of the keys to success with children is teaching them to lose the right things.

You might say, "My children are already pretty good at losing things." Children are experts at losing things, whether it's your purse or wallet or the keys to the car. Getting them to *not* lose things would seem to be a higher priority in most homes.

But your children are even more prone to losing more important things than your car keys. They're prone to losing the simplicity that God builds into all of us as He weaves us together in our mothers' wombs. At the same time, they seem to accumulate the sinful things faster than a five-year-old boy accumulates dirt.

Children start out in life with childlike faith, trust, love, and simplicity. They also start out in life with a sinful nature and a penchant for evil. They need us to teach them how to keep the first group and lose the second. Most children are taught the opposite; they're taught to lose the wrong things—like faith. They need to be taught to lose the things that *are* wrong—like sin.

Parents who really understand the walk of faith can fall for the idea that they have to take a totally blank and faithless spirit and teach it to walk by faith. But the point that parents need to understand is that their children start out already walking by faith. A very little child can't do anything else—he has a simple relationship with God and a simple relationship with you. He *has* to trust others for everything—and he does.

Jesus confirmed this when He praised the Father by saying, "I praise you, Father, Lord of heaven and earth, because you have hidden these things from the wise and learned, and revealed them to little children. Yes, Father, *for this was your good pleasure*" (Luke 10:21, emphasis added). God delights in giving wisdom to trusting little spirits. They don't have any clutter to keep them from hearing their heavenly Father.

Our goal must be to nurture this faith and simplicity that are *already there*. We must teach our children not to change in these things, but rather to go on in them. We must be extremely careful to expose our children only to those things that will build their faith.

In the final analysis, it isn't amazing that a little child can accept Christ as Savior and live in a wonderful and exemplary way. It's amazing that adults, who have usually lost their innocence and kept the sinfulness, can do these things.

Many children start out sucking their thumbs. Too many adults have been trained to suck their spiritual thumbs. They try to be a little bit faithful while they enjoy most everything that the world has to offer. These thumb-sucking Christians don't seem to understand that you can't be a little bit faithful; to be *faithful* means to be *full of faith*. You can be a person of little faith, but you can't be a little bit faithful. Your children have a wonderful gift—childlike faith—from the Lord; you need to grow it into faithfulness.

Jesus said, "If you have faith as small as a mustard seed, you can say to this mountain, 'Move from here to there' and it will move. Nothing will be impossible for you" (Matthew 17:20). Moving a mountain sounds like it would take gigantic faith, but He says that faith as small as a mustard seed will do it. What's He saying? He's saying that small, simple, no-doubt faith *is* gigantic and will get gigantic results. But you have to have it before you can get the results, and before God can grow it big.

Children already have it. We can help God grow it big. But if we allow our children to be exposed to faithless teaching and faithless lives, we shouldn't be surprised to see the simple faith squashed right out of them. It's a delicate and precious possession.

We need to use the simple trust that's already there as a weapon to help them eliminate the wrong things from their lives. It's amazing what temptations and sins can creep into the lives of even very little children. But the defense — the shield of faith — is already there too.

If we say, "Oh, this can't be sin since they're so little," we have abandoned our children to the devil's work. If we say, "Oh, I'll just tell my children to quit thinking about it or doing it, and it'll be all right," we are putting a burden on their backs that they'll not be able to carry. What we need to say is, "This is sin creeping in, and I need to teach them how to use their simple faith to resist it in the power of God."

Then we'll have taught our children to use the right things that they have to lose the wrong things that they have. And this is victory.

Lights Out!

If you've discovered anything of value about evenings, you've probably come to realize the importance of sleep. Staying awake into the wee hours used to be no problem; now, you're finding yourself dozing on the couch or in your favorite chair. For some of us, even comfort isn't required, just being motionless for thirty seconds can do the trick.

You also know what happens to you when you don't get enough sleep. You're too tired to spend time with the Lord at night, in the morning, or any other time. You sleep until the last possible minute plus twelve, and then rush into the day with your engine wide open. You have to fight back impatience and irritation every step of the way. Nothing seems quite right. Even if it did, it would still make you mad.

Folks, your little children are no different from you, except they haven't figured out the importance of sleep yet.

Now this is a big difference. How many of us parents would have to be argued into going to sleep? How many of us would display our creativity by thinking of countless ways to stay awake after our heads have touched the pillow? How many parents have you ever heard say, "Well, nuts, I guess I'll have to go to sleep?" Most of us *enjoy* sleeping. In fact, if we adults have any problem, it's that we *love* to sleep—and we are commanded not to do that (see Proverbs 20:13).

But here are these children, and they hate the whole idea. To be blunt, they think the idea of going to bed stinks. It looks like a waste of time to them, and besides, they're sure they'll miss something to which they can make a valuable contribution.

But it isn't a waste of time, and you *want* them to miss something. They need it for themselves, so that they can be physically refreshed and alert and avoid the snares that the devil has invented for the weary. They can't be champions if they're fighting a body that's out of control. It seems that no matter what time children go to bed, they usually get up at their regular time anyway—and the tiredness compounds.

And you can't parent a champion if your children are up until you don't have the time and energy to do anything else but collapse into a chair. It's an amazing relationship: *Their* sleep will bring *you* rest. You'll be able to commune with God and with your spouse, and figure out exactly what it was that you did that day. You want your children to miss this regrouping time. If they don't, you won't have one.

One thing we have learned is that kids don't normally get into bed and go to sleep. It's too much of a shock to their sensibilities and their belief that family life can't go on when they're unconscious. Even a bedtime story sometimes won't get the job done. So we always allow thirty minutes, even for ones as little as two or three years old, to listen to tapes or read books after they've gotten into bed.

What this creates is a fixed and fairly inflexible "lights out" time, rather than a set bedtime. The main advantage is that you won't have to argue and force your children into bed. If they know the lights are going out at eight-thirty, come what may, they'll have an incentive to get into bed by eight to maximize their time. If they get into bed at eight-fifteen because of their own lack of discipline and focus, they still have lights out at eight-thirty and have their time cut to fifteen minutes.

The principle of "lights out" also gives them a wind-down time. In addition to deenergizing, they can also have some time to think through the events and the lessons of the day. Your children need it no less than you.

It's important for you to insist that they do their "noodling" on their own time. Going to the bathroom, getting a drink, finding their lost poopsie-bear, giving you a hug, and so on—all of this must happen in their thirty minutes or before. With a little help, they'll be able to see that this is eminently fair, and you'll be pleased with how much "fiddle factor" can be removed from your evenings.

And don't battle the evening clean-up, either. Let them know what you expect and where things should go. Let them know that anything not put away will be picked up by you and put in *your* closet, for a week or so. Don't give things back sooner. This will become a "no problem" area.

Start dinner and the evening early enough so that the family as a whole and the children in particular have time to spend quietly and joyfully together. (This really puts the responsibility on you fathers not only to be home on time, but also to actually set the schedule for the evening.) And plan your evening so that you'll have at least two hours after "lights out" before you go to sleep. There'll always be exceptions to your plan, but keep them to a minimum for your children's sake. And yours.

If you're reading this in the evening, and you're finding yourself slipping away, I've only got one more thing to say: lights out.

Control with Gentle Power

How should you accomplish the things discussed in this chapter?

Quietly.

You lose if you debate with your children, scream at your children, or nag at your children. You lose if you're constantly playing umpire. You win if you let God keep you under control and quiet. You win big if you can bring your children under control with a look—the look of gentle power.

You can do it.

Your motto should be "No anger, no words, just looks like swords." Control them as the Holy Spirit controls you—through spiritual power.

At first, you'll have to stare at them until they stop. As you develop this, they should quiet down quickly when you enter the room. This is especially effective with dads, but moms can and must win this way.

God doesn't scream at you. Don't scream at your children.

Conclusion

Let your children know they aren't the center of the universe. End all tantrums, violent words, and aggressive actions. Teach your children how to control their tongues and carefully respect the privacy of others. Learn to see through the phony "treat us alike" idea. Help your children to lose childish ideas while retaining their childlike faith. Have a quiet, spirit-controlled bedtime.

And do it all with gentle power.

16

TRAINING THE OLDER CHAMPIONS

Your sons and daughters will prophesy,
your young men will see visions.

(Acts 2:17)

W e want to raise children who, as young men and women, will prophesy — speak forth — the Word of God into a dying culture. We want young people who will see visions of what can be accomplished in their day for the kingdom of God.

In this chapter, we'll explore some ideas that I hope will help.

I'm in Love with Me

Many young men and women are legends in their own minds.

A fine-sounding but terribly destructive idea circulating these days says that children must have a well-developed sense of self-esteem if they're to be successful. Low self-esteem can have tremendous destructive power in children's lives. The answer to this supposedly horrible situation is for them to develop high self-esteem.

So we parents, gullible as always, encourage our children to take pride in themselves and be self-confident. We encourage them, basically, to fall in love with themselves. And then we are amazed when they actually *do* these things and become "independent" — or egotistical and arrogant.

If you listen to many psychiatrists or psychologists you can get the idea that the lack of self-esteem is one of the most serious problems facing all of us, especially young people. In a way, this is true. You don't have to look for very long into the eyes of an abandoned or abused child to see that he doesn't like himself very much. There's an even larger group of young people who stay with their parents until adulthood, but who are so unloved that their hearts end up in the same shattered place.

This total or near-total disregard for self or anything else can lead to terrible tragedy, as the young person does anything to get anyone's attention. He can end up in twisted relationships, on drugs or alcohol, or even on one of the lists of suicides. His life can be full of hatred of himself, his family, God — everything.

The world, of course, has a solution to this problem: You should want your child to feel good about himself and sure of himself. You are to encourage your child to take pride in himself. As a result your child will have enough confidence to live his own life in his own way.

The problem is, these people are just substituting one sin for another. Instead of committing the sin of hating God's creation (themselves), your children are encouraged in the sin of pride. It's true that the world has too much sadness and tears and loneliness; it's equally true that the world has too much pride and self-centeredness and independence. Way too much.

In the choice of the lesser of these two evils, we as parents should choose neither.

Our real problem is that we don't understand the value of low self-esteem. You don't have to look very far in Scripture to find that God, in fact, is in the business of *causing* low self-esteem. "The Lord tears down the proud man's house" (Proverbs 15:25) is God's black-and-white statement to confirm this point.

God knows that high self-esteem is the greatest obstacle to a person coming to know Him; He hates pride, so "God opposes the proud" (James 4:6) and "the proud he knows from afar" (Psalms 138:6). He needs to force this out of your child's life if your child is ever going to get onto the higher ground of an intimate relationship with His Maker.

Because of this desire to bring all men to Him, God opposes pride in all its forms. He warns us not to think higher thoughts about ourselves than we ought (see Romans 12:3). Our lives lived in the flesh aren't going to justify very high thoughts about ourselves anyway. He allows children to come to a point of low self-esteem and crushing feelings of worthlessness. These are tools to be used by God and wise parents, and not enemies to be attacked with the God-hated sin of pride.

You *should* teach your children that they have immense and special value as beings created in the image and likeness of a perfect and holy God. They need to know that the *only* thing of eternal value in the universe is people. They should be told that they were so loved, in fact, that God Himself became a man to pour out His life so that they might live. They should be constantly reminded that an infinitely filled God emptied Himself so that they might be filled to overflowing.

But they also need to know that this connection with perfection was lost through the sin of pride—the very same thing that's being sold as the "solution" to our problems. Man did run away from God and sought to live his own way, which has led to a painful and problem-filled existence.

Pride is not only not the *solution* to the problem of low self-esteem; pride is, in fact, the *problem* that causes low self-esteem.

Scripture is plain: "Let him who boasts boast in the Lord" (1 Corinthians 1:31; 2 Corinthians 10:17). Pride leads away from God and will eventually produce an even lower self-esteem. Pride puts up a pretty good front, but it's a fleshly sham and can't last. It was pride that broke our connection with God in the first place, and the substitution of pride for low self-esteem only makes the break wider.

Low self-esteem can be used by a wise parent to bond the child closer to His God. The emptiness does need to be filled and the bitterness eliminated, and there's no one better able to do it than God. In fact, there's no one able to do it at all *except* God. Do let your child take pride, but let him take it in God.

And if your child isn't suffering from low self-esteem, teach him to boast in the Lord and he will feel as good about himself—and God—as he can ever feel. God will give your child humility that will bring him honor, and meekness that will bring him power, for "the Lord lifts up those who are bowed down" (Psalms 146:8).

Your children must be taught to believe that they can't spend the rest of their lives feeling good about themselves by their own efforts.

They must be taught that if they do, the doubts will come, and they'll fall to lower self-esteem than they ever had when they were young. Your children must become convinced in their own hearts that being proud of God is the only truly satisfying kind of esteem, and they must learn that they'll have to persevere in this if they don't want to end up on rock bottom.

Just look how low the world is. Isn't it interesting that the same world that proposes human pride as a solution to low self-esteem has lowered man to the level of an animal and given young people no reason to feel good about anything? The world's pride has produced an unprecedented epidemic of depression and self-hate.

Your children need *God*-confidence, not self-confidence. Give them this from the ground up, and they probably will never have a problem with an "inferiority complex." The reason that many of us have known so few children with low self-esteem is that many of us have never seen a child trained from infancy to devote his or her life to high God-esteem. God is in the trust-and-obey line of work. Trusting and obeying children don't have to deal with inferiority rubbish, because their minds are on God and the kingdom and not on themselves.

And if your children do hit a period of low self-esteem, for heaven's sake, don't try to cure it by giving them high self-esteem. Pitch out all of the ideas and books that serve up this destructive teaching, perhaps garnished with some Christian trinkets. Give your children the only real cure, the opposite of high self-esteem; give them high *God*-esteem.

Teach your children to love God, not themselves.

There's a lot more there to love.

The Birds and the Bees

Many of us were raised to think that dating the opposite sex is just as natural as going to church on Sunday mornings. Dating has been so accepted for so long that we have convinced ourselves that it must be an acceptable part of a Christian's life. We are fairly sure that we could even muster some Scripture to dating's defense.

Stop reading right now, go to the Word, and find every passage that justifies and supports the American normalcy of dating.

That didn't take long, did it? The whole scheme of dating that's been constructed in this culture just doesn't have anything to do with God's best for our children.

We can be so foolish. We allow our precious children to run around with individuals and groups we know nothing about until it's too late. We try to keep it out of our minds, convinced that if their choice is too horrible we'll veto it. Many Christian parents are willing to settle for their child finding a "nice" Christian to date. Some Christians don't even have this much of a "standard" and would settle for "nice."

This sounds like you're proposing arranged marriages, you might be thinking. You've found me out, but before you fall out of your chair, please hear me out.

Everything good or of value in a Christian's life is arranged by God. Everything. "Then I said, 'Here I am, I have come — It is written about me in the scroll' " (Psalms 40:7). "LORD, you have assigned me my portion and my cup" (Psalms 16:5). It's asked in Scripture, "A wife of noble character who can find?" (Proverbs 31:10). And the answer is also given in Scripture: "A prudent wife is from the LORD" (Proverbs 19:14).

So, a young person — or for that matter, an older person — has a person picked out for them by God, if he or she is to be married. Did you hear that? Picked out by *God.* So the question of the Christian ought to be: How can I come to know this person?

What do you think? Is a person going to find his or her God-picked partner by a random plowing through the masses that make up the opposite sex? Or is God more likely to give him or her leading and guidance through a God-ordained authority — like his or her own parents?

It's possible to develop the bogus notion that *any* person whom our child marries must necessarily be the ideal person from God. The rationale? God wouldn't have "allowed" it to happen otherwise. Where on earth does that idea come from? This is saying that actions don't have consequences, that Christians can't make mistakes or miss God's leading, and that whatever a Christian might do is good because God wouldn't have let it happen otherwise.

I'm not proposing that if you are married and found your partner by dating, you begin a new search for yourself using better ways. God no longer has any options for you except to remain married and to let Him make it the best that it can be. But we can be part of a generation that helps our children find an old and better way.

The way is simple. The entire subject should be laid at God's feet. The parents and their child should be in prayer, the Word, and discussion together *from a very young age,* and should all keep their spiritual eyes open so that the person that God has arranged won't be missed. Times to relate to the opposite sex should be set up within the context of families, so that both the parents and the child and the other person's parents have the same basis for discernment because they've been through the relationships and potential relationships *together.* There should be *no* disagreement between the child and his parents before anything serious is planned. There should only be an absolute certainty that this person is, indeed, the one.

Finding the person that God has picked, in other words, should be a family project. It isn't arranged — as it has been in some cultures — by the parents alone, using only cultural traditions. Marriage is arranged by God and discovered by a Christian with the loving help of his or her wise and committed parents.

There's another major advantage of doing things God's way. God's only way of birth control for the unmarried person is chastity. In a God-arranged, parent-shared "discovery" process, you can limit your teaching on birth control to chastity alone, with little or no concern that your child might need some other kind.

There are, of course, times for your children to relate to other young people. The ground rules? Generally, limit the contact to other growing Christian champions. Make sure things are done in larger groups (no one-on-one). Try to have the event at your house. And make sure that things are chaperoned.

If you have a daughter, how do you and she handle requests for dates? Have your daughter tell him he has to meet with you first. That'll ferret out the really bad eggs. If you meet with him and feel like you've been food-poisoned, tell your daughter why and given him the thumbs down. If you don't see a big problem but your daughter just doesn't want to spend time with him, tell him no, either directly or through your daughter. You can take a lot of pressure off of her, and this approach can work in other areas, like babysitting, as well.

If you have a son, the process works a little differently. Lay down the guidelines that he can only invite growing Christian young ladies. Make his first invitation to them be for dinner — at your house. Help him decide from there where this should go, if anywhere. If at all possible, insist that he meet with the girl's father early on.

Above all, give your children a vision that a godly life is more important than dating. Help them to see by your own relationships with adults of the opposite sex how they can have a deep, rich, intimate, holy, and pure relationship with young people of the opposite sex. And encourage them that being single can be a blessing rather than a curse. God starts everyone out single, so it must not be too bad an option.

Finally, give your children a vision for staying home. Work with them so they're not pressured to leave home and be "independent." Let them see that they don't have to find a partner so they can be "adult" and have their own home. Your children already *have* a home. Learn to adjust your thinking about your children over the years so that by the time they're adults living in your home, you're *treating* them like adults living in your home.

And may every one of your children joyously and comfortably stay with you, until God makes it joyously and comfortably clear that marriage is His plan.

Peers

A lot of people spend their time looking for ways to find some decent peers for their children. Youth groups, Bible clubs, summer camps — the ways are endless. In some churches, peer-group activity has become almost an entertainment business.

Your kids don't need to be entertained. They don't need to spend gobs of time with other kids their own age, either. In real life, people have to relate to people of many different ages. *You* have to relate to people of many different ages. Get your children in on the real world. How would your life be different if you only spent time with your own age group?

What draws kids to most youth groups and similar ideas? If it's the Lord, then you've got something special and you ought to treasure it. But if it's the activities, the music, the food, the chance to get away from adults, the chance to goof off with other kids — then you might not be accomplishing much of anything positive and might even be doing harm.

And don't send your kids to camps and rallies "to get saved." They might have a phony emotional experience and end up with spiritual emptiness. Keep them at home and at church to be saved. Sending them away is just a cop-out.

All that glitters isn't gold. Peers and peer groups can glitter.

But they aren't gold.

What I Did for Christ

One of the popular songs that made it on Broadway a number of years ago was "What I Did for Love." This was sung as a response to some who were complaining that their careers hadn't been as "rewarding" as they had hoped. The singer rebuked them for even thinking such a thought; she had chosen this career for love of the profession and hadn't expected anything else, and she encouraged them to look at it the same way. In a day of people choosing careers to stay away from being under authority and to grab as many material things as possible, it was a refreshing song (even though the play itself had some problems).

But the sad truth is that relatively few people today do anything career-related for any reasons other than the love of self and the love of money. This is a day when the basic question is: What pleases me? This is a day when the underlying reasons for starting a business are: (1) "I want to be my own boss" (rebellion); and (2) "I want to keep more money for myself" (greed). These aren't the kinds of reasons that appeal to God.

I was discouraged from pursuing a desired career path because "you can't make any money at that," and "you'll never go anywhere in that field." The only argument I had was that it was the direction my heart was heading in spite of the obvious problems, but it wasn't enough to stem the tide of practical arguments on the other side.

Those arguments were wrong. I've heard other parents and counselors giving the same misdirected advice. Too many people, if there isn't an obvious and immediately bountiful payback, steer others from going the way that God Himself might be encouraging, all because of what they can *see*.

We would improve this whole process just by encouraging our children to do things for *love*. Tell your children: Don't do it because it's easy, or because you can "do your own thing," or because you can rake in piles of money; do it because it's in your heart. Tell them to do it, to do it well, to do it now, and to do it without reference to those "all-important" practical considerations of position and money.

But just as this decision is too important to be made on practical points alone, it's also too important to be made on the "love" your child has for this career. We who are in the household of God need to set our criteria much higher than that. We should create an environment for our children where they can make their choices based on doing it for *Christ*, and for no other reason. Only what they do for Christ will satisfy them.

Encourage them not to do *anything* for money. What they need will be added to them if they seek God's path for them first and only (see Luke 12:31). Aside from this glorious promise, they would be much better off living in a tent with a single-car garage and doing what Christ wants them to do, than to live in a mansion and hating every minute of their labor.

What they shouldn't do for money includes schooling as well as other forms of training and preparation. The colleges are full of young people who have no idea why they're there except to have a good time on the way to an income-generating degree. Many colleges have become a home for rebellion against authority, greed, and spiritual corruption.

What are we doing to these young people? Why aren't we telling them about what's truly important? Is that all there is?

Praise God, no. It isn't all. You can give your child much more, because your God wants to give them more.

What can you do as a parent or counselor? Spend enough time with the child to learn about his deepest motivations and desires — as they relate to serving Christ and others, not *himself*. The sentences that begin with "I want" or "I need" or "I'd like to" should be immediately discounted. God isn't interested in satisfying selfish desires. He knows that the only way for this child's deepest wants and needs and likes to be satisfied is for him to give them up to his Lord and yield his life to others.

Once you see these deep motivations and desires, and take the time to observe how they're manifested through his spiritual gifts and talents, you can start to formulate a list of possible directions. Start this process when your child only has a single digit on his birthday cake, and then continue it in modified and expanded form into his teenage years.

I suggest that you keep a piece of paper called "career paths" somewhere where it will come to your attention often—in your Bible, taped to the front of your television, or in the drawer with the Milk Duds. Have a list of the current possibilities for each of your children written down, with a note or two on why this is a possibility and how this can be explored or developed. This would be a perfect thing to bring up regularly when you're out together on an outing.

As you develop this list, don't assume that your child should do what you're doing, or what you've always dreamed that he should do. But at the same time, you shouldn't assume a passive role in this process. God didn't put you there to dictate his career, but He didn't put you there not to lead and guide and influence the process either. Have a powerful influence in this area of your child's life. He knows more about his heart's desires, but you know more about life.

Make sure you include on your daughter's list the *possibility* of being a full-time wife and mother. That may not be God's choice for her, but if it is, He wants her to be a wife and mother full-time.

Be in prayer on this whole subject of career paths. I am talking about how your child will spend a huge portion of the rest of his life, and you should want it to count for God to the maximum.

One final reminder is in order. Encourage your children to remember that their primary business on earth isn't to pursue a career, even a God-inspired one; their primary business is to pursue *God*. So the song, at last, is true: What they do should be for love.

Of God.

Conclusion

You can show your children how to replace low self-esteem and high self-esteem with God-esteem. You can make their relationships with the opposite sex times of value and victory instead of sin and defeat. You can and must limit peer-group involvement to keep your children's eyes on the kingdom of God. And you can help your children find the vocation that God already has planned for them.

EPILOGUE

We have covered a lot of ground in this book. But I want to close with a simple thought, a little reminder from a fellow pilgrim: *You can do it.*

May God bless you richly in your efforts as you follow Him.

And may *every* one of your children be champions.

ABOUT THE AUTHOR

J. R. Lucas shepherds the Living Faith Church in Shawnee Mission, Kansas. He has been a management executive with several different companies, and the president of Luman Consultants, a management consulting firm.

For almost two decades Mr. Lucas has been involved with the education of children within the church. He is deeply interested in improving this process and centering it firmly within the family unit. He is the author of the Christian novel, *Weeping in Ramah* (Crossway Books), and lives with his wife and four children in Prairie Village, Kansas.

The typeface for the text of this book is *Times Roman*. In 1930, typographer Stanley Morison joined the staff of *The Times* (London) to supervise design of a typeface for the reformatting of this renowned English daily. Morison had overseen type-library reforms at Cambridge University Press in 1925, but this new task would prove a formidable challenge despite a decade of experience in paleography, calligraphy, and typography. *Times New Roman* was credited as coming from Morison's original pencil renderings in the first years of the 1930s, but the typeface went through numerous changes under the scrutiny of a critical committee of dissatisfied *Times* staffers and editors. The resulting typeface, *Times Roman*, has been called the most used, most successful typeface of this century. The design is of enduring value to English and American printers and publishers, who choose the typeface for its readability and economy when run on today's high-speed presses.

Substantive Editing:
Michael Hyatt

Copy Editing:
Susan Kirby

Cover Design:
Steve Diggs and Friends
Nashville, Tennessee

Page Composition:
Xerox Ventura Publisher
Printware 720 IQ Laser Printer

Printing and Binding:
Maple-Vail Book Manufacturing Group,
York, Pennsylvania

Dust Jacket Printing:
Weber Graphics, Chicago, Illinois